Bloom

A Novel

BLOOM

by Margaret Mitchell Dukore

Quartet Books
London   New York

*I would like to thank the National Endowment
for the Arts, which helped make this possible.*

First published in the U.S.A. by Franklin Watts 1985
387 Park Avenue South, New York, NY 10016

First published in Great Britain by Quartet Books Ltd 1988
A member of the Namara Group
27/29 Goodge Street, London W1P 1FD

Copyright © 1985 by Margaret Mitchell Dukore

British Library Cataloguing in Publication Data

Dukore, Margaret Mitchell.
Bloom.
I. Title.

813'54[F]   PS3554.U398
ISBN 0-7043-2635-3

Printed and bound in Great Britain by
The Camelot Press PLC, Southampton

For Steven

Bloom

Chapter

If you turn to page 266 of the Kerrybrook Academy for Girls 1967 yearbook, in the second row of seniors you will see a blonde girl in a poor-boy sweater and Yardley slicker lipstick. Under the picture it says, "Lola Marie Bloom," and under that it says, "Nickname: none." (That's not really true. Although most people called me plain Lola, a few jokers called me Lolita [well, what can you expect with a name like Lola], my P.E. teacher called me Bloom simply because that's what it said on the pocket of my P.E. shirt. Since I wasn't one of her hot stars on the hockey field, she never bothered to find out Bloom's first name.)

Under "Nickname: none," it has my senior quote. It wasn't bad compared to some of them. Most of the quotes were from *The Prophet*, *Peanuts*, Shakespeare, or the Beatles. Mine was from e.e. cummings, but it wasn't an obscure quote. Since high school, I've heard it read at two weddings, one christening, and a speech contest I went to in college. The only reason I decided to use it was simply because we were studying e.e. cummings in English the day the quotes were supposed to be turned in, and I thought it sounded "neat." I had absolutely no idea how appropriate it would seem to me when I looked back at my life and tried to figure out what actually happened to Lola Bloom. What happened to the little girl on the bike in Coronado or the strange-eyed teenager sitting on the lawn at Kerrybrook in San Diego . . . tried to figure out why the rest of the world walks around normally, and why I . . . . Well, it will take more explaining for you to get the whole picture. I don't just want to come out and say I'm crazy . . . or even that I was crazy. If I came out and said that right at the beginning, you would write off the things I did and thought as the antics of a mentally ill woman. In a way they were, but having come out of it, maybe I'm a little richer for it (good way to write off "bad experiences"—say they made you "stronger" or "richer"). You'll have to judge for yourself. At first I wasn't going to tell you that everything turned out all right, but people can enjoy a story more if they know it turns out okay in the end. As a kid, I enjoyed horror movies much more the second time when I knew they'd turn out all right. So settle back, and I'll try to explain what happened to Lola Bloom, "Nickname: none."

My yearbook quote was "You shall above all things be glad and young. For if you're young, what ever life you wear it will become you."

I had to laugh at some of the other pictures. On the right of me is Constance Bonner ('Nickname: Connie"). Her quote is "People who need people are the luckiest people in the world." Three years ago, she had her two kids taken away from her because she was a child abuser. One child had a fractured skull, and when my mother sent me the article from the San Diego paper, I shivered thinking of Connie Bonner spiking the volleyball and leading the prayer service at chapel. Then comes Agnes Brady ("Nickname: Bunny"), and her quote is "Surf's up!" Now she has some high-level secret type job in the Reagan administration, and it was reported to me that when she came back for the fifteenth reunion, she had a Secret Service man with her.

And Lola Bloom? Well, as I said, I have to explain. I've tried to find certain events in my life . . . certain moments, experiences, feelings, relationships, years, etc., to tell you about, so you might understand what I did. It might also help you understand why the life I wore didn't BECOME but became ME, and how hard I had to work to finally make my life BECOME me.

Anyway, I'm getting way ahead of myself. At this point it's hard to understand what the hell I'm talking about, but be patient. I need to tell it in my own way. Then maybe you can understand why I'm still alive, why I'm not a child abuser, and why I'm not a high-level secret appointee in the Reagan administration (or ANY administration for that matter).

I could start at the beginning and tell you about my childhood in Coronado, California, or about my summers with my father in Kahaluu, Hawaii, but I really don't think I should start there. You'd just close the book. I remember reading somewhere that when Nabokov taught creative writing, he had everyone start right off writing their autobiography, and anyone whose first sentence started off with, "I was born . . ." failed. It's bad enough when you have to start from the beginning with colorful or famous people like Elizabeth Taylor or Henry James, but if I said, "Lola Bloom was born in 1949," you wouldn't read further, and then you'd NEVER understand.

I'm going to start by telling you about my husband, Grant . . . my relationship with him. There's a good reason for this: most of the people who know me (especially my mother), think what happened was Grant's "fault." They actually believe that I was perfectly normal . . . an ordinary, sane person until I met him, and that he somehow forced me into insanity. I claim (and I know) that my craziness was one of the things Grant loved about me. I'm not saying that was good, or that he was good for me, but if I had just been Jane Doe with a sweet and stable personality, Grant wouldn't have noticed me, let alone been mad for me.

Grant Rosenberg was (and is) brilliant, but his brilliance wasn't what attracted me to him. When I would do odd things, Grant was the one who DIDN'T look at me strangely. He celebrated whatever I chose to do with a lust and joy you can't imagine. Actually, I think he was just as crazy as I was, but he was stronger . . . then. He was not self-destructive (or so I thought). He was somehow able to leap over the trenches of depression that I fell into head first. He had the ability—most of the time—to pull me out of the holes I buried myself in, and when my crazy euphoria hit, he kept me up there . . . ran with me so I sailed again like a kite. When the despair would hit again, Grant wouldn't be dragged down into it as I was. He would be opening more champagne, pulling me off the floor, and forcing me to run on the beach at midnight, or dance in Kapiolani Park under the tropical moon surrounded by bougainvillaea and honeysuckle. Grant Rosenberg: my husband. I kept my own name because Grant though it was pretty. He thought the name Lola Bloom reeked with languid sex. He'd watch me blow smoke slowly out of my mouth, and he'd look me straight in the eyes and say, "Lola Bloom, Lola Bloom," the way Eilert Lövberg probably said, "Hedda Gabler, Hedda Gabler." The first time he said my name like that, suddenly "Nickname: none" didn't matter. Suddenly it was the best thing. Suddenly being Lola Bloom meant something more than before.

Well, face it, Grant was amazing. He usually only slept about four hours a night because there "wasn't any fun in sleeping," and he never got tired. He had the energy that Lola—the depressive—envied and admired: admired because he was my amazing lover and envied because depression often involves envy. You think about a whole world of people out there who are NOT counting up the Seconal.

Grant could drink a fifth of Bombay gin and feel "just fine" in the morning, and would be roaring off on the motorcycle for beer and the newspaper while, at a slug's pace, I slowly put the coffee in the Norelco Express, laboriously, one plastic scoopful at a time.

In the car, Grant never wore a seat belt, drove like a madman, and will probably never get in a car accident. He smoked three packs of Dunhill cigarettes a day, and I'm sure he'll never get cancer. He was brilliantly crazy, with a Ph.D. from Cambridge in mathematics and astronomy, but he made his living by drawing a cartoon character called Mr. Macho. Once a week, he'd do a *Mr. Macho* strip, and once a week it was nationally syndicated in almost every paper in the country. *Mr. Macho* came out YEARS before *Real Men Don't Eat Quiche*. Mr. Macho not only wouldn't DREAM of eating quiche, but refused to eat quartered club sandwiches because they were too wimpy. Mr. Macho drove an International Scout II, a Blazer, and a pickup truck. He had two Doberman pinschers and a pit bull terrier. He called women "girls" or "cutsie pie" or things like that, ate at truck stops, went hunting and bragged about hitting an "eight pointer" straight between the eyes. He drank Bud, watched boxing, played poker, etc. You get the picture. Grant made the strip so FUNNY that in a country full of feminists, he hadn't even got one piece of hate mail. Everyone loved Mr. Macho the way everyone loved Archie Bunker.

Since *Mr. Macho* only took up about an hour a week, Grant had the time and space to be the amazing one . . . the lover . . . the drinker . . . the sweet, sweet man who was so gentle, so funny, that in an interview he could get away with saying that the kind of women he liked were "blonde women who knew their place and knew when to shut up." Grant, of course, got a laugh on that line, when anyone else would have had tomatoes thrown at him.

If I ever slipped and fell into one of the trenches of depression that Grant always seemed to sail over, he would do things like pick me up naked, put me in his restored 1957 red Chevy convertible, and drive me to the top of Mount Tantalus at full speed and play Buddy Holly tapes. By the time we reached the top, I was usually a little better. Almost ritualistically, I'd shake up the champagne and spray it all over his head. He would kiss my breasts, my mouth . . . kiss me all over. We'd lick the champagne off each other, and he'd fill his mouth with the Korbel (or on my truly black days, Moët & Chandon) and slowly kiss me . . . letting the champagne flow from his mouth into mine. Some got lost and ran down between my breasts; some I would swallow.

Then Grant would drive home very slowly . . . down the green winding road that slithered down Tantalus heights to civilization in Honolulu. Then he'd zoom up St. Louis Heights, and I'd turn around and kneel in the convertible and watch Diamond Head get smaller and smaller as we wound our way up the hill to our house . . . the house I loved because I loved the man in it.

He would put me to bed and stroke my hair until I was asleep, and in the morning, if the devils in my head were still disturbing me, he'd cook me something I loved like a cream cheese omelet with Mexican salsa. He would bring it to the bed and gently feed me as if I were a little child. In a sense he was right: in a depressive state, I was so overwhelmed by life that I might as well have been an abandoned three-year-old child standing in the middle of the H-1 freeway.

He would talk to me so sweetly that I'd eat a little. He'd stroke my hair, make love to me, and kiss my eyes. He'd do this until I was able to gradually push myself up into the daylight, and there I would stay for a while . . . walking on eggs . . . waiting. I'd slowly tidy the house, quietly go to the market, and quietly cook, read, sleep while Grant—the raconteur, the comic, the dreamer—would tell me funny stories, make funny comments, make love to a quiet woman . . . waiting too. We were both waiting.

Then it would happen. The euphoria would set in. I could feel it coming like a rush . . . the excitement that only a drug addict can understand. This rush just came, and not only was I not buried in a trench, I was flying . . . , straight up into the clouds like Wonder Woman or an MX missile (Wonder Woman when it was a good high and an MX missile when, at the end of the marriage, the euphoria turned to anger).

We would get wonderfully crazy during the euphoric periods. We'd buy two bottles of Moët & Chandon and take them to a bowling alley, drink out of the bottles, and watch the hard hats stare at us as if we were rare creatures from another planet. That was another reason why I loved Grant. He *was* a rare creature, and instead of being a crazy woman panting and frightened in a corner, I too was amazing. When he not only accepted my madness but celebrated it, neither of us regarded it as dangerous.

"Lithium," said Jake O'Shea, the psychiatrist the hospital assigned me later on. "You should have been on lithium."

"I was willing to pay any price for my euphoria," I said. "The way a drug addict will steal and kill just to get his fix. Yeah, my black holes, dark days, painful tears, sleepless nights, terrifying dreams, and the sense that my life was worth less than a female cockroach were still worth it."

"But you had Grant to lean on then," he said. "What would you have done without him?"

"Probably have actually killed myself. I needed him, and that made me feel totally overwhelmed and frightened at what other people call life." He just stared at me and wrote something on his notepad. "Do you drink?" I asked him.

"Uh . . . yes . . . some."

"Well, let's say on New Year's Eve or your birthday you decided to get wonderfully and excitingly drunk, and the absolute knowledge that you're going to get a hangover doesn't either stop you or keep you from whooping it up at the party."

"I don't exactly 'whoop it up'—as you say—'at a party.' I understand your point, but a hangover is a lot less serious than death."

"Not if you don't want to be alive," I said.

But that was later. That was after Grant left me. I couldn't help wondering if I had gone the lithium route ten years ago, if Grant would have even wanted me. Would the lovemaking have been the same? I also wondered if I hadn't had Grant, would I have been THIS crazy? Well, sure, I was already crazy when he met me, but without someone feeding both the devils and the angels in me . . . encouraging both the earthworm and the eagle, I might just have been interestingly crazy rather than dangerously crazy. Who knows? On the other hand, as I said, without Grant, I might be dead. I'll never know the answer to that.

I met Grant right after I graduated from the University of California at Santa Cruz (I graduated from Kerrybrook in 1967, and, wrapped in my Indian gauze shirt and my love beads, I was pleased with the idea of a mellow, laid-back college that didn't give grades). Ever since my parents were divorced, my father had lived in Hawaii, and I usually spent the summer with him. If I hadn't met Grant, I might have happily gone on to graduate school in Boulder, Colorado. There was no particular reason I chose Boulder. Everyone said it was pretty. A lot of friends from Santa Cruz were going there . . . some to avoid the draft . . . most to avoid the shock of the real world.

My father was a minister, and his church was located in lower Manoa Valley just close enough to the city to miss most of the rain. When his church was in Kahaluu on the other side of the island, I liked it better, but then you never know what you miss until you don't have it anymore. To be honest, I never liked ANY of my father's churches.

Now my father is another whole story, which I'll get into later. What I'm trying to do now is to get you to see that Grant wasn't totally responsible for what happened. Yeah, sure, he encouraged me . . . allowed me to smash dishes and throw the pieces out the window, stamp on champagne glasses, and run outside naked in the rain, knowing he would catch me before I was arrested. He was fascinated by me, and his fascination was only more fuel. Each time I dreamed up another odd and drunken thing to do, he would join me if it was at all safe, stop me if it was dangerous, but laugh and kiss me as if I was a rare bird, and Lola Bloom ("Nickname: none") did so want to be a rare bird.

One time I came right out and asked Grant why he did love me, and he took my face in his hands, gently kissed my eyes, and said, "Because you are Lola Bloom, and because you're my passionate and drunken lover, because you are you . . . unique." He smiled his Clark Gable smile and said, "And because everything you say truly blows my mind."

The first time he saw me was the night I had filled a thermos full of vodka right out of the freezer in the kitchen of my father's church (safer to keep it there than in the gleaming waxed kitchen of his house in Mililani Town). I downed almost half a bottle of it and then got on the bicycle my father used in his clown shows and rode down to Waikiki looking for madness.

I rode fast . . . as fast as I could. It was all downhill, so sometimes I'd take my feet off the pedals and coast. Some people stared at the crepe paper and balloons on the handlebars. When I got into Waikiki, it was harder going—partly because the vodka had caught up with me, and partly because of the crowds. I still rode as fast as I could, weaving in and out between bunches of Japanese tourists in matching muumuus and aloha shirts, sunburned tourists from the Midwest, cops, hookers, and the local crowd coming out of the eight-thirty show of M*A*S*H.

When I came to the fountain in front of the Ilikai hotel, I suddenly remembered the box of Cheer I had in the basket on the bicycle. That afternoon

I'd taken the bike (crepe paper, balloons, and all) to the laundromat, and while the clothes dried, I drank gin from a 7-Up can and danced to the Muzak version of "Raindrops Keep Falling on My Head." I had not met Grant yet, and I was euphoric at the goddamned laundromat listening to 1001 Strings. That definitely isn't normal. Grant didn't meet a healthy, normal person that night.

I polished off the vodka—still pretty cold—and took the Cheer from the basket and dumped it into the fountain. As the bubbles rose, the crowd grew. Some cameras clicked, and I was surrounded by the loud colors of the tourists' newly purchased flowered Hawaiian wear. The bubbles spilled over the edge of the fountain. Sometimes a little clump of them would break loose and fly off like a snowstorm in reverse. I watched more bubbles rise, and tilted my head back, looked up, and there was Grant, bearded, with a Dunhill cigarette hanging out of the side of his mouth. I looked at the other faces—the tourists. They were all staring at me as if I should be put away. Then I looked at Grant again, and he was smiling this radiant smile. The bubbles continued to spill over the edge of the fountain, and Grant smiled right down into my eyes and slowly applauded.

Then, just as the security guard from the Ilikai came running out, Grant grabbed my hand and led me around the corner. He started off just walking fast, and then soon he galloped. Most people run; Grant galloped. His motorcycle was parked (illegally, of course) in the Kaiser Hospital parking lot. As the security guard came around the corner, Grant lifted me up as if I were made of nothing more than the last bite of cotton candy, set me on the back of the motorcycle, jumped on, and zoomed out into the street just as the guard came running into the parking lot. We drove fast by the crowd at the bubbling fountain, and more security guards started chasing us and yelling at us. Grant broke about a couple hundred traffic rules, and roared straight up St. Louis Heights to his house, which looked right down into Diamond Head.

Grant had intense blue eyes, wore orange and black striped socks with faded blue jeans, a dress shirt, and a necktie.

From the living room of his house, the city looked like those little Italian Christmas tree lights blinking on black velvet. The house was old— probably built in the late twenties. The inside was painted completely white except for the roses Grant had painted on the ceiling over the mattress he used for a bed. There were lots of colored cushions around in various sizes and shapes, and no other furniture except a built-in kitchen table that looked like it had come straight out of a diner . . . like you should always eat cheeseburgers at it. I gathered Grant thought so too, because he had a small jukebox on it, a napkin holder, and those catsup and mustard dispensers they always have in diners.

"I love you" were the FIRST words he spoke to me. "I'm Grant Rosenberg, and I *loved* your bubbles and your bike."

"My God, the *bike!*" were the first words I said to him. "It's my father's. It's gone."

"You have a *father* who rides around on a bike with balloons and streamers on it?"

"He uses it in his Clowns for Christ show."

"Your father's a *clown?*"

"No. He's a minister who . . . dresses up like a clown. He's a member of the Order of Red Rubber Noses. There really is such a thing."

Grant laughed. "Kind of like the Johnny Carson of the church, huh?"

I laughed too. "Did you know that there's *actually* a clown depression clinic in Arizona? And if you're depressed you go there and for some enormous amount of money, they dress you up in a clown suit, and I . . . guess . . . cheer you up."

"You're kidding!"

"No. Really not." I smiled. "What would you do if you were depressed and someone made you go there?"

"Instantly kill myself," he said cheerfully.

I was beginning to love him.

"Wait here," he said. "The refrigerator is full of champagne," and then he jumped up and disappeared out the door. I heard a car start and went back to the window. One tiny boat made a spark of light in the black space that was the ocean. In about twenty minutes, Grant was back. He came bounding in the door carrying a balloon and a streamer. "Got your bike!" he shouted.

"You got the *bike?*" I was amazed. "You mean it wasn't stolen?"

"Who would steal a crummy bike with goddamn balloons on the handlebars? I think the security guards left it out there as a decoy to see if they could catch the madwoman who dumped the fucking Cheer in the fountain."

"What did you tell them?"

"I didn't tell them anything. I just drove up on the curb, reached out, and grabbed the bike and threw it in the convertible. Simple." He leaned forward and kissed me. "What's your name?" he asked, stroking my hair.

"Lola Bloom," I said.

"Dickensian," he said. "You're sexy, and Lola Bloom is a sexy name. You should be named Lola Bloom." He kissed me again. "You've been drinking vodka," he laughed. How different from the tone of voice my father and his wife Sally used when they said, "You've been drinking vodka."

He sprang up—almost like an awkward cat—and practically danced into the kitchen. "I've got two kinds of champagne," he said. "One is better, and one is prettier to look at."

"I want the pretty one," I said.

He laughed and popped the cork on the prettier one. Then he opened a cupboard filled with Woolworth dishes and Corning Ware and took out two fluted champagne glasses from Tiffany's. I knew then what his priorities were, and I liked them.

We went out to his rickety back porch and sat with our legs dangling over the side, clinked glasses, drank champagne—some from the glasses and some right out of the bottle—and blew smoke rings with the Dunhill cigarettes.

We made love on the close-to-collapsing back porch. He took off my U.C. Santa Cruz sweat shirt. I took off my jeans, and he took off my silk panties that my mother, Helen, had bought for me at I. Magnin.

"Nice," he said holding them up to the moon.

— 15 —

"They have to be dry-cleaned."

"You have to *dry-clean* your *panties?*" he asked, amazed.

"That's what I said when my mother bought ten pairs for me, and she sighed and said, 'Find a cleaner who will send the bill to me,' so I did."

"What about the sweat shirt?"

"Oh, I wash that myself."

"Good." He smiled.

I stood there naked, looking at the lights and feeling the cool—but never cold—breeze blowing against my breasts. Grant gently kissed the back of my neck. I turned around, and he let me slowly undress him. He spread out clothes to cover the porch. He kissed my body all over, and then it started to rain. Hawaii is so astounding. One minute you could see the moon and the next it would be raining a fine, warm Hawaii rain. From one side of a house you could see stars, from the other, sheets of rain.

Grant, my sweetly drunken lover, laughed, and kissed my damp breasts . . . my damp nipples. I kissed his neck, his ears, his chest, his penis, and his knees. As he traced my spine with his finger, I said, "I'm crazy, you know."

"And I love you for it," he said and kissed me . . . his tongue on mine . . . under mine . . . his arms gently pushing me down onto the damp clothes.

The fine, warm, misty rain fell. It felt like the time in Coronado when I once attached a fine-spray garden sprinkler to the kitchen sink and stuck the hose out the window and drank straight tequila while the warm mist sprayed over me.

I jumped up and ran into the house and went to Grant's bed. I pulled all the flowered sheets off it, and brought them—with the pillows—to the sweetly wet rickety back porch.

The rain was still falling. I reached for the bottle and swallowed a huge mouthful of champagne. The sheets and pillows were beginning to get wet. Grant kissed me again, and I could feel myself, wet, between my legs.

Suddenly I remembered I was having my period, and I tried to become a little sane for a minute. "I'm having my period," I whispered. "Uh . . . do you care?"

He wrapped his arms around me as tightly as he could. I could feel his erection against my stomach. "Lola Bloom," he said, "you could have every contagious disease known to mankind, and I wouldn't care. No, darlin', I don't care."

I pulled out my Tampax and joyously tossed it over the rickety railing the way you see people let go of homing pigeons and wondered if it would get caught in a lawn mower someday.

"You're crazy, Lola Bloom," he shouted and poured the rest of the champagne all over me. I put my legs apart, my knees up. I put my head down on the damp pillow and let the rain wash the champagne from my face. Grant entered me, then sat up, pulling me with him.

We laughed and fucked and cried and drank until I was ready to come. "Slowly, slowly," he said, and I shivered and came. He came and held me tight, and we lay there holding each other as tight as we could, on the flowered sheets wet with champagne, rain, semen, blood, sweat, and tears.

"I love you, Lola Bloom," he said. And we never left each other.

Now this was the first night I had laid eyes on Grant. How could Helen, my mother, even hint that I was a model college coed and normal adjusted child whom this man had somehow—by some strange voodoo power—turned into a madwoman. No, he was just a madman who fell in love with a crazy spirit he felt at home with. As I said, he encouraged and allowed my madness, but good old Helen truly believed (because she WANTED to believe) that Grant was like the husband in *Gaslight*. No. No. Not at all.

Chapter

2

Yeah. They say people always choose wrong the first time around. My mother definitely thought I chose wrong, but even if Grant WAS responsible (which he wasn't) for my suicide attempts, I still don't think I chose wrong. It was just that there was something wrong with me. A normal person wouldn't say that beer bottles on the floor of a '57 Chevy were one of the contributing factors in the mushrooming love she was feeling for someone. But I DID fall in love with those beer bottles, with the man who didn't believe in health food. (He once said he felt sorry for fruits and vegetables because they didn't have a chance. Cows and pigs could at least run away.) I fell in love with someone who wasn't a cliché, a man who celebrated and lusted after all the qualities in me that either scared everyone else or simply made me "Nickname: none" in the Kerrybrook Academy for Girls yearbook.

Together Grant and I created the third level of irony. Only a few select people we knew got what I always called "the cosmic joke." The third level of irony is GETTING the cosmic joke, realizing that it is all funny. Even during my blackest days, I somehow knew it was funny that this tiny woman on this tiny planet in this huge universe was thinking that her death would make one damn bit of difference.

But that was the dark side. We used to try to explain the light side of the third level of irony to people, and either they loved it or they looked at us oddly and tried to invite us over for some nerdie thing like coffee and dessert and a literary discussion of *The Elephant Man* or to watch the rerun of *Roots* with them. Some people are incapable of making the leap to the third level. The kind of people who carefully wax their 1978 Datsun hatchbacks, the people who won't go to a bar unless it has Boston ferns hanging in it, the people who read *Passages* and live by it, or the people who think *Das Boot* was a deep and profound film—as opposed to a good old-fashioned submarine movie, which it was—just because it was in German. Even if Grant and I gave our simplest explanation, there weren't too many people who got it. We explained it to my mother when she visited and was HORRIFIED at our priorities and couldn't understand why we would spend sixty dollars on a bottle of champagne and get our clothes at K-Mart or Goodwill.

"We live on the third level of irony," I said simply, knowing Grant would take over with our pat explanation. Helen just looked at us as if we were a couple of teenagers who had just said, "Gag me with a spoon."

"It can all be explained with plastic toys," said Grant.

— 20 —

"Plastic toys," repeated Helen, giving me the I-told-you-he-was-weird-all-along look.

"You see," said Grant, "the ordinary people and the stupid people, the people who 'suck beers' while they watch Monday Night Football and the masses of unenlightened people you see wandering around shopping malls, well, these are the people on the first level of irony."

"What does that have to do with plastic toys?"

"First-level people go to Woolworth's and buy pink plastic toys made in Taiwan for their kids. Then the normal people who believe they are enlightened and have their coffee specially ground, the people who eat microwave-oven-heated quiche with pasta salad, the people you find hanging around on redwood decks, or"—he flashed Helen one of his winning smiles—" the folks around the bar at the Coronado Club." Helen rolled her eyes. "These," he continued, "are the second-level-of-irony people, and they would never *dream* of dropping into Woolworth's or K-Mart and buying pink plastic toys for their kids. They go to places like Ghiarardelli Square in San Francisco or the Ward Warehouse here and buy their kids hand-carved wooden trains, leather Winnie-the-Poohs, Creative Playthings, Raggedy Ann dolls with hand-embroidered faces and natural cotton bloomers . . . . You know what I mean."

"I think those sound like very nice things," said Helen.

"That's what I mean," said Grant. He smiled again, and even Helen had to admit that when Grant smiled at her it was practically impossible not to like him. "Then there are some," he continued, "like us, who are on the third level and know that the kids really *like* the pink plastic toys made in Taiwan from Woolworth's better."

Helen looked confused. "But you don't have children," she stated.

"That was just an *example* . . . one people can most easily relate to."

"Well," said Helen, ending the conversation, "I would *never* give a gift from K-Mart to a child."

There were a few people who "got" us, got the joke of life. They were the ones who would sit with us on the rickety back porch and watch the sunset turn Diamond Head into a silhouette just like you see on all the postcards. They were the ones who instantly understood about me . . . how I was sick . . . and didn't care. "Lola's down" was instantly understood as "We love you, but don't come around and try to cheer her up." They were the ones to whom drinking and drugs were not steps down a dark ladder to addiction but a weekend ritual—a sacrament, if you will—a joyous encounter with other people who understood that you could go to the Bistro for dinner and spend a hundred dollars and just feel stuffed, or you could spend a hundred dollars on an occasional celebratory gram of cocaine and buy a celebratory bottle of champagne, and in fifteen minutes you were so happy you could run down to the 7–11 store and get some Velveeta cheese to eat on the beach with your champagne in a silver bucket, your glasses from Tiffany's, and your beach mats from Sears and watch the sun sink into the ocean.

We always watched for the green flash. We had long debates as to whether or not it was a myth.

Supposedly just the second the sun dips behind the horizon, there is a green flash, so we would all watch for it, never see it, and chalk it up to the myth that had become a reality because myths are things people on the first and second levels of irony want to believe.

It was sure a good thing the *Mr. Macho* comic strip was in almost every major paper, because it is rather expensive to be crazy. (It's MORE expensive to be crazy on the second level because you have to buy sectional couches and food processors and home computers, too.) Getting up to get to your nine-to-five job would put quite a damper on Grant's euphoria, and I . . . . Well, the way I was then, a job would have been impossible. You can't tell an employment agency that you're a manic-depressive and that some days you won't be able to get out of bed. That scared me sometimes, because I had no idea what I'd do if Grant left me, but then I would do something horrible like make a drunken fool of myself at a party, and there would be Grant, not judging me, but smiling with the Dunhill hanging out of his mouth the way he did when I put the soap in the fountain, and I'd feel sure he wouldn't leave me. He needed to be needed; he needed my craziness as an excuse for his, and—and I know this is true; I'm not remembering wrong—he loved me, and it was for what I was, not for what he hoped I would become.

Grant and I lived together for two years, and got married one day just because we decided to while eating the worst chop suey we had ever tasted in the neon pink concrete Hee Hing Chop Suey.

Naturally, we had a third-level-of-irony wedding. You see there is this department store in Honolulu that has a different wedding dress in the window each week. They are your basic white wedding dresses with stiff veils, all different versions of the classic plastic-bride-on-top-of-the-wedding-cake dress. Now, your first-level-of-irony people would go to the Ritz and buy a stiff, looks-ALMOST-like-real-silk, virgin-bride dress, and your second-level people would never DREAM of buying a dress from the Ritz window. They wear Laura Ashley Victorian dresses, resurrect their grandmother's dress, wear peasant dresses with wide-brimmed straw hats, wear dusty pink mid-calf designer dresses, or ANYTHING just so it reflects their true personality and taste and DOESN'T look like it came from the window of the Ritz.

But we, of course, were on the third level.

"I've got it," I said taking a bit of shrimp Canton that was so sticky you didn't even have to know how to use chopsticks to eat it—it just STUCK to the chopsticks.

"What?" asked Grant, taking a bite of wonton, making a face, and gently putting the other half back on his plate.

"The second we finish dinner, which I guess is about now, I want to rush to Ala Moana Shopping Center and buy whatever wedding dress is in the window of the Ritz. I mean, no matter *what* it is. That's going to be my dress!"

"You've gotta have the old veil too, you know," laughed Grant. (He was great. I mean, he was serious and knew I was serious, and everyone else would have thought we were kidding.)

We had taken the motorcycle and had brought hundred-proof vodka to drink with our chop suey, so drunkenly but truly in love, we zoomed over to the Ritz fifteen minutes before closing. I must admit I don't blame the saleswoman for looking oddly at a "slightly intoxicated" couple who rushed in and said, "We'll take the dress in the window in size eight." Easiest sale she's ever made, but she DID call the MasterCard company TWICE just to make sure our card wasn't stolen.

The dress, of course, was white, the veil gathered into a little crown decorated with fake pearls and fake lily of the valley. The dress was the true example of the stereotype that instantly pops into everyone's mind when they hear the words "wedding dress." Grant loved it. He said I looked like the Snow Queen of Culver City, California. I immediately wanted to wear it home, but then we figured that it might get tangled in the wheels of the motorcycle, so holding the pale pink Ritz box, we roared up St. Louis Heights singing "Oh, Promise Me" loud enough so we could hear each other over the roar of the motorcycle.

When we got home, I hung the dress on the hook in the bathroom, and Grant and I stuffed it with tissue paper, turned it around backwards, and hung the veil on the top part of the hook, so it looked like we had a bride standing facing our bathroom door. Then Grant opened some Moët & Chandon, and we lit twenty-five candles and put them all over the bedroom. We made love under the roses on the ceiling with my legs wrapped around his neck and his hands gentling holding my ass . . . and the room spinning . . . the candles flickering . . . and the leftover Hee Hing chop suey in its carton by the bed.

After the obligatory post-coital cigarette, we finished the champagne and the chop suey, and fell asleep clinging to each other. "I love you, Lola Bloom" were the last words I heard before falling asleep.

We were married the next week. Maryanne Raymond was my bridesmaid. She was one of our friends who had achieved the third level. She'd been everything from a blackjack dealer to a top-less dancer to a piano teacher. One day she just woke up and decided to come to Hawaii, and got a job teaching one dance course at the university and was a cocktail waitress at some bar with a Ta-hitian theme where she had to wear a sarong. We debated whether or not she should wear the Torch Room sarong for the wedding, but she insisted that she immediately go down to the Ritz and buy whatever bridesmaid dress was next to my bridal gown.

"It's perfect!" I said when she came back with a stiff pink fake-silk bridesmaid dress with sort of a pillbox hat with a tiny pink net veil sticking out the back. "It's *perfect!*"

Grant went to King's Bakery and ordered a three-tiered wedding cake (with the plastic bride and groom on top, of course), and he had them write on the bottom layer, LEVEL ONE, on the mid-dle layer, LEVEL TWO, and on the top where the plastic bride and groom were standing, LEVEL THREE. Of course Mr. Sakai at King's Bakery had absolutely no idea why he was doing this, but

Grant just said, "Trust me," so he shrugged and wrote what Grant asked.

He rented a tuxedo and wore it with his orange and black striped socks he had worn the day I met him and a "Dewey for President" button we had found one night in the gutter outside Shakey's Pizza Parlor on Keeamoku Street. He bought me a huge fake white orchid corsage to wear with my window-of-the-Ritz dress, and for "something blue," I found some blue satin pointed-toe 1962 shoes at the Goodwill. From Maryanne I BORROWED some pink net stockings, and for "something old," I wore the silk panties that had to be dry-cleaned and that I had worn the night Grant met me. I also wore a garter we had bought at Farrell's Ice Cream Parlor (thinking it was ironical that we had NEVER bought ANYTHING at Farrell's except one of their Gibson Girl garters). I had a huge bouquet of gardenias which, after the ceremony, we floated in our rented punch bowl filled with Purple Jesus punch (the kind that tastes just like grape juice but is almost pure alcohol, and that fraternity boys in college used to get sorority girls drunk on), and we floated them in the fishbowl full of gin, and ate crab and caviar in the park by the beach as we drunkenly and dutifully watched for the green flash as the sun sank into the goddamn Pacific.

Chapter

So, simply, we were married for eight years. We got a little calmer, but not enough to worry us . . . make us think that somehow we were less amazing. Every week Grant would turn out another *Mr. Macho* comic strip, and I . . . well, I . . .

What did I do? Of course there were still the days when I couldn't move from bed, but they didn't happen too often, just as the better-than-on-drugs euphoria didn't happen as often as I'd have liked it. For a year, I even went into remission, but—like cancer—I knew it would always come back to haunt me, and it did.

I must have done something with myself. I mean, I cooked. I learned to be quite a wonderful cook and would prepare elaborate picnics for our friends: cold Cornish game hens stuffed with cranberries for an early supper in the woods at the top of St. Louis Heights; pheasant with orange sauce for a picnic supper by the ocean; cold poached salmon with hollandaise sauce for a picnic supper by the fountain in Thomas Square. I cleaned the house. Yes, that was a necessary daily ritual as Grant and I always made such a mess each night. I must admit I loved the decadence of waking up under the roses with empty champagne bottles by the bed, overflowing ashtrays with roaches and cigarette butts, the flowered sheets damp with champagne and semen, the sink piled with dishes from whatever elaborate meal I had prepared the night before. It never was a discouraging sight because it gave me a reason to be alive during the day, washing dishes, sheets, preparing for another night of madness. Yeah, the condition of the house each morning at least reminded me we had lived the night before.

But then there were those days when I realized I was nothing . . . wasting my life for love and drunken madness. On the other hand, love and drunken madness were my two favorite things. At least Grant was bringing laughter to millions of Americans who chuckled over Mr. Macho. After we were married, his agent sold the idea of a Mr. Macho doll to Mattel. It came dressed in jeans, Jockey shorts, and a white Marlon Brando T-shirt, and you could buy football uniforms, baseball uniforms, hunting shirts, bowling shirts, soccer shoes, and so on. You could also buy all kinds of accessories like a pickup truck, a hunting dog, or a fishing pole. Grant and I both agreed that the doll looked a little wimpy to be named Mr. Macho, but then Grant reminded me that G.I. Joe always looked wimpy, even in his camouflage outfit. It was something about the wrists. I bought a Barbie Doll so Mr. Macho wouldn't be lonely, and I put them on the top shelf of our built-in bookshelves. Grant's agent then negotiated a contract for a Mr. Macho coloring book. He wanted Grant to do a few comic books, but we had more than enough money from all the other Mr. Macho shit, and he didn't think it would be worth the effort. He sold the rights for an animated television special, and since we didn't have a television, we watched in a bar down the hill in Kaimuki.

Two wasted lives, I thought. Nothing would change if Mr. Macho suddenly disappeared. Nothing would change if Lola Bloom suddenly vanished. I knew I should be out doing something that would matter, but I had trouble figuring out what exactly did matter. Grant, the brilliant and amazing one, drawing a little cartoon that wrapped up people's garbage the next day, and Lola Bloom? Lola Bloom was crazy, and each year the dark trench of depression grew wider and days of euphoric joy grew shorter. Still, even after I tried to kill myself and Jake O'Shea would say, "You should have been on lithium," I continued to say that I had been willing to pay for my highs with my lows.

"Your 'lows,' as you call them, almost cost you your life," he said.

"No, you're wrong. It was the highs that almost cost me my life."

He looked bored, as he often did. "Pardon?"

"My life was nothing except my craziness. I couldn't leave Grant . . . because I loved him so much, and because I was crazy, and staying with him only allowed it. You see, I wanted to die in the middle of all that happiness. . . . I knew in the back of my mind that I'd be low again soon. I wanted to die with the wind in my face, laughing, rather than lying in bed, staring at the roses on the ceiling."

"Roses on the ceiling?"

"Grant painted them . . . yeah, Grant."

In some ways I feel sorry for Grant. He'll always live with the guilt that my near death was because he left me. In the last year of our marriage, I had a high that lasted two months. It was not the first high that Grant watched rather than joined. I'd dress in odd costumes and speed down the hill on the motorcycle. Sometimes I'd run through Waikiki asking every sailor if he wanted to fuck me, but even a sailor eighteen years old and just back from three months at sea could sense the danger or see the craziness in my eyes, and would back off. Sometimes I'd remember it in the morning, and sometimes I wouldn't.

I'd run down Lewers Street dressed in Grant's blue silk scarf and a Goodwill evening dress and toast the crowds in Waikiki—the hookers, the pedicab drivers, the Japanese tourists with their expensive cameras and watches. Even without drinking, I felt more ready to conquer the world than if I had just been injected with heroin and cocaine. I'd talk to the drug addicts along Seaside Avenue, and they all thought I was on drugs. They would complain to me about how everyone tells about the "bad" about heroin and the rush of fiery peace. They assumed I had just been injected as no one (unless they are on drugs or in a manic-depressive high) can be as thrilled as I was with the plastic flower leis and tourists from Iowa. I'd chat with them for a while and move on, each of us with our highs—mine from the poison in my mind and theirs from the poison of heroin.

As you can imagine, all this wasn't easy for Grant. On one hand, he felt responsible for encouraging me each year to go one step further during the time when the euphoria was still fun for him. He was good to me, he took care of me, and when he stopped enjoying me, he didn't stop loving me.

That last high period I had before Grant left me was the longest one I'd ever had, but it was definitely not the first one Grant hadn't shared with me. For the past year, he had been standing at a distance . . . trying to talk me down, make me calmer. Then the euphoria would turn into uncontrolled anger. Grant would just stare at me sadly while I stood there and called him a cocksucker and a motherfucker. I'd scream at him that if it hadn't been for him, I might have done something with my life. I hated him for being successful, wonderful, handsome, and funny. I'd shout that I was tired of being his sidekick, "the woman Grant lives with," the blonde who knew her place, that crazy girl Grant's involved with, Grant's wife, Grant's wife, Grant's wife.

He wouldn't fight back. He just looked sadly at me. During that angry part of the high, I stormed out the door with no shoes on and ran all the way down the hill to Kaimuki Town. I was terrified, because I knew I'd go back. I was scared because

I had no other choice. It didn't occur to me that GRANT might make a choice.

I bought a quart of Mickey's Fine Malt Liquor and drank it as I trudged back up St. Louis Heights, not crying and still angry. I let myself in. Lying on his back with his head on one of the colored pillows, Grant was listening to Rosemary Clooney on the stereo.

"You forgot your shoes," he said, tossing my rubber thongs at me in a sharp rather than playful way.

I didn't say anything, but went into the kitchen and got very, very drunk. After an hour or so, Grant came in and poured some Bombay gin into a tumbler with no ice. He drank it down as if it were Kool-Aid. I unbuttoned my shirt, and he knelt down on the floor and kissed my breasts. After I was naked, he bent me over the kitchen table and gently kissed me all the way down my spine. He picked me up, and we fucked on the beige ceramic tile I had lovingly cemented to the once-ugly kitchen floor. It was the first time we had made love that Grant didn't say, "I love you, Lola Bloom."

The next morning, we were both quietly hung over . . . each respecting the other. I slowly and quietly made coffee in the Norelco Express while Grant automatically made two Bloody Marys.

We sat on either side of the kitchen table that looked as if it belonged in a diner, and I didn't feel the usual bonding I felt after a wild night of drinking, sex, and drugs. I felt almost as if Grant were a stranger . . . the guy you pick up at a bar and have to face over coffee the next morning. No. It wasn't the same. I felt stranger than when we WERE strangers.

"I thought yesterday about leaving you," I said as calmly as I could.

"At least you came home last night," he said coldly.

"What do you mean?"

"What about the night before last?" he asked quietly.

I tried to shake off the haze of the morning to remember. Yes, I remembered walking through Kaimuki, and I remembered buying a quart of Bombay gin at the liquor store that used to be the Still and have chilled Korbel but had changed management and now only had chilled André.

"A memory for details, but not for important events," sighed Grant.

"Huh?"

"I found you lying face down in the grass in the playground of Liliuokalani School."

"You *found* me? You brought me home? I didn't come home?"

"I knew you hadn't gone far because you didn't take the car or the motorcycle. At four I went to look for you."

"I don't remember . . ."

Grant got up, lit a Dunhill, and stared out at Diamond Head for a few minutes. Finally he said, "Why did you think about leaving me?"

"Because . . . because I love you, and I don't want to do this to you anymore."

Grant looked confused. "Then don't," he said.

This time I stared at him. "Do you think I do this *on purpose!*" I practically shouted.

"Well, 'on purpose' wasn't exactly what I meant."

"What do you mean?"

"I love you, Lola. I wouldn't stop loving you if you became . . . uh . . . a little more like a regular person."

"*You're* not like a regular person!"

"But I'm not hurting anyone or myself."

"But . . ." I paused. In a moment of clarity, it is easy to say, "Sure, I'll try *really* hard not to be crazy," but if you *are* that way, moments of clarity have nothing to do with the other side. Just like the dark, depressive side of Lola Bloom (which Grant secretly loved too, because it gave him a feeling of power when he was able to pull me out of it) had nothing to do with the Lola Bloom who danced in the rain, tossed flowers into the bathtub, and stood up in the convertible.

Since I knew that wasn't what he wanted to hear, I finally said, "I . . . well, maybe I can . . ."

Grant sighed. "Look, I can't take this anymore. When I first met you, I was fascinated by you . . . blown away. Then I realized that it wasn't just Lola Bloom having fun. It was *real:* you were crazy. . . . But by then I loved you for it, we were married, I was attached to you, and, fuck it, you were still fun. Then it turned scary. There was the anger instead of the wild abandon. When you were okay, I had to deal with your fears about yourself. Then your highs became too frightening for me to join, and your lows . . . well . . ." He paused. "I don't deserve to be lashed out at when all I've tried to do is help you."

"Help!" I screamed. "*Help!* Jesus Christ! I start smashing dishes against the wall, and instead of grabbing me and telling me to cut it out, you open a bottle of champagne, toast the broken pieces, and hand me another plate! That's like giving Charles Manson ten thousand dollars everytime he killed someone. It's not help, it's . . ." I floundered. Grant was just staring at me. "I kept on doing these things, partly because I couldn't help it, and . . . well . . . I thought you loved it."

"I did love it. I don't anymore," he said quietly.

"This is the way I am. This is me. What are you doing? Are you asking me to change?"

"You're fucking right I am!" Grant yelled. "Okay, if this is the way you're going to be, if you *assume* your craziness is the only unique thing about you, then no *wonder* you lie on the bed for days at a time in despair!" He softened. "It's *not* all you've got. You are a brilliant, beautiful woman who's wasting her life by saying, 'Hey, I'm crazy. Isn't that great?' Lola, being sane does not mean being boring."

"That's easy for you to say. You're famous, you have money, and you're educated. All I have is you and a degree in English from U.C. Santa Cruz. What the fuck good is that going to do me! My life is nothing but . . ." I was going to say "you," but I stopped myself in time.

"Your life isn't me or your degree from Santa Cruz. You're life is what you do when you get up in the morning, and if you want to continue to do it here—with me—I don't want any more crazies. I don't care if I sound unfair, but I just can't take another second of it!"

"Well, I'm not *going* to get any better!" I screamed. "I don't want to be ordered by you or anyone else to shape up or ship out!"

Grant was quiet as he stubbed out his Dunhill and lit another. "Okay," he said sadly, "if you're convinced you won't get better, then you simply won't. Someday you're going to jump out of a window, and I'm sorry Lola, but I don't want it to be my window you jump out of. I'm sorry."

I stood silently. All I was wearing was one of Grant's shirts. He pulled on his pants, put on a T-shirt, and said absolutely nothing. In complete silence, he took about half an hour to pack two suitcases. I backed into a corner of the bedroom. The orange and black striped socks in a ball were stuffed in a corner of the suitcase. It was like one of those dreams you have, where you can't wake yourself up, but you know you're dreaming. Many times nightmares made me scream for Grant to wake me up, but the scream was always in the dream and not really coming out of my throat. Now, my voice was silent, but I wanted to scream, "Wake me *up!* Wake me up!"

It was so strange . . . so sudden. I mean, I'd known Grant was unhappy, but it never occurred to me that he would just leave. It wasn't like him. He would talk to me about it, then cry, and then we'd make love and it would all be okay. . . . But there he was sticking T-shirts into the Samsonite suitcase. It was like a scene out of a bad movie.

Just as he was about to close his second suitcase, he quietly walked over to me and unbuttoned his shirt that I was wearing. I started to breathe again. We would make love, and then he'd unpack. When the shirt was off and I was standing naked in the corner, Grant silently folded it and PUT IT INTO THE SUITCASE, leaving me naked. He clicked the lid shut. I shivered. He walked over to me and kissed me on the forehead. "I love you, Lola Bloom," he said quietly.

I remained silent. Tears were literally streaming down my checks and running onto my breasts.

"I have to save myself," he said. "Since you refuse to save yourself, I have to save me."

He picked up the suitcases and walked out the door. The screen shut behind him. I walked to the screen door and saw him toss the suitcases into the convertible. He drove away slowly, and it was so strange because I had never seen Grant drive slowly before . . . ever.

I turned around and stared into the house. I toyed with the idea of just ending it right there, but I didn't have enough drugs, and it is kind of hard to slit your wrists with a Trac II pink plastic Daisy Shaver. Instead, I went to the refrigerator and took out a bottle of Moët & Chandon, opened it, and drank the whole thing right from the bottle.

I wasn't even drunk when I finished the champagne. I was still naked, and even the thought of putting on some clothes literally overwhelmed me. Was this really curtains for the marriage? The rent was due, and I only had a hundred and sixty-eight dollars in my checking account. Then I realized that even if I HAD the money, the thought of being organized enough to write out a check and get it in the mail on time was totally frightening.

Wasted Lola Bloom: she not only didn't have the money to pay the rent, she wasn't even exactly sure where to send it if she did.

I stared out at the mango tree across the street. A father and two kids were picking mangoes, probably for the mother to make chutney. Because they were so straight, I envied the Char family across the street. Mr. Char was a loan officer at First Hawaiian Bank, and Nadine, his wife, was a bookkeeper for Kamaina Electric in Kakaako. They had two kids and a boxer dog, and picked mangoes on the weekend so Nadine could make chutney and mango bread, and the kids had bikes, and Harry Char washed the car on weekends and mowed the lawn, and they were saving up to buy a boat. I sat and hugged my knees. They would never call the weeds in their yard their "natural vegetation": they would never drink champagne in a bowling alley: they would never hang their Christmas tree upside down from the ceiling; they'd never go to the roller rink in a rented tux and an evening dress; they'd probably live longer than I would; and they'd never . . . probably never ever . . . feel so positive their lives were wasted.

I decided that Grant would come back. He would KNOW THAT I—I hate to say this, but it's true—couldn't function without him. Could I be happy with a man who thought that?

I slowly walked over to the bed, and for the next three days, I lay there. Once the phone rang, but I was in a half-sleep and by the time I figured out what was disturbing me, the phone had stopped ringing. Occasionally, I went to the bathroom, but since I wasn't eating anything or hardly drinking anything, I either slept or stared at the roses on the ceiling. Dead. I was dying, and I knew it.

On the fourth day, I woke up in terror. There had been another nightmare: Grant was standing naked with his back to me, and when he turned around, I saw that it wasn't Grant at all . . . just a man with a distorted, horror-movie kind of face. Not a particularly unique nightmare, but terrifying just the same. When I woke up, I wasn't sure where I was. I looked at the bed and sometime during those three days, I had started my period. I crawled out of bed and put on a T-shirt. Blood. Blood when I met Grant. Blood the day he left. Cycle completed.

My hands shook, and blood ran down my legs. The shadows of the leaves outside on the white wall looked like ink blots come to life, and every time a breeze blew the tree, they seemed to move toward me.

It's funny, but I wasn't afraid of the night: it could cover me like a comforter, and the moon is soothing. It was the days that scared me. Even if you didn't look at the sun, its light was everywhere, and if you did look at it, even your eyelids couldn't completely shut it out. It burned and penetrated you.

That morning the light was somehow different in the house. I couldn't figure it out: everything was the same . . . except that Grant was gone.

But that was another strange thing. When I

perceived the light to be different, I didn't even think about Grant. The future—with our without Grant—was incomprehensible. There was no such thing as future. Even if Grant DID come back, I knew it was the future that scared me . . . future in general, not future without Grant.

For the next two days I didn't sleep at all. I sat at the diner-like kitchen table and stared out the window almost the entire time . . . looking down into Diamond Head, looking at the ocean. On the first day the ocean was very blue—darker than the sky; on the second day there was a strange haze, and the horizon line melted into the sky. Sea and sky were one. I registered that everything looked lovely. I felt almost peaceful, but it only reinforced my solid knowledge that there was nothing I wanted, nothing that would make a damn bit of difference.

On the third day with no sleep, two Mormon missionaries came to the house on bicycles. With literature in their hands, wearing white shirts and black ties, they tapped on the panes of glass in the door. They knocked urgently and smiled and waved at me through the glass panes. They gestured for me to open the door. Menstrual blood was all over the cushion of the window seat. It took every bit of energy I had in me to plastically turn up the corners of my mouth, but I still sat motionless on the window seat. Finally they went away. Since there was no Tampax in the house, there was blood all over the carpet and kitchen. It really looked as if the Manson murders had been committed there.

Well, as you probably have guessed, I tried to

kill myself that day. This first suicide attempt was such a cliché that I'm embarrassed about it. True suicidals would just laugh at me. As I said earlier, it is pretty hard to kill yourself with a disposable Daisy Shaver, but after the Mormons left, I suddenly remembered that we had a single-edge razor blade in the cigar box where we kept our drugs.

I got the box from Grant's file drawer. Inside there was a little grass, but nothing else except a cocaine straw and the single-edge razor blade.

I was pretty stupid to think that suicide for me would be as simple as slitting my wrists. It wasn't.

I carefully sliced the veins, and, still wearing my bloodstained T-shirt, I sat hugging my knees and leaning against the bathtub.

The carpet in our bathroom was from the Sheraton Waikiki Hotel. It was so hideous it was funny. Only people on the third level of irony could appreciate it.

One afternoon Grant and I had been walking in Waikiki drinking Myers rum out of a silver flask. We decided to get loaded and sit in the lobby of the Sheraton Waikiki Hotel and be amazed by all the bizzare tourists in their new bathing suits, cut lower than last year's, so they would have a strip of leftover tan, a strip of new burn, and a strip of white, all together looking like Neapolitan ice cream. We went behind some bushes in the garden of the Royal Hawaiian and smoked some dope, and then I ran—Grant following me—with my arms outstretched, into the main lobby of the Sheraton Waikiki. The carpet was lime green with two other shades of green ferns and leaves all over it. Hanging from the ceiling were wicker baskets with bright pink plastic flowers dripping over the edge. The furniture was all overstuffed and covered with shiny vinyl that matched the carpet exactly. The wallpaper had pineapples and flowers in stripes.

Grant and I sat on a fern-patterned vinyl love seat and watched a wedding couple from Japan walk through the hotel. They had been married in Japan, but she still wore her white dress (not unlike my wedding dress) . . . all the way from Tokyo on a 747 in a wedding gown. The back was all crushed, and her hand trembled as she signed in at the desk.

We laughed at the decor and smiled—almost tearfully—at the wedding couple, and then we went up the escalator to look at all the banquet rooms. In one room they were cutting out a square of carpet to put in a dance floor.

"I want it!" I said. "Let's steal it!"

We crouched in the corner until the workmen went on a break, and after polishing off the Myers rum, we rushed over and rolled up the square of lime green and dark green fern carpet, and then casually we carried it down the escalator, smiled and nodded at the people at the front desk, walked around all the fake Greek columns, past the Greek statue (misassembled so the wrong arm was up) that stood in the middle of hibiscus bushes, and right out onto Kalakaua Avenue.

Grant had carefully cut it so it fit our bathroom "almost as good as wall-to-wall." Definitely a third-level carpet: the stupid people see it and say, "Oh, wow! Art deco!" (or if they didn't even know that much, they'd say it was "neat" or something); the smart people would think it was the most hideous bathroom this side of Hawaii Kai; and the third-level people—the brilliant and amazing ones—would think it was funny and therefore wonderful. If you can get a laugh—or at least a smile—every time you go to the bathroom, you're doing much better than most of America.

There was already quite a lot of blood on the carpet from my period. I couldn't lie in a warm bath because the bathtub was broken. Well, the drain didn't work. We had always been "meaning to have it fixed," and now that I'd be dead soon, it was comforting to think that I wouldn't have to worry about bathtub drains, dinner, going to Timber Town to buy a garbage can, medical insurance, having a new muffler put on the car (mufflers and garbage cans are so necessary and so boring and you get absolutely no satisfaction out of them), or the future. None of that made a damn bit of difference now. The shower worked just fine, but I knew that bleeding to death in the shower probably wasn't a good idea, so, like an idiot, without even putting a blanket over me, I leaned against the bathtub, hugged my knees, and watched the blood trickle down my arms and mix with the menstrual blood on the carpet.

Amazingly enough, there were no tears. The feeling of despair left. I would never have to move from this spot; I would never have to tell Mormons I wasn't interested; I would never have to watch Grant be brilliant and full of energy; I would never wake up wondering what I had done the night before. I didn't even have that cliché thought: "Boy, will Grant be sorry when he finds out." I didn't even think in terms of Grant's remorse, or guilt, or pain. He was simply one tiny part of the whole picture. . . . The life of Lola Bloom—the life Lola Bloom wanted to leave. I wanted to be dead. I didn't care if he was sorry or not. Dead was what I wanted.

Suddenly, I realized that this was the exact wrong time to do it. After knowing Grant for ten years, I knew he'd come back, if not to me, to make sure I was all right. He couldn't take the not knowing. I still was dead set on dying, but I wanted to die when I was happy. I wanted Grant to know it had NOTHING to do with him and everything to do with knowing that I did not want anything in life except to be crazy Lola Bloom, and it's pretty depressing to know that the one thing you want— the insanity—is the thing that is killing you, and that the one thing about me that attracted Grant to me so strongly ten years ago is the one thing he is afraid of now. It's hard to face the fact that the one unique thing about you not only is destroying you but isn't doing anyone else one fucking bit of good. My life was only a haze of liquor and laughter, and I hadn't the energy or the desire to change that. If I died now, it would be too simple. Grant would think it was because he left me. That was the ONE thing I didn't want him to think. With great effort, I got up and bandaged my wrists. I staggered over to the kitchen table and stared over the catsup, mustard, and napkin dispenser and jukebox at Diamond Head and the tiny lights of Kaimuki, wondering how all those tiny little people in those tiny little twinkling cars managed to live life like the Char family, and why Lola Bloom, thirty-four years old, would not even be able to hold down a job at Baskin-Robbins.

I think it was two days I sat there. I thought I hadn't slept at all, but I must have, because suddenly I felt a hand on my shoulder. I woke with a jerk and cowered in the corner. I looked up, and Grant was staring at me, holding one of our floor pillows covered with blood. Without a word, he picked up my hand and looked at the blood-soaked gauze twisted around my wrists. He looked at the pillow.

"That's blood from my period," I said calmly. "The only blood from my wrists is on the Sheraton Waikiki carpet."

"I got scared that you . . ."

"That's why I stopped it," I said. "I didn't want you to think I'd done it because of you. If it ever happens, you'll know life did it to me, not you."

Grant took out a Dunhill cigarette, lit it, and leaned against the refrigerator. He didn't look well at all. "I think we need to talk," he said. I didn't answer. "I haven't changed my mind, it's just . . ."

I paused. Where would I go? Even if I went to Maryanne's, I couldn't stay there forever. I couldn't go home to my father; that might finish me off faster than if I got a room at the Y and stared at walls. I didn't want to ask Grant for money to go to Page, my sister in California. Where would I go?

"Are you okay, Lola?" he finally asked.

"I'm not dead," I answered in a monotone.

"Why did you have your period all over the house?"

"I didn't have any Tampax."

"Oh," he said simply. I guess he figured that was about as reasonable an explanation as any.

I wished I could have felt a rush of safe relief seeing his face, but I knew I wasn't safe, it had nothing to do with Grant.

"I gather you're not back to stay," I finally said.

"I did say I couldn't take it anymore," he said.

There was a long silence, and I felt the tears come. Lola Bloom had blown it: I lost the only man I'd loved, and wasted my life.

I wiped the tears away with the back of my hand.

Grant silently finished his cigarette, looked around for an ashtray; not finding one, he tossed it into the sink.

"I love you, Lola Bloom," he said softly. "I'll always love you, but . . ."

"I don't want to hear the 'but,' " I snapped. "I know. You can't take it anymore. I refuse to make the effort to get better just to make life easier for you. Is that what you think?" I waited and then said, wiping the tears away, "I have no idea *how* to get better." I put my head down on the table and sobbed. Grant stroked my hair and looked at my bloody T-shirt and the blood on the table bench.

"Take a shower," he said gently.

With great effort, I got up and went into the bathroom and took off my T-shirt, caked with—literally—blood, sweat, and tears. I tossed it into the wicker wash basket. Grant followed me in and took off his clothes. I loved to watch Grant undress. He was over six feet tall, and since he didn't exercise or jog or do any of that health shit, his body looked human. It didn't have that sculpted, unnatural, muscled look. He had a large penis, and he wasn't all tan the way everyone else in Hawaii is. I think Grant and I were the only people on the island who didn't "touch up their tans" every weekend and/or run. Once when Grant and I were walking along the beach looking at people rubbing oil on themselves and turning over just to catch the rays at the right angle, Grant said he believed the degree of intelligence one has is instantly detected by the amount of suntan you have. I rolled up my sleeve, and he kissed the white inside of my forearm and told me that meant I was a genius. He pointed to a guy with a toothpick in his mouth and a perfect dark tan, who looked as if he should be roasting on a spit. We laughed and decided that I, being the whitest on the beach, was the smartest, and so far that afternoon, that guy was the stupidest.

There was not another man in the world like Grant. How could I go out into the world with normal people? I needed to watch it with Grant. We were the only two who looked at it the way we did . . . like we were watching through one pair of eyes.

I turned on the shower, stepped in, and felt the water getting warmer on my breasts. Without a word, Grant stepped into the shower behind me. He soaped me gently, and then I stood directly under the shower, with water streaming down from my hair, and soaped him. He turned me around and licked the back of my neck and buried his face in my wet hair. He gently pushed my legs apart with his knee and entered me from the rear. Then he put his arms around me and his hands on my breasts. I wondered how many things in this world had been solved by sex. Then I wondered how many things sex had destroyed. Sex was so interesting, it was ALMOST worth staying alive for, but not quite.

Grant kissed my ears and neck. "I'm going to start," I managed to say and shivered and came. Then I knelt in the water and made him come in my mouth. I swallowed the semen and wrapped my arms around his thighs. Without drying, we got out and lay on the blood-covered bed and smoked a Dunhill and looked up at the roses on the ceiling.

"Someone," Grant said, "should invent a special post-coital cigarette that comes in a box like the Tampax box."

"What do you mean?" I asked.

"You know how Tampax has cellophane over it that says 'Tampax' on it, and when you take it off, it's just a plain and tasteful box?"

"Yeah."

"Well, someone should invent a brand of cigarettes called Post-Coital but have it say it only on the cellophane, so when you take off the cellophane, it's just this tasteful blank box that looks great on the nightstand."

"I think you're back to stay," I stated in a monotone.

He smiled at me. "Why do you think that?"

"Because you've come up with another of your get-rich-quick schemes. Things are back to normal."

It was true. Grant was ALWAYS coming up with

get-rich-quick schemes that were too complicated or involved too much work to carry out. One was the crawlers. You start up the fad of crawling instead of running; you make a fortune on the *Complete Book of Crawling;* you make a fortune off all the equipment like knee pads and hand pads, and he was sure people would buy the idea because our natural state should be on all fours; then we would have fewer health problems. Yeah, he wanted to turn all runners into crawlers. *Mr. Macho* was the only scheme Grant had ever seen through, and *Mr. Macho* made him enough money, so it seemed like a little too much effort to try to piece together his elaborate plans. One of our favorites was what we called the University on Tape—sort of the advanced form of those radio credit classes some universities have. This would be your entire education on tape, and you could get a degree from select universities in the country, provided you met their entrance standards. For example, a degree from the Yale tapes would cost you more than a degree from the University of Hawaii. Just think, everyone—who could afford it—would have the opportunity to take political science from Henry Kissinger or creative writing from Joyce Carol Oates . . . even after they were dead. "If only we'd caught Nabokov in time," I said. Grant wanted to go the whole hog and be sorry we didn't catch Shakespeare for playwriting. Because Grant and I would be the highest administrators, we would rake in the most profit. As part of our university, we figured that living in Hawaii was the perfect opportunity to offer courses in every aspect of running a hotel, down to the towel washers, so we would buy a hotel and turn it into a hotel school where all the employees PAID to learn rather than got paid, and then we'd also charge the tourists who stayed there, but we'd be always full because we would charge less than other Waikiki hotels, so the guests wouldn't bitch about being practiced on. Whenever we brought up this idea at a party, no one—except a few third-level people—got the joke.

Since Grant was back to planning another get-rich-quick scheme, it seemed like we might be back into our old pattern. Did I want to be?

"You know," he said, "I bet in our lifetime all wars and all athletic competitions—even the Super Bowl—will be played on giant video screens."

"That means a twelve-year-old could get an athletic scholarship at our University on Tape," I commented.

"Or be a general in the U.S. Army, for that matter," added Grant. He stood up and got some more champagne, and we drank until it got dusky. We lit a few candles, and made love again, and fell asleep on the bloodstained sheets.

Things were back to normal. So GRANT thought anyway.

Serious suicide takes either more guts than I had or—in my case—more planning. Real gutsy suicidals just jump off buildings, drown themselves, or pour gasoline all over themselves and flip on a cigarette lighter. I figured if I had a gun, I might be gutsy enough to shoot myself in the head. I had read somewhere that being shot in the head doesn't hurt because the brain has no nerves. Like when they do brain surgery, they just use anesthetic to slice the skull, and when they hit the brain it's PAINLESS. Patients are often AWAKE (that gutsy I'm not) and see splashes of colored light as the surgeon probes for the tumor. Death with a gun would probably be one long green flash. No pain. Green light, then nothing.

I didn't have a gun or the nerve to go out and buy one, fill out a license, have the guy in the gun store think I was afraid of robbers or into hunting. Then I'd have to learn to load it, and I don't know how many people would be thrilled to help someone with a history of suicide attempts learn to load and shoot a .38. Even if I DID buy one and learn to use it, I wouldn't want to go out in the woods somewhere to shoot myself because I wanted to die looking at Grant's roses on the ceiling. If I shot myself in our bed, it would just be too grotesque for Grant to come home to.

It was simple. It had to be with drugs, that was all. I hated the thought of having a cliché suicide, but everything else I could think of involved too much risk of coming out alive, unable to walk, with brain damage or—worse—pain. There was enough pain in my MIND for one person.

My suicide plans became a quiet obsession. After three days of quietly cooking for Grant, drinking a little less than I usually did, and making love with Grant until the early hours of the morning, I finally got around to taking the bloody sheets to the laundromat with my usual gin in a 7-Up can. In all my despair, I actually enjoyed going to the laundromat. When Grant and I first met, he'd bring martinis up there for me along with what he

called his caviar special. It consisted of Mc-
Donald's hash browns topped with sour cream and
caviar. He said it was the three-levels-of-society
special. People who don't know shit about food buy
those hard little squares of McDonald's hash
browns; EVERYONE—from the lowest Bulgarian
peasant to the czars of Russia—eats sour cream; and
the gourmets and the rich eat caviar. To have this
and a martini in the Manoa Laundromat was definitely a third-level experience. Also, I was a regular there. Granted, being a regular at the Manoa
Laundromat isn't exactly the same as being a regular at the Russian Tea Room, but it was nice when
Estelle, the attendant, would start my washer with
her key and just let me give her the money, so I
didn't have to have the degrading experience of
stuffing the quarters in. Estelle was pretty interesting: small, Chinese, and of indeterminate age—
somewhere between forty and death. She sort of
looked like the dwarf in *The Year of Living Dangerously*, wore designer jeans, took phone messages
for me, and smoked thin cigars. Since Grant and I
usually made a horrendous mess every night, I was
usually there at some point every day. This time I
hadn't been there for a week, and Estelle, ironically, said she thought I'd died. She didn't know,
of course.

As I sat watching our flowered sheets being
slowly tossed around in the dryer, I suddenly had
an inspiration. You see, as with the gun, I knew
fucking well that a person with scars or bandages
on her wrists can't just go to her doctor, say she's
having trouble sleeping, and then ask for a prescription for forty Seconal, but suddenly—right

there in front of the Pepsi machine—I figured it all out.

I felt strangely peaceful as I folded the sheets. It was truly comforting to know that in a few days I'd be dead. I happily contemplated all the things I was going to miss: nuclear war (*I* would die looking at roses painted on a ceiling; everyone else would be fried instantly, hideously burned, throwing up with radiation sickness, or running around with their skin hanging in shreds and all the morphine in the city blasted away), over-population, bread lines, old age, cancer, Grant . . . I stopped for a moment. I truly did love Grant, but I hated life more than I loved Grant. When life seems so black and endless when things are going RIGHT, you get terrified of what it would be like if things went WRONG. Yeah, it was nice to know that I was going to be dead soon. And it would be when Grant and I were happy, so Grant would never have the guilt (or his ego fed) that I did it because of him.

I put the sheets in the box on the back of the motorcycle and calmly drove home.

During the next three days, I paid visits to literally EVERYONE we knew—or rather everyone who wouldn't be totally surprised and floored at the sight of recluse Lola Bloom standing at the front door.

Maryanne was spraying her plants and listening to Sarah Vaughan on the stereo. She looked vaguely surprised when she saw me standing outside the door.

"Uh . . . hi. Come in."

"I just . . . well . . . thought I'd drop by.

Grant's . . ." I was about to say Grant was drawing, but since Grant drew every week, and I never visited anyone, that would sound a little fishy, so I said, "Oh, Grant and I had a fight—nothing major—but I just thought I'd leave him alone for a while."

"Sure," said Maryanne. She made some herb tea for herself and gave me a bottle of Mickey's Fine Malt Liquor. After about fifteen minutes of forced conversation, I pretended I had to go to the bathroom, went, and locked the door behind me. I opened the medicine cabinet and looked for drugs. Any drugs. There were two bottles of Valium (of course), some Motrin for menstral cramps, the end of a bottle of Tylenol Number Three with codeine, some antibiotics, and a half of a bottle of Dalmane.

I dumped everything—including the antibiotics—into a jar I had in my purse and left the empty bottles. It would probably take her longer to notice the drugs were gone if the bottles were still there. I wasn't *stupid*.

Then I proceeded to make the rounds of all our friends, pretending each time I had to go to the bathroom, and then dumping all the drugs anyone had into my jar. By the time I got home, I was sure I had enough drugs to kill King Kong.

I had to wait all day before I could figure out a way to be alone in the house long enough to die. Finally, I remembered the wedding Grant and I were supposed to go to in a bamboo forest the next day on top of Mount Tantalus. Carolyn and Hugh were good friends, but they were "too sixties" to have reached the third level. I mean, in 1983 they

— 55 —

still took LSD, still listened to Buffalo Springfield and Peter, Paul and Mary, still had beaded curtains in their doorways, still had an Indian bedspread on their bed, and were getting married in a goddamned BAMBOO FOREST that required a six-mile hike. Grant and I had accepted the invitation (a) because they were friends and (b) because for nostalgia's sake a real sixties wedding might be amusing.

Since he knew that anything that involved exerting myself physically was painful, Grant didn't suspect anything when I said I didn't want to go.

"Shit," he said, "I know hiking isn't your number one thing and you're afraid people will think you're turning into a jock if you wear your running shoes, but this isn't Girl Scout camp, this is Carolyn and Hugh's *wedding!*"

"They've been living together since before you and I got married." I paused. I knew if I waited any longer, SOMEONE was going to figure out what happened to their drugs. At least I had got my biggest haul from someone who was on vacation. First I had been disappointed, but his house-sitter had let me use the bathroom anyway.

After the wedding everyone was going to a Korean restaurant in Kaimuki and then to Maryanne's to "get drunk and loaded," so I knew I'd have a long time alone, but after today someone would probably figure out that everyone else's drugs were gone too, and I'd be locked up.

"It's not the hiking," I finally said. "I'm really feeling sick . . . kind of like I'm going to throw up. How would it look if I vomited in the middle of 'for better or for worse'?"

"I'll stay home and take care of you," Grant said simply. (See, he did love me.)

"Carrie and Hugh don't want to get married without *you!* They're crazy about you. They won't even miss me."

"Come on, stop it," he said. "You've got to give up that female cockroach bit. You're not just my sidekick, my straight man. You're a whole person, and Carrie and Hugh invited *us*—not just me."

"I *said* I felt like I was going to *throw up!*"

Shit, I thought. What if Grant did stay home and take care of me? Any moment one of our friends could say to another, "Someone ripped off my drugs," and the other would say, "Funny, someone ripped off mine, too." If worse came to worst, I could go off somewhere where no one would find me, but I did so badly want to die safely under the roses.

"Obviously, I'm not *that* sick," I said. "I'm not throwing up yet. I just don't feel well enough for the hike."

"Okay, I'll go on the hike, hear the marriage vows they wrote themselves, skip the dinner, and come back."

"*Go to the goddamn dinner!*" I yelled, then realized I was sounding a little too eager to be alone. "Look," I added, "if I feel better, I'll come for the dinner, okay?"

"Okay," he said. He put on his jacket. "I'll take the motorcycle so you can have the car." He came over and kissed me tenderly on the mouth and said—as he always did when he left me, even for an hour, even for good—"I love you, Lola Bloom."

He went out the door with his bouncing walk and his perpetual vitality. He leaped on the motorcycle, waved, and roared off down St. Louis Drive.

I knew the party wouldn't be over until one or two in the morning. Since Grant was always the last one to leave a party, I thought I probably had enough time, and even if I wasn't quite dead when he came back, he would probably say to himself, "Oh, passed out again," strip off his clothes, fall into bed, and pass out beside me. Yes, I would have time. I hated the thought of Grant waking up next to a dead body, but at least there would be no blood and gore.

I remembered some words to a Joni Mitchell song, "Do you want to contact someone first . . . send someone a letter?" I knew for sure I didn't want to leave a suicide note. You only do that if you want to make someone feel good and sorry for what they've done to you, and no one had done anything to me. I'd done it all to myself. Contact somebody? I thought of Dillon, my father. Jesus, I didn't even want to have DINNER with Dillon. I didn't even want to contact him when I was feeling fine, so WHY would I even think I'd want his to be "the last voice I'd ever hear." My father was a clown minister. His second wife—not my mother, thank God—had started a company called Chuckle, Incorporated, and they BOTH dressed up as clowns and did religious birthday parties. Sometimes they even dressed Free, their two-year-old kid, like a clown, too. Sally had rewritten the major Bible stories so they could be performed by clowns, and they charged something like a hundred dollars a birthday ("Happy face balloons, five dollars extra"). Dillon would put on this damn clown outfit and go to hospitals to cheer up terminal cancer patients. When Grant's sister Alex was dying of cancer, we flew to California to see her. Strange . . . I envied her—not for the pain but because she was lying in the room she was going to die in. Anyway, Grant made jokes and sang songs for her, and I sort of huddled in the doorway not knowing what to say or do. I arranged daisies and watched her cheeks get hollower each day, watched her shudder in pain if someone accidentally bumped against the bed. The last thing she said before she died was in answer to Grant's question. "Hey, Alex," he asked gently, "I'm curious. How would you feel if right now at this moment some bozo in a clown suit leaped into the room with a bunch of happy face balloons to cheer you up?" Alex had looked up and said with her usual cynicism, "I'd *kill* him." She died twenty minutes later, with one final shudder, then peace. No, I did not want to contact my father.

I thought about calling old Helen, my mother, in Coronado, but she would think it strange. I never called her. She would call me every couple of weeks and ask if we had bought furniture yet and stuff like that. After we had been married two years, she gave up on that and figured we never would. She visited us once and announced that Grant was turning me into an alcoholic, and wouldn't listen to the simple medical facts that no one TURNS you into an alcoholic: either you are one or you aren't, and there is a difference between being an alcoholic and being addicted to booze and being a heavy drinker and being someone who just likes to drink, and I tried to get Grant off the hook by pointing out to her that I drank just as much before I met Grant as after. She also didn't like our house (she didn't understand "funky") and actually offered to buy us one in Kahala, and had absolutely no understanding as to why we liked THIS house, which sagged so the eggs slid to one side of the frying pan. When she visited, I even rented a bed, because I wasn't stupid enough to think Helen would get off on sleeping on a mattress on the floor, but after looking around the place, she had said, almost desperately, "Take me to the Kahala Hilton!" So we loaded all the Gucci luggage into the Chevy. She also had no idea why we thought it was "fun" to drive around in a '57 Chevy. She offered to buy us a new car and didn't understand when I tried to explain that Grant and I didn't belong in a brand-new Chevy Citation hatchback. She didn't say anything about my being crazy, but then I had ALWAYS been crazy, and she had chosen—I guess for the sake of self-preservation—to ignore it all these years. No, I didn't want to contact my mother.

My sister Page was a television actress. She was three years older than I was and started out her lucrative—if not brilliant—acting career doing a commercial for, ironically, a razor. At first, she didn't even GET the commercial, but the model they intended to use cut her leg on the second take, so she was instantly out, and Page—the backup model (I guess people cut themselves a lot in razor commercials)—shaved her beautiful leg, and she was off and running. Also the fact that she was the granddaughter of Irving Adrian, the producer, probably didn't hurt her career either. Although he died long before Page went into show business, it was common knowledge that she was his granddaughter.

Should I contact Page? She was the star of a hit television series called *Classified Ads*. Each week she played a lovable kook like Rhoda who answered some kind of classified ad, and "adventures followed." Sunny—her character—lived a life RULED by classified ads. She had obtained her apartment, everything she owned, her job, her ride to work, and so forth through classified ads. Usually on the series she answered a lonely hearts ad, and some bizarre man would be the guest star. I picked up the television section to see what Page was going to be doing this week. It said, "*Classified Ads:* Sunny answers an ad from a hot-shot lawyer looking for a woman who likes country music and quiet dinners, and Sunny discovers the lawyer is the class nerd from her high school years." The show was often in the top ten. If you are a third-level person and have to live in a world where people make shows like *Classified Ads*, *Three's Company*, and *The Love Boat*, and they actually reach the top ten, no wonder third-level people go crazy. For the purpose of self-preservation, Page probably had to remain a second-level person.

Grant was lucky: he was healthy crazy. I was just sick crazy. Did I want to contact Page?

Page had come out to Hawaii once to guest star on *Hawaii 5-0* before she got the *Classified Ads* series. She had stayed at the Kahala Hilton Hotel and let us drink the booze from the bar in her room at the studio's expense. She thought that Grant was "a hunk" and "a real comedian," and told him that *Mr. Macho* was definitely her "most favorite" comic strip. (I don't think Page ever read the comics, but I gave her credit for trying to make Grant feel she was interested in his work, even though Grant— being a third-level person—figured she probably never read the comics.) After she left he told me he thought she was quite brilliant but most certainly a second-level person. I sort of gave old Page the benefit of the doubt. I figured you HAD to be— as I said—a second-level person to be a television actress. I couldn't imagine saying—with a straight face—all the things Page said on talk shows. When you asked her about ANYONE in "the business," she always said, "Oh, he's a really nice guy and a really great person to work with." On the Johnny Carson show she actually said that *Classified Ads* had "a lot to say to women today" (I mean, that's close to saying that *Sheriff Lobo* or *Happy Days* had "a lot to say to women today"), and on the Mike Douglas show she said that Bob Goldstein, the producer of *Classified Ads* (who I personally knew Page thought was "the biggest bastard in the business"), was "like a second father to her". When she said that, Grant and I, being third-level people, hooted, and Grant said, "God, a clown minister and Bob Goldstein as her two father figures!" When she called to ask how we thought she had come off on the show, we dished her so much about saying Bob Goldstein was like a second father to her that when she went on *Merv Griffin*, she went back to saying he was "a really nice guy and really great to work with."

Yeah, you had to force yourself to be a second-level person to survive in television and, I knew now, in this world.

Should I contact Page? Would there be any publicity if Page Bloom's do-nothing sister ended up dead? I didn't think so. I'd be lucky to even make the obituary page of the *Honolulu Star-Bulletin*. I thought about Page's long hair blowing in the wind on her sailboat off Marina Del Ray and about how she had taken me to Joe Allen's and introduced me to John Travolta and Roy Scheider without even acting embarrassed about the fact I was related to her and was still wearing sixties bell-bottom jeans and an Indian blouse. I thought about her laugh, her insecurity about herself even though *Variety* had called her a "major new talent." Yes, so I SHOULD contact her—of course not to say good-bye, because you can't call up someone three thousand miles away and say, "This is good-bye." Especially Page, who had a tendency to go hysterical or to ignore or laugh off anything she didn't want to hear to PREVENT herself from going hysterical. I could just see her holding up production for a week, going berserk or saying, "Come on Lola, babe. You don't mean that." Sweet Page . . . Sweet Page, who told me, when I was twelve, WHY I was bleeding every month, when Helen had said it was "just something I would have to live with for about forty years" without telling me ALL women had to live with it and why. Sweet Page arranged for me to meet John Wayne before he died. Even though we both thought he was a conservative bastard, we both knew how many Saturday afternoons I had spent in dark theaters loving him. Sweet Page, who walked off the set and was ready to fly to Hawaii when Grant called her and told her about the wrist-splitting episode. Page sent me clothes. Sweet Page often cried at night because—being on the VERGE of being a third-level person—she knew deep down that a million actresses could play Sunny on *Classified Ads* and that the show wouldn't change the world, make her sister well again, or even put a new or original thought into anyone's head. Sweet Page, who knew it wasn't fair that she got thirty thousand dollars an episode while families only a few miles away from the studio were starving or on welfare. Yes, I should call Page, say something cheerful—not manic or depressive—so she would know I was happy when I died and know that it was not because Grant didn't want me or because Page was a fucking success while Lola Bloom not only didn't contribute anything to the world but made the world harder for the people who did.

I called the number of the phone on the set. "Is Page Bloom shooting or in her trailer?" I asked. Naturally I got the whole bit about who is this calling and how did I get this number. Finally, they rang Page's trailer, and of course Page didn't answer it, but it was least Anna, her assistant, rather than some dumb makeup person. It's really rotten luck when you're suicidal and the one person you'd like to contact is one of the hardest people in the world to get hold of. Anna (who at least knew who I WAS) said that Page was there, but to "make it quick" because she was going to be called on stage in a second.

"Hi, Lola, babe," she said in her familiar trained voice.

"Hi," I said carefully. "Uh . . . what classified ad are you answering today?"

"Well"—she laughed a little—"this week I answer an ad that says, 'Sweet, friendly dog free to good home,' and it turns out to be this enormous Great Dane that wrecks my apartment and makes me split up with the guy I met through last week's ad, which said, 'Will do any reasonable odd job,' so I get rid of the Great Dane, and then I realize that I miss him, so I rush to the pound and pick him up and bring him home again. God, you should see this dog they have! This is the first scene I've ever done with an animal."

"Are they going to have a Great Dane on *every* episode from now on?"

"I don't know. I haven't seen next week's script." She paused, then said a little sadly and defensively, "But this episode has some terrific one-liners in it, and . . ." Her voice trailed off. She knew I wasn't the audience on the Merv Griffin show. She knew she didn't want to (couldn't) justify *Classified Ads* to me. "So what's new with you?" she asked, her voice perking up again.

"Oh, I'm okay. Grant's thinking of getting a motorcycle with a sidecar."

"Why does he want to . . ." Again her voice trailed off. Too many times she had made the mistake of asking Grant or me why the hell we did whatever it was we did at the time. When she came to our wedding and saw our costumes, she had asked, "Why in the fucking hell?" but after that she just gave up. She at least (unlike Helen), accepted and just didn't bother to understand why, and she was smart enough to know she probably wouldn't.

"So anyway," she said, "why the midmorning call?"

"I was thinking about you," I said.

"Are you drinking?" I tended to call Page when I was drinking and Grant wasn't around to enjoy it with me.

"No," I said calmly. "I just wanted to say that . . . that . . ." This time MY voice trailed off.

"What?"

"That I'm happy, and . . . I love you."

"You're drinking," Page stated. "Love me, I believe, but *happy?* When you're depressed you aren't happy, and when you're not depressed, you're too crazy to bother to call me and tell me so."

"Well, there's always a first," I said.

"Truly?" she asked hopefully.

"Truly."

"That's terrific! [Everyone in Hollywood in 1983 said "terrific"] You sure you're not drinking?"

"No, really not. I . . . ."

"Oh, sorry, Lola," Page cut in. "They want me on stage. gotta go. Love you too. Bye."

I slowly hung up the phone. Page's voice would be the last voice I'd hear.

I unplugged the phone in case some of our concerned friends discovered their drug bottles empty and tried to phone and also because I was afraid some salesperson would phone. If you've just downed a lethal dose of drugs, you don't want to be interrupted by someone asking if you'd like your carpets cleaned for $9.95 a room.

I bolted the door in case someone got scared and decided to come over. I didn't stop to think that a ten-year-old child could break into the house without any trouble. The front door was square glass panes, and a pane could be broken with a small fist very easily.

Then I went to the freezer where there was a fifth of hundred-proof Stolichnaya vodka. If you're going to go, you might as well go drunk. Committing suicide sober takes more guts than I have. If even going to the LAUNDROMAT sober took more guts, I thought, there certainly wasn't any reason to live. If I HAD more guts, I wouldn't need to die. If I were stronger, the future wouldn't terrify me so. But it did. Fact. Lola Bloom's time had run out.

I filled a 7–11 store Big Gulp cup to the top with vodka and went into the bedroom and propped myself up on enough pillows so I could drink the vodka but still be at the correct angle to see Grant's roses on the ceiling.

Very systematically, I swallowed pill after pill with the vodka. The Valiums were great because you could swallow five or six at a time. Motrin was candy coated, so it slid down the throat. Seconal slid down in capsule form. Tylenol Number Three with codeine stuck a little, but the Stolichnaya vodka washed them down, one pill after another. I swallowed the first few without emotion. Then as I took the rest, the tears started to come. Lola Bloom would be gone. A few would feel touched, sad, or guilty, but most would just say, "God, that's too bad. Lola Bloom was really screwed up," and in a couple of weeks, they would forget. Page would come for the funeral and try to keep it out of the press that Page Bloom was Lola Bloom's sister. If she didn't manage to keep it out of the press, the funeral would be a circus where people who didn't even know me would come to stare at Page and ask for autographs. The one disadvantage in not writing a suicide note was that I couldn't say I didn't want a funeral or, if they insisted, that I didn't want my father to do the service. Unfortunately Dillon, the fucking clown minister, would probably do the service in a clown suit with his wife Sally and their two-year-old kid, Free, dress up as clowns, too. Helen would dress up like a mannequin in Saks, and Grant wouldn't go because it would all be too sickening for him. Would he miss me or be relieved that his "problem" with his psychiatric patient had been resolved for him?

My eyelids were getting heavy, but I peacefully thought that it didn't matter. It really, truly didn't matter if they flew in the Reverend Sun Moon to do the service and Prince Charles and Lady Di to break the ground. Lola would no longer exist, and therefore never care about the embarrassing antics of others . . . never care about anything again. It doesn't matter, I thought peacefully. I finished most of the pills before the roses on the ceiling began to spin and change colors. First they turned from burgundy to coral. Then they spun, changing shapes. My eyes couldn't focus anymore. I turned my head to the side and saw the violets on the pillow . . . spinning roses. . . changing violets . . . the beautiful knowledge that nothing mattered anymore. Not one fucking thing.

Chapter

4

Do you have ANY idea what it is like to wake up when you expected to wake up dead? If you reach the point when life and future are scarier than the chance that all those ministers like Billy Graham might be right about hell, you don't want to wake up. I mean, since no one knows the truth about death, there just MIGHT be a hell you could burn in forever. I didn't really believe that, but of course, who knows? It might be a possibility. What I had hoped for was nothing: to cease to exist, to be under general anesthetic for all eternity. I doubt the theories about how you might be born again in Bangladesh, and anyway, I had already done my female cockroach bit on the planet Earth in Hawaii and California. What I wanted was nothing, no feeling, no mind. So you can imagine what a bummer it was to wake up when I was supposed to be dead.

The first sensation I had was this blinding light. It was like lightning that wouldn't stop . . . a strobe light in slow motion. Five or six blinding flashes—then the pain. My head felt like it was being repeatedly bashed in with a ball-peen hammer. I took a breath to yell, "Make it *stop! Make it stop!*" but my mouth was dry, and the room was spinning. I looked for the roses, but everything was white and bright. I was still spinning . . . then blackness for a few seconds, and then the feeling that I had to throw up. I heaved and heaved, my eyes shut, but nothing came up. My mouth felt like sandpaper. I heaved, the room spun, and my head ached. This wasn't the way it was supposed to be. I either wasn't supposed to feel any pain ever again, or I wanted to wake up to bands of angels and Jesus, Clark Gable, Humphrey Bogart, John Wayne, and President Kennedy all saying, "Welcome to paradise, Lola Bloom." I wanted to hear them saying, "You were right, Lola Bloom. Life isn't what it's cracked up to be. Come! We have martinis already made [the thought of Jesus drinking a martini sort of amused me, even then]; let some cold gin run down your throat! Let's celebrate your drunkenness! Here in heaven you don't have to hide in tiny, dark bathrooms and throw up while all those people with nicknames drink Perrier water and judge you!" If there was a heaven, this was not the way it was supposed to be. I wanted either (most likely) simply nothing . . . or heaven . . . not pain, sickness, and life.

"She opened her eyes for a second," said a bored-sounding female voice.

With great effort I opened my eyes again, and the white room was still spinning. I tried to say that I wanted to puke, but a rasping sound came out of my throat.

"Lola? Lola?" said the female voice.

People ALWAYS choose the wrong time to use your first name. Nurses always call me Lola and make me feel young and helpless, while box boys in Safeway call me ma'am and make me feel like a used housewife. Saleswomen in stores look at my check and call me Mrs. Bloom, but nurses always call me Lola. I thought I must be in a hospital.

"Lola?" repeated the female voice.

I finally managed to say it: "I feel like I'm going to puke."

I was quite groggy, and my head felt more and more like it was going to split wide open, and all the devils locked inside it all my life would come pouring out and attack me.

"You just had your stomach pumped. Can you open your eyes?"

Carefully, I opened them again. The room was still whirling, but not as fast as before. The woman WAS a nurse in a white nylon pantsuit.

"I didn't die," I stated rather than asked.

"You're a lucky woman," she said. I looked at her name tag and tried to focus my eyes to read it. Grace Takamoto, R.N. Lucky. Everyone's idea of what is lucky and what isn't is different. Lucky I didn't die. Lucky. Shit.

"Grant?" I asked, wondering how the hell I had managed to live. I felt just like shit. "Grant? Did he find . . ."

"A friend of yours called the ambulance. The driver had to break into your house."

"Which friend?"

"I don't know. All they told me was that she found some drugs missing, knew you were suicidal, called another friend, and he went and looked and found HIS drugs missing, and when they couldn't get an answer at your house, they called the police and an ambulance." (If only I hadn't done that high school wrist-slitting bit, then Lola wouldn't have been thought of as suicidal.)

"Fuck."

"Now, please, Lola," she said gently. I felt a little sorry for her as she had to work with people like me, and could never really understand.

"And Grant?" I asked. She looked a little puzzled. "My husband? Why isn't he here?"

"Oh, your husband. They don't know where he is."

"He's in a bamboo forest," I mumbled. She looked a little confused. "At a wedding," I added. She frowned. "Hiking," I said. Now she was completely mystified.

"Uh . . . your friend will keep trying to contact him. He should be here soon."

"No!" I almost shouted. At that point my stomach gave another heave. "Water," I rasped. "I need water."

She handed me a paper cup. "You'll probably just throw it up," she said comfortingly. "Why don't you want to see your husband?"

I took a gulp of the water, and yes, Grace Takamoto was right. I instantly threw it up. She mopped my chin.

"He . . . he . . . I didn't do it because of him. He doesn't love me when I get crazy. I don't know how to get better. He's going to be pissed off at me for . . . he . . ."

Old Grace looked a little nervous. "A psychiatrist will come in to see you later . . . discuss your options. It would be a good idea if he talked to you and your husband together."

"*No!* I don't want to see Grant! He told me no more crazies. . . . He'll try to cheer me up!"

"So what's so bad about that?" asked Grace.

"It will only remind me that I'm incapable of making *myself* happy," I said.

Grace Takamoto smiled a lame smile and left the room. I looked at the bed next to mine. An ancient Samoan-looking woman was lying unconscious with a tube in her nose. I tried to sit up and pull the curtain, but as I lifted my head, the room reeled again. I hoped the woman next to me would stay knocked out.

God, I had failed again. Lola Bloom couldn't even kill herself right. When ordinary life is so hideous and scary, just *think* of what life is like after you've discovered you can't even kill yourself.

I dry-heaved again, and then the crying started. I didn't want to be "normal." Fact. Grant was tired of craziness. Fact. And the world has no use for someone who doesn't want to do one fucking thing except drink and die. Definite fact. Lola Bloom is sick, I thought. She's dying. They should put her out of her misery.

In that sterile white room, I was breaking. I felt sick, in pain, and panicked. I managed to sit up and reach for the water. The room was only rocking slightly now. I carefully poured some water from the yellow plastic pitcher by the bed. With the room seemingly rocking, it was hard, but I did it. I drank slowly, heaved, dropped the glass, and threw up water all over myself and put my face in the pillow, and sobbed and sobbed and sobbed.

I must have drifted off to sleep, because suddenly I heard Grace Takamoto say, "You have a visitor." I jumped. I wouldn't have wanted to see Robert Redford at that moment. I slowly opened my eyes and turned over in bed, and if you thought I wanted to be dead BEFORE, well, at that moment I wanted to be dead TEN TIMES MORE than I had when I methodically took a lethal dosage of drugs.

Standing there next to the unconscious Samoan woman was my father, Dillon Bloom, dressed in a white clown suit with red polka dots on it and a huge red bow tie. He had an enormous freaky-looking red smile painted on his white face and a Ping-Pong ball nose with a Bozo wig. In his hand he carried a bunch of balloons with happy faces and butterflies on them.

"Lola, baby!" he said as if he were greeting me back from my first semester at college instead of a brush with Mr. Death. He tied the balloons to the foot of my bed, hugged me, and got white greasepaint all over me.

FORTUNATELY, he didn't say something like "Did you hear the one about God and the mental patient?" or anything like that. Grant hadn't told him about the wrist slitting, but had made a wry comment to me about how Dillon would probably come in with a hat and cane and say, "Did you hear the one about God and the razor blade?"

I stared at him without words. He hitched up his red and white polka-dot clown pants and sat down on the bed.

— 74 —

"Why did you do it, Lola?" he asked seriously. I had to laugh. God, to have a fucking
CLOWN sitting on your bed asking you a serious
question when the freaky red smile refused to go
away was so horrible it was funny. "Lola, babe?"

"I hate life," I stated (talking to a clown about
anything serious is simply ludicrous). "Is that good
enough for you?"

"How can you hate life?" He laughed stu-
pidly. "Look at the beautiful world God made for
you. Look at your handsome husband. You have
a mother, sister, and father who love you. You're
so pretty, and you live in Hawaii. Do you know
how many people would love to live in Hawaii?
We're the 'loveliest fleet of islands anchored in any
ocean.' That's what Mark Twain said."

"Fuck Mark Twain. I can't *believe*," I said flatly,
"I simply can't believe you went to seminary and
they didn't tell you that saying shit like that not
only doesn't make a suicidal feel any better but
makes her feel worse."

I remembered Grant's way of cheering me up.
It started because Dillon actually would say the bit
about how "I cried because I had no shoes until I
saw the boy who had no feet," so one day when
Grant and I had a flat tire on the H-1 freeway in a
rainstorm during rush hour, Grant said to me
ironically, "I cried because I had no *feet* until I saw
the man in the Chevy with a flat tire." We used
that a lot, more to make fun of Dillon than to actually cheer ourselves up, but usually making fun
of Dillon did wonders for the morale. "I cried because I had to stand in line for two hours at the
department of motor vehicles, until I saw the

woman who had to talk to a clown about a suicide attempt." I was sure Grant would have said something like that . . . if he'd been there. Somehow, he always could make me laugh, or at least smile on the darkest days. Having a goddamn clown tell you that you should want to live because you're a hop, skip, and a jump away from Waikiki makes you wish you had a gun: first to shoot him, then yourself.

"Where's Grant?" asked Dillon, sounding a little ticked off that I had, even in my hazy state, put down his whole cheerful speech.

"No one knows. He went to a wedding in a bamboo forest and hasn't come home."

"You mean he doesn't *even know?*" said Dillon, soberly twisting his Ping-Pong ball nose.

"No," I said, "and I don't want him to know." I was too weak to get up, but I desperately wanted to be home when he got there. "He'd leave me if he found out."

"I can't believe you would have stayed married for eight years to a man who would *leave* you if you tried—"

"I love him," I stated. "I'm hard to live with. Even Jesus Christ himself would have trouble living with me."

"Hey," said Dillon as if he hadn't heard. "Look at this." He took one of those long skinny balloons out of a pocket in his polka-dot clown suit, blew it up, and twisted it into the shape of a heart. "What does this mean?" he asked as he handed it to me. Not having a pin around, I calmly bit the balloon, and it popped, sticking little pieces of rubber to the white greasepaint he had got all over my face.

"Now, look, I'm sorry," he said. He took a Magic Marker pen out of another pocket and drew a heart on the reverse side of one of the happy face balloons, untied it from the foot of the bed, and tied it to my wrist. I stared at it sullenly. "Lola?" he said. I didn't answer. I couldn't answer.

"Give that to Grant when he comes back. You can't tell me he doesn't love you."

"He does love me." I said simply.

Dillon didn't answer right away. He stood up and reached into another pocket. I almost screamed, *"Don't!"* but I didn't have the energy. He whipped out one of those whistle blowers with the feather on the end. "I know you need to rest now," he said. "Just remember when God created this world he gave human beings the ability to laugh. Let's try to remember it. Also remember he is with you all the time."

I didn't bother to say that I had laughed for the past ten years. Grant was one of the funniest people I'd ever met, but that had nothing to do with this. I almost made the crack that if I had succeeded with the suicide, I'd be a lot closer to God than Dillon was, but I decided that was a bit much. Dillon's orange Bozo wig slipped slightly as he leaned over to kiss me. After straightening it, he blew on the whistle blower, tickled my nose with the feather, and skipped—I'm not making this up, SKIPPED—out of the room.

I knew I had to get out of there, home to the roses, and forget the whole thing. To hell with my fear of pain. When I couldn't take it anymore, I'd just have to find a sure-fire way to end it . . . find some skyscraper to jump off of or get up enough nerve to hang myself. Surviving a suicide attempt, facing the music for what you tried to do, is worse than whatever pain might be involved in a sure-fire way.

Very shakily I got out of bed, but there was no sign of my clothes. I opened the closet and saw there was a muumuu (probably the Samoan woman's) in there. I quickly put it on over my hospital gown. It was huge on me, but when death is on your mind, fashion sort of takes a back seat.

Just as I slowly opened the door to the room, I realized that I was directly across from the nurses' station. Grace Takamoto looked up from her *Woman's Day* magazine and reached for the phone.

"If you *ever* try to leave again," she said in a voice that had lost its caring quality, "we will have you restrained, and that is no fun."

Fuck, I wasn't looking for FUN. I wanted to die. I took off the muumuu and went back to my bed. My head still ached, and my body felt as if it had just run the Boston marathon. Then I heard Grant's voice. "I'm Lola Bloom's husband." He sounded scared and breathless. I wondered who had told him what. I could act normal if I needed to, so ignoring the fact that the room began to sway a little, I sort of sat up.

Grant came in with his usual springy step. His eyes were still beautiful, but full of tears.

"Hi," I said in a rather low-key voice.

"You took drugs from Annie, Fran,

Maryanne, and God knows who else," he stated, then burst into tears and put his head on my breasts, and while I stroked his hair he cried and cried and cried.

Finally, when he was able to speak, he looked up at me and said, "You promised . . . you promised there'd be no more . . ."

I held his head. "You're so strong," I said, "so amazing, wonderful . . . and . . . and I feel like that insect . . . a small insignificant insect who wants to die before someone steps on her and squishes out all the guts she has."

"Shit," said Grant, "if you really *are* that female cockroach of a woman you keep describing yourself as, and if I really *am* so fucking wonderful and brilliant, why the hell do I love you? What the shit am I doing with you?"

"I suit your purpose. Next to me, your sidekick, you feel even stronger."

"You're full of it, Lola."

"Okay, you loved me because I was entertaining until you found out that I wasn't just flamboyant . . . that I was . . ."

"If it was only the euphoria I loved," Grant interrupted, "I would never have spent all those hours taking care of you when you couldn't get out of bed. I lived with you for two years before we were married. I knew what I was getting into. I loved *you*. I still love you. I loved you so much then, I thought I really could take this seesaw life forever. After ten years, I found out no one can. I was burned out." He paused. "But . . . but I'll stay with you because—"

"Stay with me!" I shouted so sharply that it made me heave again. "You're making me sound like some kind of fucking responsibility."

"You *are* a responsibility, dammit!"

"Well, I don't *want* to be a responsibility. I want to be a lover, a wife . . ." I started to cry. "And I *always* felt I was a responsibility, and that made me crazier, and I can't get better if I know you're hanging around because I'm a responsibility. But with you, I'll . . ." I paused. "If I don't get better, I'll always be *someone's* responsibility, and I can't get better unless . . ." I stopped crying. For the first time in a long time I didn't want to die. I wanted to be well and happy for the man I loved. I knew I'd have to leave him for a while. What I needed to do was kill the frightened, useless Lola Bloom, and maybe—without Grant—I could kill the scared child, Lola Bloom, without killing myself.

Grant put a finger to my lips. There were tears in his eyes again. "I love you, Lola Bloom," he said.

"That's what you say when you're leaving me."

"I won't. Don't worry."

I stroked his hair for what seemed a very long time. Finally, I said, "You've got to."

"Huh?"

"You've got to . . ." I paused for a second. I still felt sick, and I wanted to cling to his shirt and make him promise never to leave me, to always take care of me, but I knew that that couldn't be. "You've got to . . . leave me."

"I'm not going to." He looked at me as if I really WAS the helpless child of my depressions. "Lola, you can't . . ."

"Can't manage without you. That's what you're going to say. Well, I've *got* to learn to manage without you because . . . because . . . . Well, I know I'm sick, but . . . well, I'm not stupid. I've read about manic-depressives, and we don't get better, but we can be stabilized, and . . . ."

"I thought you didn't want to be stabilized. We talked about lithium, and—"

"I didn't want to do the lithium bit because I thought you wouldn't love me if . . . . Well, you see, you make it too easy for me to be crazy. I have to try it without you. I have to."

He sat for a long time holding my hand. Finally, he said, "I do love you, and I don't know about splitting up, but on the other hand, you do *need* to get better. You *shouldn't* be dead, and I shouldn't have to come home to blood and rolled-up eyeballs. But I guess I'm not helping. Yeah, I do love you when you're crazy, but I know you're a person and not just an interesting novel." He got up and walked to the window. I tried to join him, but the room was still sort of rocking. I lay back. After a long time he said, "You tried to kill yourself this morning, and a few hours later, you decide you want me to leave you. Just think about it a little longer."

"If I do, I might change my mind, and we both know . . ." I didn't finish the sentence. It's hard enough telling someone you HATE to get the fuck out of your life, and not only did I not hate Grant, but I loved him as a lover, a friend, a brother, a father, and a husband. I looked at him leaning against the windowsill, and saw the lights of Honolulu blinking behind him. It was a different view than we saw from the house, but it was the same city. I knew I either had to cry or laugh, and I'd done enough crying for the day. I wanted Grant to make me laugh before he left me.

"My father came to see me," I said, knowing that the subject of Dillon always made Grant laugh.

Grant smiled for the first time since he came into the room. "He didn't wear . . ."

"He did."

"Fuck. I'll *kill* him," Grant laughed.

I pointed to the balloons tied to the foot of the bed. Grant turned around and saw them for the first time. "I think I'm going to be sick," he said, smiling.

"Think how you'd feel if you were *already* ready to throw up before he even showed up."

"He came to his daughter's bedside after a suicide attempt wearing a goddamn *clown outfit?*"

"He twisted a long skinny balloon into a heart, but I bit it."

"Amazing."

I held up my wrist, and Grant untied the happy face balloon with the Magic Marker heart on the other side. I saw him glance at the razor scar from the earlier suicide attempt. His eyes were sad for a second. He reached into his pocket and pulled out his Swiss Army knife and flipped out the corkscrew. Then, one at a time, he popped every fucking happy face balloon. He took a corner of the sheet and whiped the white greasepaint off my face.

Grace Takamoto came rushing in, not having the slightest idea why she'd heard a series of bangs.

"Just popping balloons," said Grant.

Good old Grace looked a little sorry for me. "Your father left one at the nurses' station," she said. "I'll bring it to you."

"Thanks," said Grant cheerfully before I could say anything. Grace returned with the balloon, and Grant popped it while it was still in her hand. I laughed. Grant had made me laugh! Grace looked seriously worried, and Grant casually closed his Swiss Army knife and put it back in his pocket. Grace sort of backed out of the room.

"She's probably going to work on seeing if she can get you locked up too," I commented.

Grant smiled, and Grant—forever the raconteur—started to tell me about the wedding in the bamboo forest and why he didn't get back until dusk. I knew from his tone of voice that he was trying to force cheerfulness, and, well . . . one of the reasons I had managed to live as long as I had was that Grant actually COULD cheer me up. I mean, he couldn't accomplish the biggie—make me love life in general—but he had always pulled me out of my dark holes.

"Well," said Grant, ignoring the No Smoking sign and lighting up a Dunhill, "we all hiked about six miles up into the Koolau Mountains to get to this bamboo forest that Hugh and Carolyn had their hearts set on to get married in."

"What did they wear?" I asked. (Because we always made jokes about how they were "so sixties," we always asked each other what they had been wearing the last time we saw them.)

"He wore a Nehru jacket."

"A *Nehru jacket!* Nobody wears—"

"You're forgetting that the last record they bought was the Beatles' *White Album*, and Carolyn actually plays "Blowin' in the Wind" on the guitar at parties."

"Got you."

"Anyway, *no one*—except Carolyn and Hugh— was the least bit revved up about the hike. Mary-anne was practically limping, but Carolyn and Hugh in their Indian sandals were doing 'just fine.' Well, we finally got up to the bamboo forest, but that wasn't quite good enough for Carolyn. She wants to find this special spot where she and Hugh first fucked, so she goes zipping off the trail, and all ten of us follow her dutifully, and in about fif-teen minutes, we're *hopelessly* lost."

Since I was feeling a little better, I could say with a little of my old cynicism, "I wish Annie had been invited. She must have been the one who found the empty drug bottles and called the am-bulance. Then I'd be hopelessly dead, and I wouldn't have to go through that boring proce-dure of getting my life back together . . . or the pain of having to say good-bye to you."

"Please, don't talk about that now."

"It's going to happen. We're hurting each other too much."

"It's a good thing Annie is such a shitty hiker. She's even worse than you are. She wouldn't have gone to the wedding if she'd been the maid of *honor!*" He stubbed out the Dunhill, took a flask from his hip pocket, and poured some gin into the yellow plastic cup. He handed it to me, and for probably the first time in my life, I shook my head.

My stomach felt so awful, I couldn't even drink
. . . couldn't even THINK about drinking. "Tell me
the rest of the story. I love your stories," I said.

Grant took a swig of the gin and tenderly
brushed a strand of hair out of my eyes. He smiled,
but there were tears in his eyes. "We were *hopelessly* lost for like *six hours*. We wandered through
ironwood forests, along ridges. Maryanne is afraid
of heights and actually freaked out, and Hugh had
to throw some water on her from his canteen to
get her to shut up. Finally, we bumped into a couple of Sierra Club volunteers who told us to follow
the red flags, so we followed the red flags for about
two miles, and then they suddenly stopped. We
went around some trees to see if they continued,
and we discovered that not only had we followed
the red flags in the wrong direction, but looking
for the next one made us lose the red flags altogether.

"As it was just beginning to get to be dusk, we
just *happened* to stumble onto a dirt road that led
to a house *with a phone*. So we all gulped down
water and used the phone to call people for rides.
If I hadn't called Jake, I might have called Annie
and learned about the drugs sooner . . . and have
been here sooner, but Bob was the one person who
you forgot to hit. *Anyway*, after we finished calling, Carolyn and Hugh suddenly remembered that
they had forgotten to get married, so that guy from
the Church of the Holy Trinity—who still wears his
hair in a ponytail and still wears his robes to Ala
Moana Shopping Center—married them right there
in the house, and the only person who cried at the

wedding was the lady who let us use the phone, so Hugh and Carolyn let her sign the license as one of the witnesses, and then she served us all guava juice and cookies."

I smiled. I realized what had just happened. Grant—because he was Grant—had made me smile only a few hours after I had tried to bump myself off. I knew I couldn't live like that. It's like being a drug addict. I couldn't manage life without Grant, and the addicts couldn't live without heroin.

"I love you," I said.

"I need you," he said. "I'm scared of you. I want you. I don't want you."

"You've got to leave me," I said simply.

Grant didn't answer. He just took me in his arms and clung to me. Good old Grace Takamoto came in with a sleeping pill in a cup. "Try to swallow this," she said. "If you throw it up, we'll give you an injection."

"Amazing," I said flatly. "They pump all the pills out of your stomach and then just give you more."

"It's time for you to go, Mr. Bloom," said Grace.

"I'm Mr. Rosenberg," said Grant, getting up.

"Humm, too bad," Grace mumbled as she walked out. "Bloom is such a pretty name."

"That's why she kept it, goddammit!" yelled Grant, but she didn't hear. "I love you, Lola Bloom," he said to me and kissed me tenderly on the mouth and walked, with his dancelike steps, out the door.

I turned off the lamp and looked out at the stars. I remembered Grant waking me up at four in the morning and leading me out to our rickety back porch and showing me the Southern Cross. From Hawaii, you can actually see the Southern Cross. I did love Grant, and it's hard to let go of so much love and so many years in an instant, but then I remembered that twelve hours earlier, I'd been prepared to give up a life.

The sleeping pill was just beginning to take effect when the phone rang. I jumped and let it ring a second time. Friends would know better than to call, so it had to be either my mother or Page. I looked at the time and figured it was just after eleven in California. I didn't want to talk to Helen, but there was a chance it might be Page, so I picked up the phone on the third ring. It was Page.

After many tears she demanded, rather than asked, what I was going to do.

"I don't understand?"

"You can't go through the rest of your life scaring the hell out of people, drinking, and waiting for . . . God knows *what!*"

"I know."

"Huh?"

"That's why I tried to kill myself."

"You have other options. I know you don't like the idea of taking lithium, but if you smoothed out some of those highs and lows, you could put your life together."

"I know."

"You *know?*"

"Yes. I asked Grant to leave me."

"But you can't get along without—"

"I've got to *learn*. Grant feeds my madness."

"You've got a point there. I never did like the way he cheered you on the night you rearranged the furniture in the Thai House and gave Valentines to everyone in there."

"It was Valentine's day."

"Yes, Lola, I know, but everyone—"

"I'm not everyone, and that's what Grant loved, and if I'm going to be anything but dead, he's . . ." My voice was starting to break. I cleared my throat. "He's got to leave."

"I want you to save your life, but you're sounding like a housewife who has just read her first issue of *Ms.* magazine."

"You don't want me fucking *dead*, do you? He wouldn't love me if I was on lithium. I'd bore him out of his mind."

Page sighed. "Do what you have to do to save your life, Lola. Because I love you, okay? That's one good reason right there."

"Why?" I asked, genuinely interested. I really had her there. "You'd feel terrible for a few weeks, but then you'd get on with your life and wouldn't miss me much. We hardly see each other. I . . . don't . . ."

"You're my *sister*, and you're a human being, and you're smart and pretty . . ."

"I've known that. I want Grant, I need Grant, you have no idea how fucking hard it is for me to give him up."

"I do," Page said seriously. "And I think you're even stronger than you think you are."

"I hope so."

"I love you, Lola."

"I love you too."

I hung up the phone slowly. The room was beginning to look fuzzy. I wanted to get up and run naked in the wind. I didn't want to get a "good night's sleep" like a good girl and be strong and save myself. I closed my eyes, sad because I knew there would be a morning, and I'd have to start being strong. It's more entertaining to be crazy.

Chapter

You bet your ass there was a morning. First, a cheerful good morning at SIX, then something on a tray they CALLED breakfast, and then Grace Takamoto's morning replacement, Nadine Kim, asked me if I'd like to take a shower.

"Do you have a razor?" I asked just to scare her a little. "I'd like to shave my legs."

"Well, I'm afraid they said that . . . uh . . . What I mean is . . . well, one of the nurses could . . ."

"Never mind. I was just trying to shake you up."

"Pardon?"

"No, I don't want to take a shower." I was still groggy from the whole experience. Little Nadine gave me the menu cards to check food preferences on, and I felt so out of it that I didn't even know what I was checking. (It turned out to be true, because when the lunch tray arrived, on it was a covered plate and a bowl of Hawaiian lomi salmon. "Oh," I thought, "I must have ordered a Hawaiian plate lunch," so I took the cover off the plate, and on it sat one lonely boiled potato with parsley on it. Yes, I had definitely been out of it when I'd checked the menu. Every meal was a similar surprise.)

Little Nadine pulled my curtains shut, and from what I heard I gathered that she was bathing the unconscious Samoan woman.

Dillon and Sally arrived at about nine. FORTU-NATELY, they weren't wearing their clown outfits. Sally did have a butterfly balloon, which I stabbed with the fork from my breakfast tray and said simply, "Thank you."

"You didn't have to do that, Lola," said Dillon, who was always quite protective of Sally because he knew Page and I thought she was just this side of being a total idiot.

"Lola, honey," said Sally, "you are *so fortunate* that that friend of yours . . . . What I mean to say is it would have *crushed* me and *destroyed* your father if you had died!"

I decided not to dignify this with an answer, so I just stared out the window.

"We're going to pray for you every night," she continued. "What was . . . ? What made you so desperate?"

"The devils in my head," I stated.

"Now, don't even joke about that, Lola."

"I'm not joking. I saw *The Exorcist*."

"Lola, *please*," said Dillon again.

Sally took out a notepad from her purse and drew a line down the middle. "Now, let's list all the good things in your life on this side." She printed "Good" in kindergarten printing, "And we'll list the bad things on this side, and I'll bet ya five bucks you'll have many more good things than—"

She didn't get to finish because, without a word, I took the paper and silently tore it in half.

"Please, Lola," said Dillon, a little softer and looking worried. I guess his clown minister training hadn't covered people who don't think clowns in hospitals are cute, or people who can't relate to optimists.

"Page told your mother not to come," said Sally with a slapped-on smile. "She made a plane reservation as soon as she heard, but Page talked her out of it."

"Oh, yeah?" That was the first cheerful, cheering-up thing Sally had said to me all year.

God, my mother. Helen Bloom. I guess it's time for some basic facts about my relationship with Helen. You know, the it-always-goes-back-to-the-mother bit.

In a short sentence, she hated Grant for allegedly turning me into a hopeless, crazy alcoholic. She never even bothered to get to know Grant, and I was pissed off by the fact that I was lying here in Queen's Medical Center, and she would definitely see that as absolute proof of her suspicions. Even a quack psychiatrist knows that suicides go back further than a marriage at twenty-five. It could be any number of things all jumbled up; in some cases it is chemical, in mine it was both. It could have been the fact I was "Nickname: none" in high school; it could have been that I lost my virginity to Mr. Shaftner, my English teacher, in the bushes; it could be that I came from a fucking broken home;

it could be "alleged" jealousy because Page was a big television star and Grant was a famous cartoonist while I had trouble getting the next-door neighbors to remember my name; or it could be that something was wrong inside my brain (like something is wrong in the body of someone who has a heart condition) that was activated by a combination of events. Why do people blame manic-depressives for their illness when they don't blame diabetics for theirs? Who knows? It's just that there were so many things year after year that had turned me from the smiling baby in the antique picture frame on Helen's dresser into the woman with frightened eyes who stared out the window of Queen's Medical Center and watched the ships enter Honolulu Harbor.

Helen married my father in 1945 in San Diego, California. They bought a neat little 1930s California-type house in Coronado across the bay from San Diego. Now they have a bridge across the bay, so there isn't much magic about Coronado for me, but when we were little, they had huge old slimy ferryboats. Page and I ALWAYS remembered to bring bread crumbs, and we'd jump out of the car as soon as it stopped on the ferry. We'd toss the crumbs to attract the sea gulls. Sometimes a navy ship would pass near enough for us to wave at the sailors.

Page was born in 1946, and I was born in 1949. At that time, my father sold insurance just like Robert Young in *Father Knows Best,* and my mother wore white gloves and aprons and pearls around the house just like Beaver Cleaver's mother. We had bikes, skinned knees, ballet lessons, trick-or-treat, Mickey Mouse Club, Brownie Scouts, swimming lessons at the Hotel Del Coronado pool (where supposedly the Duke of Windsor met Wallis Simpson), and basically (I hate people who say "basically" a lot) all the things that parents in the fifties thought were essential to making the kids happy, normal, healthy adults. Obviously, just a fantasy.

The shit really hit the fan when my grandmother died. As she was driving along the Pasadena Freeway in Los Angeles one day, her Mercedes just exploded. I mean, she was just driving along with a full tank of gas, and the damn thing just exploded like a neutron bomb. No one ever figured out why. Terrorists? Hell, no. I mean, she was just a nice little old lady, not connected to crime or drugs or anything.

Now, my grandmother lived in Beverly Hills and was the widow of Irving Adrian, the legendary movie producer. When Helen's mother's car exploded, the entire Irving Adrian estate (except for the Mercedes, of course) went straight to Helen Bloom. At that time, Page and I were too young to comprehend just how much money ten million dollars was, but we did get the message that as long as we lived with Helen Bloom, we'd never have to shop for clothes at Sears, never have to buy stuff on sale, and never have to eat at Howard Johnson's ever again.

Helen instantly put our nice little three-bedroom, two-bath house up for sale and bought what was just this side of being a mansion on Margarita Avenue. It even had one of those little blackamoors holding a ring to hitch your horses to in front of it. Dillon removed the old darkie the first day we were there.

I think Dillon was the happiest of all about the Irving Adrian estate. Even after the inheritance taxes there was still a bundle.

One night after we moved into the big house, Helen was in bed reading, and Dillon climbed in beside her and started nibbling her ear. Old Helen is actually one of those people who say, "Not tonight, dear, I've got a headache," and she doesn't understand or realize that she is being a cliché. Usually, Helen was a regular second-level person, but in the area of sex, she was down at level one. People on level one actually say, "Not tonight dear, I've got a headache." Level-two people are terrified of being a cliché and say anything *but* "Not tonight dear, I've got a headache." Third-level people say it because it's funny. Anyway after "Not-tonight-I've-got-a-headache" didn't work she tried the You-have-to-get-up-early-for-work excuse, and Dillon stood up naked and raised both arms over his head and said, "No!"

"No?" Helen was pretty confused.

"I'm not going back to Grand Pacific Insurance. I quit."

"You *quit?* Whatever for?"

"Why should a man with ten million dollars go into the Siberian salt mines of Grand Pacific Insurance?"

Helen gathered her bed jacket around her. "Uh . . . just because you should. Husbands are *supposed* to work."

"Jesus, you couldn't have thought I *liked* working at Pacific Insurance. It was just my *job!*"

"I never thought about liking or disliking a job."

"Maybe because you never had a job." He sighed. "I'll go to work here," he finally said. "I've dreamed of roses all up and down each side of the driveway. I want to fill the garden with daisies; I want to go to lunch in a white suit at the El Cortez Hotel and not give a damn about being back to the office and punching the clock; I want to be able to get up and look at the stars at midnight and watch them until dawn; I want to make love to you without worrying about setting the alarm; I want to go to Lola's school May Day program and sit with all the mothers and snap pictures."

Helen stared at him as if he had said he wanted the atom bomb tested in Coronado. "You want to do *what?*"

"I never mentioned anything like Rolls Royces, Caribbean cruises, or silk shirts!" Dillon almost shouted. "But I don't think I should have to go back to policies and wrongful death suits!"

"You can just forget about quitting," she said. "How would it look if I had an unemployed husband!"

"I had an unemployed wife, and that didn't seem to bother *you!*"

The shouting went on so long and loud that Page and I both heard it. This was in 1954 when Page was eight and I was five. Neither of us could understand why Helen was so livid about Dillon's sudden interest in horticulture, but it was really true that in the fifties, if a guy lived off his wife's money, he was simply being a leech rather than "not being macho." I know if Helen, Page, and Dillon all kicked off, and I inherited the ten million dollars,

I wouldn't have cared if Grant had wanted to quit doing *Mr. Macho*, but this was Helen, and this was 1954.

"How can you want to do this and still consider yourself a *real man!*" Helen screamed.

"It takes a *real man*," Dillon shouted back at her, "to have the guts to do it."

"Or," said Helen icily, "a leech."

Seeds for divorce were definitely planted.

Years later Page wondered if Jane Wyatt would have thrown Robert Young out of the house if he had stopped selling insurance, and I pointed out to her that Robert Young only did it to support his family like Dillon did, so he'd probably want to quit, too.

"Well," she said, "Robert Young always looked pretty cheerful when he came home from work, and Dillon always looked like he had just been run over by a Rototiller."

"Well, anyway, Jane Wyatt wasn't the only daughter and soul heir to the Irving Adrian estate."

When Helen discovered that Dillon was really SERIOUS about growing roses (she figured it out when about fifty rosebushes were delivered, and she called Dillon's office, and they said he no longer worked there), she filed for divorce.

At five, you just think of your parents as parents, and unless they throw platters at each other in front of you, you don't perceive "marital problems." Of course there were other problems in the marriage, and Helen was just using the I-want-to-plant-roses notion as an excuse. I do know there were differences as to what they should do with the money, just like that TV show where some guy gets a million dollars and each week someone's life is ruined by "having too much money." Shit. Dillon wanted to buy a yacht and actually have us take a year off from school and sail the South Pacific. Page and I thought that sounded just great, but Helen, of course, nipped that right in the bud by giving us a look that indicated she thought that was the most jack-shit idea in the history of mankind.

Dillon really didn't feel too upset about the divorce either, so there MUST have been other problems, and the fact that he moved in with Sally, the secretary for the real estate woman who sold us the big house, THE VERY DAY Helen kicked him out of the house, indicated to us—or rather to Page, who told me—that Dillon had probably been "shaking the springs" with her and was glad Helen kicked him out for wanting to grow roses and not for fucking around.

Then Dillon and Sally just disappeared. Vanished. Helen never mentioned him, and if we did, she would shrug and say she had no idea where he was and that she had no respect for a man who didn't communicate with his own children.

Helen, unfazed, continued on with the life she was brought up in. She went to "the club" for lunch, bridge, tennis, and so forth, gave cocktail parties and dinner parties, had her hair done, bought jewelry, furniture, and a Rolls Royce.

We had no idea where Dillon and Sally had gone. The only thing we knew was that Helen had settled five hundred thousand dollars on him. Having no conception of money, I had visions of Dillon traveling the country as a hobo with a stick over his shoulder with his belongings tied in a cloth. The first Halloween he was gone, I dressed as a hobo in memory of him. Helen had bought me a very expensive bunny outfit and was a little pissed off. When I told her it was because Dillon was probably a hobo, she explained to me exactly how much five hundred thousand dollars was, and that shattered that fantasy, but I still dressed as a hobo, and the next year the bunny costume was too small, so Helen gave it to the Goodwill.

It was the next Halloween that I first seriously thought about death. Helen had put us in the most expensive school in San Diego, Kerrybrook Academy for Girls, and they had a Halloween party at which they gave a prize of a Whitman's Sampler to the person with the most original costume. I had this idea that Page and I would go as a clothesline; each of us would be a pole with a rope tied to our necks. Then we would hang all kinds of clothes on it and split the Whitman's Sampler. Page wasn't too hot to trot on that idea (she wanted to be something boring like a princess), but she was bright enough to perceive the idea as original. That night I had a nightmare that we were walking down the middle of Margarita Avenue with Helen's Dior dresses and Chanel suits hanging from the rope. In the dream, a motorcycle cop came screeching around the corner and rode straight toward us. One of the Dior dresses flapped in his face, and he rode right into the rope at sixty miles an hour. I saw Page's face turn blue as the cop kept weaving back and forth with the Dior dress covering his face, and I felt—in the dream—the noose tightening around my neck. I couldn't breathe, yet

I felt no pain as the cop dragged us behind his motorcycle. I tried to take a breath, and I woke up shaking. I looked up at the canopy of the bed and thought about dying and all the stuff I'd miss if I died. It was at that moment that I realized there wasn't really ANYTHING in life that I would truly mind missing. At six, you don't think of drinking, drugs, and sex as anything you would EVER do; college sounded boring; and I already knew that Kerrybrook Academy for Girls was boring, and Page had told me it didn't get any better each year, as I had hoped it would; getting married sounded boring, because after the wedding, what else is there left to do? Having kids sounded boring because you had to be pregnant and have a gynecologist do all kinds of horrible stuff to you, and then the kid might not even like you. The only two things I realized—at six—I REALLY wanted to live for were that someday I hoped I would learn to ride a motorcycle and that someday I would get to meet John Wayne.

As I lay in Queen's Medical Center with Grace Takamoto guarding the door outside, I thought ironically, No WONDER I tried suicide. I already knew how to ride a motorcycle, and Page had arranged for me to meet John Wayne before he died.

It wasn't until I was ten and Page was thirteen that Helen broke the news to us that Dillon was a Congregational minister living on a banana farm in Kahaluu, Hawaii. I mean, she just didn't announce out of the blue that Sally and Dillon had lived off some of the money while Dillon went to seminary in San Francisco, then went to Hawaii and bought a banana farm in Kahaluu. He let it go to weeds because to his horror he learned that if you actually want to GROW bananas, after each tree bears fruit, you have to go out and hack it down so it can grow again and bear more fruit. He and Sally started their church (the clown bit would come a little later—in the early seventies, of course).

Even though Page never reached the third level of irony, she wasn't stupid. One day she noticed that when we were home from school, or on Saturdays, Helen made sure she always got her greasy hands on the mail before we did. Since we were too young to receive love letters she might want to censor, Page just wondered. One Saturday after she told me this, we sat on the curb and waited for the mailman, and Helen came out and nervously stood beside us. There was nothing in the mail but bills and a letter from Page's pen pal in Ohio and a note from Kerrybrook Academy announcing the annual father-daughter dinner.

"Why don't you want us to see the mail?" Page asked directly.

"You just saw the mail," answered Helen, doing her very best to sound preoccupied.

"But . . . but . . . you came out and waited *with* us. You don't like to walk all the way to the end of the driveway."

"I always hope for letters from friends," she snapped.

"That's not so," stated Page.

"What's not so?"

"You're hiding something."

Old Helen looked at us. Her lips were sort of trembling. "You'd never be able to understand," she said. "You . . . can't, you see."

I was actually feeling sorry for her. I'd never seen Helen cry, and now her eyes were a little misty. "I can't keep it from you forever," she said, and then she sat right down there on the grass in a Pucci dress.

"I don't . . . uh . . . didn't want . . . uh . . . you to find any letters"—she paused—"from your father."

"You know where our father is?" asked Page coldly.

"Yes," she stated, and then burst into tears. Page and I sat on either side of her and stroked her back.

"Let's get off this grass," she managed to say as she began to feel the dew soak through the Pucci silk. We helped her up, as she wasn't as used to getting up from the grass as we were. She was very shaky, and we each held an elbow and walked her down the long, curving drive to our house.

"Where! Where!" I kept insisting during the walk.

"Shut up, Lola," said Page. "She'll tell us. . . . She'd *better* tell us."

"I . . . can't," she almost whispered.

"You'd *better*," said sweet, pretty Page in a threatening tone of voice I had never heard her use before.

Instantly I assumed he was in prison for molesting children or raping poor Mexican women.

"Is he in jail?" I asked.

Helen stopped walking. Suddenly the thought hit her that if we DIDN'T know where he was, we would assume the worst. I couldn't think of anything worse than being in prison for something horrible like torturing victims.

"Is he dead?" asked Page.

"He couldn't be *dead*," I said, "or Helen wouldn't be so worried about getting a letter from him."

We reached the house, and Helen glided onto the back veranda that overlooked the pool, and seemed very interested in what the gardener was doing to one of the rosebushes.

"Tell," stated Page.

"You know why we . . . we . . . uh . . . got divorced?" asked Helen, sinking into a white wicker chair, taking out a cigarette from a silver box on the wicker table and very shakily lighting it.

"Because he didn't want to work?" I asked.

"Because he was screwing around with Sally," Page said definitely.

"*Page!*" said Helen, gently shocked.

"Well, he *was*."

"I'd rather have you say 'having an affair.' "

"Same difference," said Page casually. She leaned against the balcony. "Well," she finally said, "that's no major deal. I mean, I can see why you threw him out of the house . . . not wanting to work *and* screwing . . . uh . . . having an affair, but *why* keep him from *us*? He's not a child molester or anything."

"He found God," said Helen simply.

Page and I stared at each other. "So?" Page said.

"He became a minister and moved to some godforsaken place in Hawaii called Kahaluu."

"So?" This time it was from both of us.

Helen shakily lit another cigarette. "You don't understand. It . . . well . . . it wasn't the fact that he . . . had an affair. *I* was going to be the one to save him. Don't you understand?"

"No," we said, more confused than if she'd told us he was in prison and she was embarrassed.

"When I met your father, I had finished Mills College. I was Irving Adrian's daughter, living in Irving Adrian's house in Beverly Hills, doing . . ." She nervously took a puff of her cigarette. She didn't cry or anything, but her eyes got damp. "Doing nothing. Just going to the right parties so I could get married. I didn't need a career. My father was worth millions of dollars, and . . ." She burst into tears, which really scared us. "There was nothing I was even interested in."

"Couldn't your dad get you into a movie?" asked Page sympathetically.

"Lord, no! I knew how he regarded actresses. They were either . . . mistresses . . . or talented . . . or someone's daughter, and I wasn't talented, and I didn't want to be 'someone's daughter,' and there was *no way* I was going to be a mistress. . . . I mean, I *knew* there were hardworking and talented women out there who made it without a single connection, but no matter *how* talented I was, everyone would always say that I was Irving Adrian's daughter."

"But what does that have to do with why you never told us about our father?"

"I met Dillon at the U.C.L.A. library. I'd gone there to get some information on graduate schools because I was terrified of another day of doing nothing, and there he was . . . playing a guitar on the steps." (When she told us this it was 1959, and she had met my father in 1944, so it wasn't like now. You didn't often see bearded men on library steps with guitars.)

"But his song," she continued, "was pretty . . . well . . . raunchy. I was fascinated. I found out he was a *communist*, and that word always brought shudders around the movie industry. It was before McCarthy, but still . . ."

"McCarthy?" I asked.

"One of the reasons your father tore up his card and started doing something ordinary like selling insurance."

"I don't get it."

"You will in time." She looked terribly nervous. "He was an atheist and just about everything else that my father—even though he was one of the pillars of the decadent film business— wouldn't want for me . . . so I . . . ran off with him."

"That day?" Page looked pretty impressed.

"No, after about six months, and my father cut us off, and well . . . it was what *I was going to do:* my mission. I was going to save him. I was going to turn him around and show my father that . . ." Her face got suddenly very hard and determined—a look we'd never seen in Helen's eyes before. "I had been *right,* and he was a good man. When I was pregnant with Page, and there was a lot of anti-communist talk in the country, I did manage to get him to tear up his card, get a straight job—at Pacific Insurance—and live rather obscurely, because even though my father cut us off financially, he never stopped loving me. We called . . . wrote, and if it ever got out that Irving Adrian's daughter had married a communist, he might have been finished in the movie business. As it turned out, later they did get wind of it, but he died in fifty-one, so they just let it lie." She nervously lit another cigarette. "I made him tear up the card, but I couldn't make him shake his beliefs . . . and the God thing . . . . Well, he wouldn't even listen to it."

"I remember," said Page. "As a matter of fact, he *didn't* believe in God. You and Dillon used to fight on Sunday mornings when you took Lola and me to church."

"It went deeper than that," she said. "He was a *militant* atheist . . . *militant!*" She dabbed at her eyes again. "He said if I didn't stop taking you to church, he was going to call the Committee on Un-American Activities and tell them that Irving Adrian's daughter had married a . . . . But then my father died, and he couldn't do anything."

"But you just said he found God," I said.

"I don't know *what* Sally did. I don't know. It was bad enough he preferred her in . . . well, preferred her, but . . ." Helen started to half sob and half heave, "but *I* was going to be the one to save him!"

"That's still no reason to keep him from us," said Page.

"Then I realized that it was this militance I sort of loved. Then I got confused. Then I got an unlisted telephone number, and . . . I threw away his letters to you. Now he writes only occasionally, but I didn't want you to know how badly I had failed . . . I guess." She looked at us lamely.

"You kept us from our father because you didn't want us to know how you had failed!" screamed Page.

"I know it was wrong, but—"

"Shit! That was *criminal!*"

"Don't say 'shit,' Page."

"Criminal!" she screamed again.

"I just thought—"

"You just *thought.* If you hadn't slipped up and been so obvious about the mail we might have thought that either our father *hated* us or that he was a drug dealer or a child molester, or that he just didn't give a damn!"

"I mean, I—"

"You are a real bitch," said Page icily.

"You watch what you say," said Helen, trying to be strong. Then she weakly burst into tears again.

Page looked over at me. "Are you going to just sit there and say *nothing?*" she yelled at me.

Helen looked up at me—I guess for some kind of compassion or something.

"I want to see my father," I said, calmly.

Chapter

It was the summer of 1959. Dillon Bloom, pastor of the Kahaluu Congregational Church, picked us up at Honolulu International Airport in a VW van that said on the back, "Darkest Kahaluu, Oahu, Hawaii, U.S.A., Earth, Solar System, Universe, Mind of God." We had had a tearful conversation with him on the phone the week before (Helen let us call him) when, occasionally, he lapsed back into the old Dillon Bloom and called Helen a bitch and a cunt. Then he would remember he had found God and learned peace, and would say we should try to "understand her." In a way, I guess, we did. It isn't easy being the only child of Irving Adrian, but on the other hand, it is a lot easier having ten million dollars than, say, to be some Mexican with nine children in a shack in Encinada.

In 1959 Dillon was a true, straight-looking Congregational minister (the long hair would come in about '66, and the clown bit in about '72).

Hawaii sure didn't look like it had in *Blue Hawaii*. We drove by used car lots in relative silence. It is hard enough to think of something to say to a father you haven't seen in five years LET ALONE a father who had turned from a radical atheist to a straight insurance man to a Congregational minister living on a banana farm.

As the car turned toward the mountains, Hawaii started looking a little better. Things got greener. (Dillon did have the wit to point out to us that all the postcard pictures of Diamond Head were taken in the middle of the winter, and that it was truly brown in the summer.) Then we went through two tunnels. Since it was our first time in Hawaii, Dillon sort of acted like a tour guide. He told us how you used to have to drive over these mountains, before the tunnels were put in, on a narrow road that went along the edge of the cliff, and the wind was so strong that sometimes VW bugs just got blown over.

"God . . ." I said enthusiastically, so he would think I appreciated his story.

When we came out of the second tunnel, both Page and I agreed that, no, the postcards weren't lying. Hawaii was the most beautiful place we had ever seen. The mountains on the other side of the island were more like cliffs rising thousands and thousands of feet in the air. It was cloudy where we were, up in the mountains, but you could look down on the ocean and Kaneohe Bay, and the water was a bright blue-green from the sun on it. The air was warm, wet, and sweet. Dillon broke the mood by telling us that they were building a new tunnel closer to Kahaluu, so that it would be more accessible.

"Then maybe it won't be 'Darkest Kahaluu,' "

I said, and Dillon laughed for the first time during our visit.

He said it would be quite a while because they had just had a major cave-in in the new one, and Page looked rather nervously at the tunnel we had just come out of.

To get to Kahaluu in 1959, you had to drive all around the rim of Kaneohe Bay. The tide was out, and small boats were beached on the sand. As the water got deeper way out, it had changed color since we had looked down at it from the mountains. It was now a sparkling dark blue. "You never see the ocean exactly the same color any two times," Dillon told us.

"You mean like there aren't ever two snowflakes alike?" I asked.

"Exactly," said Dillon getting a little less nervous.

We drove through some jungle and then came out on the edge of the bay again. Dillon pointed out what looked like a strip of mud with a hedge growing on it that blocked off a portion of the bay. He said it was an ancient Hawaiian fish pond. We drove through some more jungle, and then we hit civilization again. Well, what I mean is, we came to a store called The Purity Grocery Store. It was a shack with two gas pumps in front of it.

"That's a pretty dumb name for a store," Page commented.

"It used to be a dairy," said Dillon.

"Oh," we said, thinking that that didn't make it much clearer.

The town of Kahaluu consisted of the Purity Grocery Store; a semi-fast-food restaurant that served such bad hamburgers that it really made any 1983 McDonald's seem like Windows on the World; my father's church attached to Sally's gift shop; Kahaluu School; and (since most people drive THROUGH Kahaluu rather than stay there) three filling stations.

Kahaluu really was pretty unbelievable. My father said he chose to live there because of the "bucolic beauty." Well, he was right on that stand. The clifflike windward side of the Koolau Mountains rose in a dark green semicircle around the town. Acres of banana trees sloped up the foot of the cliffs. The mountains, as Page said, actually looked like "pleated cliffs," and in some of the pleats ran waterfalls. Chickens walked, unconcerned about the van, on the edge of the road. Goats grazed in the mushy, wet green pastures. Wide-eyed barefoot children waved, recognizing Dillon's van. Nearing the edge of what Dillon said was his banana farm, a stream twisted and turned.

Dillon told us he had heard somewhere that it was the third worst poverty area in the nation.

"But it's so *beautiful*," said Page questioningly.

"Kahaluu's poverty is well disguised," Dillon said. "You see, instead of being poor in a rotting, freezing Chicago tenement, you're poor under a green tree, near flowers, and a few steps away from a panoramic view of the mountains and ocean. You're poor in a place where the temperature doesn't get below seventy degrees or above eighty. Your kids can swim in the bay, so it's all very pretty, but starving is starving just the same."

"Starving is better than being cold *and* starving," I pointed out, and Dillon agreed.

We drove up the winding road to his house on the banana farm that had "gone to weeds." If he hadn't told me they were weeds, I would have thought we were driving through one of the lushest, greenest, sweetest spots on earth. He told us that when Waikiki started being a big tourist deal in the fifties, the poverty in Kahaluu became a little more visible. As we drove a way up a hill, he pointed out a group of crumbling houses in the distance.

"As hotels were built," he said, "the developers took the beach shacks that once stood in Waikiki and put them on flat-bed trucks and dumped them right over there in the middle of Kahaluu. A lot of the folks then were living in rusting Quonset huts left over from World War Two, and were instantly attracted by the sight of a real house at a very low rent. What they didn't realize was that the houses had just been set down and no one had bothered to connect the plumbing. Well, Kahaluu doesn't have a sewer system, but no one even bothered to dig a cesspool, so all the water and all the shit just ran out into the yards."

"That's what happened in *The Jungle*," said Page, who was always proud of her superior knowledge of literature. "They sold the Polish meat packers houses like that."

"Yeah," I said.

"You haven't read the book," said Page.

I shrugged. "They can't still be like that *now*, can they?" I asked.

"Oh, no. The board of health made the owners dig cesspools and connect the plumbing, and

they watched all the other houses being moved in."
We broke out of the jungle of banana trees, and
on either side of the road were more decaying
houses that stretched along the beautiful "bucolic"
road that led up to Dillon's banana farm.

"Sally isn't home," Dillon said. "She's at the
store. I'll just take your bags in; then I'll give you
a tour of Kahaluu, treat you to a hamburger at
Nakasone's Drive-In, and show you the inside of
the infamous Purity Grocery Store."

When we got back down to the town, he first
stopped at the store, which I soon realized could
have got rid of all its groceries and sold beer, potato chips, Hostess cupcakes, ice cream bars, Cokes,
and motorcycle magazines, and done a fine business. Even people who had to take a bus did all
their serious grocery shopping in Kaneohe, a larger
town about five miles away. The store had rusted
gas pumps in front of it that looked as if they hadn't
been used since the other three stations were built.
It looked like their sole purpose was that they were
a place for old Filipino men to lean against and
converse in Tagalog.

"Look at that," said Dillon pointing to an ancient Chinese woman with a shopping bag limping toward the store. "Look at her feet." Her feet
were tiny. They had obviously been bound. She
was very old and teetered painfully toward the
door. "Five years from now you won't see that
anywhere in the world," he said. "Even in China,
the bound-feet women are all her age or dead." I
stared in amazement.

Then we went across the street to Nakasone's
Drive-In, but after sniffing the greasy air, Page and

I decided to pass on the offer of the hamburger. Instead I had a chocolate milkshake, which was made with canned milk and sucked dogs.

Then there was Dillon's church, which catered to the poor of Kahaluu (a little self-righteously, I must admit). The church was built of dark green wood and stood back from the road. It had a new timber steeple that looked like it had been tacked on as an afterthought. Red torch ginger grew around the steps, and a part-Hawaiian man was mowing the grass. He waved as Dillon got out of the van.

"Eh, dees your keeds, Rev?" he asked.

"Yeah," said Dillon so proudly that I almost felt good in spite of the milk shake. "This is Page," he said, pointing to Page, who was showing—at thirteen—definite signs that she was going to be a blonde "looker" in a couple of years. "And this," he said, pointing to me, "is Lola. Lola, Page, this is Kimo Kamahale, one of our church volunteers."

We smiled and nodded.

"You like see moi?" Kimo asked us, and before we could answer, he said, "You not taste see moi yet?" We shook our heads, so he dug into his pocket and extracted something in a cellophane bag. He took one out. It was about the size of a grape and gray and hard and wrinkled. Yuck.

"Looks like something a rat laid," Page commented out of the side of her mouth. "Are you supposed to *eat* it?"

"The local kids," Dillon cut in, "like it better than candy."

"What is it exactly?" I asked, thinking if I kept

talking long enough he'd forget that we were supposed to taste it.

"Lee Hing Mui," he stated.

"Oh . . ." I said. "I mean, what's it made of?"

"Dried plum." Well, that didn't sound too bad. I guess Page didn't think so either because she bravely tossed one into her mouth.

"Ah . . . ha . . . ah . . . a . . . , and *salt!*" Page managed to say and spit it out. "God, this tastes like a ball of salt."

"Oh," said Kimo jokingly, "no one likes unless they like born here."

"Then why did you give it to us?" I asked, genuinely curious.

"I thought you maybe like were deeeferent."

At that remark, I bravely took one and stuck it in my mouth.

"Watch da seed," said Kimo.

Yes, Page had definitely been right. It tasted like a ball of salt and sugar mixed together. I could feel tears welling up in my eyes, but even then Lola Bloom wanted to be special—or deeeferent, as Kimo said—so I ate the whole thing, slowly, and spit out the seed. Page and Dillon stared at me in total amazement. "Um . . . pretty good," I said casually.

"Hey," said Kimo. "You *are* deeeferent!"

Dillon led us to the gift shop that Sally ran to help support the church. Judging from the looks of Kahaluu, I figured the collection plate turned up about a dollar ninety-eight a week tops.

In front of the store were eight gigantic neon-colored tiki gods that looked like they had been lifted from some Trader Vic's somewhere and spray-painted. "They're to attract tourists driving around the island," said Dillon, seeing Page wrinkle up her nose. Poor Dillon, after not seeing his daughters for five years, this is how they reacted to his tourist attraction. "We're the only highway through here," he added lamely.

Inside the shop Sally was sitting behind the cash register on a stool. I had only seen her once before when we were buying the Coronado house, and being only five then, I hardly remembered her—just a blonde lady behind the desk of the real-estate office. Now—although she was my stepmother—she was STILL just another blonde lady behind a cash register. Her hair was neither long nor short, she was neither beautiful nor homely, neither tall nor short, and later I learned that she was neither totally boring nor interesting.

Later on in life, after I had slit my wrists and was letting them bleed on Grant's Sheraton Waikiki carpet, I had had an image of myself as simply "a Sally." That might have been why I did things like throw soap in the fountain. I had thought that because I WAS a Sally, I had to force myself NOT to be, and maybe that was why I drank—it gave me the synthetic courage to be that rare bird I had always wanted to be.

I imagined that Sally wasn't too thrilled to have us around for the summer. She smiled, but it was the kind of smile you give customers if you wish you were working somewhere else. She was stringing shells to make a lei.

Dillon introduced us to her, and she said that

Page had "nice hair," and that I had "nice eyes," and I said that was a "nice lei" she was making.

"The children of the congregation collected shells with me when we were on retreat in Waimanalo," she said. This was going to be a swell summer, I thought. I glanced around the store. Besides a number of other odd shells, there were some Japanese glass ball floats, which Dillon told us had floated all the way from Japan. They were used to keep the fish nets from sinking, and often one would get loose and the currents would carry it straight to Hawaii. Sally also sold hideous ceramic angels, odd jars, first-day-cover stamps, and stuffed birds. As I peered into a Mynah bird's glass eye, Sally explained that the birds were always smacking themselves to death against the plate-glass windows of Dillon's house, and, not wanting to waste perfectly good dead birds, she would take them to a taxidermist and have them stuffed. "One of our best-selling items," she said, proudly.

She also sold some fairly pretty glass wind chimes, mobiles, cactus plants, and postcards. My favorite was a Hawaiian beauty, nude from the waist up with gigantic breasts, and on it it said, "Greetings from Hawaii: Land of Pineapples." She also had beach towels with surfers and shit on them, and pineapple juice in a water cooler.

Dillon told us that he preached every Sunday to "from three to ten people."

"Not exactly Saint Peter's in Rome," said Page.

"Well," he rationalized, "if you go through your whole life and only change one person's life for the better, you've accomplished something."

Sally smiled that vacant smile again and said she'd drive us back to the banana farm. She was wearing a long yellow and red print muumuu. She gave us each a little cone-shaped shell for a present, and, wondering exactly what we were supposed to DO with them, we thanked her. We drove in a beat-up jeep along the junk-littered, jungle-winding road that led up to Dillon's banana farm—or rather up to Dillon's "property," which once HAD BEEN a banana farm. We rode silently, not being able to think of a single thing to say to Sally.

Both times, later in life, when I tried to kill myself, the memory of that ride came back. Sally, supposedly a nonperson, had somehow managed to change Dillon's entire personality—who was to say whether it was for the better or worse?—and Dillon was saying that if you changed even ONE person's life, your life was worth something. As I methodically stuffed sleeping pills down my throat, I had thought: Lola Bloom, the nonperson, made Grant's life WORSE, not better, and had changed no one's life while living, and might not even by dying.

Sally dropped us off at the house at the end of a long driveway. She gave us the key and told us she had to get back to the store and then drove off into the jungle. Page slapped a mosquito, and I surveyed the house: medium-sized, falling apart.

"Holy cow!" was all I could say when we walked in. I mean, there was Jesus shit all over. They had this rug right there in the front hall with Jesus holding out his hands to little lambs on it with a red background. Feeling kind of funny about stepping on Jesus's face, I kind of walked around it. There were several Bibles lying around, and in the kitchen was a plaque hanging from the wall that said, "The Lord is my shepherd, I shall not want." There were more crosses around the house than you would need for a year-long trip to Transylvania.

On the dresser in the room that was to be ours was a lamp in the shape of praying hands. "God bless us all" was all Page could say.

On the other side of the room was a large picture of Jesus hanging on the cross—well, not exactly of Jesus. It was a close-up of his hand with a nail in it. "She's gotta be kidding," I said. "She expects us to wake up every morning and look at a picture of a hand with a bloody *nail* in it?"

"Hey," said Page suddenly (Page was good at changing the subject at the right times), "I've got a song for you." Page had a neat singing voice. She started doing the J-Fred and sang: "The B.I.B.L.E / Yes that's the book for me! / I stand alone on the word of God / The B.I.B.L.E.!" We both hooted, and then Page taught me the steps to the J-Fred, and we danced and sang "The B.I.B.L.E." all through the house.

Maybe you're beginning to see what happened to Lola Bloom. Maybe you're understanding a LITTLE more where I came from. The story could have been tragic. I could have died at thirty-four, not even knowing why I had lived.

That first summer in Kahaluu I asked Dillon HOW the hell Sally—a nonperson who didn't seem to have a manipulative bone in her body—had accomplished what strong-willed Helen had not: to turn Dillon from a MILITANT atheist to a Jesus freak. I didn't tell him that Page had told me to "grill him like a cheese sandwich," because she was positive that was the first question old Helen would ask at home the second we got out our baggage claim stubs.

Dillon smiled. "She let me get drunk," he said, simply.

"Huh?"

"In trying to turn my life around so old Irving Adrian would accept me, Helen screwed it up by trying too hard. Before we were married, I was a *major* drinker—sometimes even had "lost nights"—but Helen put a stop to that. I figured there was no moral issue at stake. I mean, it wasn't like trying to get me to believe in God or Christianity, so I agreed to cut way down."

"I still don't get it."

"Every time I reached for a second or third drink, Helen would give me one of her famous sideways glances . . . her disapproving look." He frowned at me. "Although I didn't verbalize it at the time, I actually married your mother for her money. I figured old Irving would kick off soon, and the inheritance would be worth a few years in the salt mines of Pacific Insurance."

"Did you love Sally?"

"At first it was just sex, then I found God, and then I loved her."

"But Sally isn't sexy," Page put in. I could see her point. At thirteen Page was already close to being a "10" and had about twice as much personality as Sally did.

"You haven't slept with her," said Dillon simply. As I got older, visions of exotic positions flowed through my mind.

Page shook her head, and Dillon went on. "Sally was real sweet. At first I was glad she wasn't good for me. Liberated from Helen, I'd drink at least a fifth of Jack Daniels every day. I had half a million bucks to blow, so we lived, I drank and grew roses.

"But how did she get you to find God?"

"Sally never brought up the subject of my drinking. If I woke up and didn't remember the night before, she would say, 'Oh, everything was okay, don't worry about it.' She was pretty religious herself, but I really thought I had a good deal because she didn't try to push religion on me the way Helen did. Well, my 'lost nights' got more and more frequent, and finally it got to the point that I woke up in Mexico not remembering *anything* about the last *four days.* I was afraid I'd lost Sally, and I rushed home, and there she was with a minister."

"Sally was sleeping with a *minister?*" Page asked, totally amazed.

"She wasn't *sleeping* with him. She was talking to him, and when I came in, it was really beautiful. There were no harsh words; they both embraced me. I started listening to him, and . . ."

"You ended up in seminary."

"Exactly."

The next month was rather uneventful as there was literally NOTHING to do in Kahaluu. A couple of times Sally and Dillon drove us into Kaneohe for

Chinese food, and every Sunday, I'd put on a pretty dress, socks, and Mary Janes, and Page would put on a pleated skirt, nylons, and white pointed-toe shoes with tiny heels, and we would go to Kahaluu Congregational Church. Since an organ was financially out of the question, there was a beat-up upright piano. We'd sing "Joyful, Joyful We Adore Thee" and "Holy, Holy, Holy" every Sunday. At first I thought they were the only hymns the pianist knew how to play, but I later learned that Dillon believed in democratic churches, so he told the congregation to write down the names of the hymns they'd like to sing, and everyone put either "Joyful, Joyful We Adore Thee" or "Holy, Holy, Holy," and since everyone knew them, that meant Kahaluu Congregational didn't have to fork out for hymnals. Every Sunday they sang them. Page used to try to harmonize to spice things up until someone said, "Eh, you stop dat. I no like you spoil da joyful song," so end of creativity in church.

Dillon's sermons were always about "change," and how "change was always possible." No WONDER his church wasn't mobbed. I could just imagine some poor Samoan woman on welfare with six kids, in a shack with no plumbing, getting all the kids dressed up and coming to church to hear that "change was possible." If Dillon had been any good at all, he would have figured out a way to say exactly HOW change was possible.

The only other kids who lived remotely near the banana farm who would have anything to do with us were the Hammonds—the only other *haoles* (Caucasians) in the valley. Mia, their mother, was overweight, chain-smoked, and was drunk all the time on King George IV scotch. Their father lived in Honolulu and "worked for the electric company" (doing exactly what was never made clear to us). Chrissie was my age, and Bob was a year younger than Page, and I don't think they were any more fond of us than we were of them. Kids never have any choice. You always have to be friends with the people your parents happen to live near. The one thing they had going for them was they had horses. Babe and Huapala weren't exactly Seattle Slew, though. Each was at least twenty years old, and not only did you have to practically beat them to even get them going, but you could just leave them untied in the driveway and come back the next day and they'd still be there. Page, who was more athletic than I was and had actually had a few riding lessons, thought they were a drag, but I was rather fond of them. I could sit behind Chrissie on Huapala's bare rump, slap her a few times, and then we could both close our eyes and let her walk through the fern forests. She knew all the trails, had no strength or desire to run away, and always got tired after a couple of hours, and would just amble on home. When we felt her stop, we'd open our eyes, and there we would be, right in front of the Hammonds' junk-filled garage. Chrissie would dump some food and alfalfa in a tub, and occasionally we'd brush her off or pick pebbles out of her hooves, and then we'd go in the house and get some Twinkies or Pepsi and shoot the breeze with Mia, who—except for an occasional change of clothes—looked like she really never moved from the couch at all. She'd always have her bottle of King George IV and be leisurely smoking her cigarette. She seemed neither happy nor unhappy. If she'd been drinking some, she was often rather entertaining: telling us stories of when she was in 4-H in Kailua in her teens and how she was the Hawaii Junior Calf-Roping Champion. It was pretty hard to imagine Mia (who Page said reminded her of a whale at Marineland) quick enough and light enough to rope and tie a calf. Occasionally, she'd ask one of us to change the channel on the television. (She watched game shows all the time, but didn't even try to guess the answers. I couldn't IMAGINE watching a game show and not trying to guess the answers.) The Hammonds "didn't have two dimes they could rub together," so the kids always wore the same jeans, and Mia bought junk food with food stamps and some of the money Bob and Chrissie's father gave her.

Page commented once that she felt sorry for Mia because she had "nothing to look forward to," and I—for the first time—admitted to Page that, besides learning to ride a motorcycle and meeting John Wayne, I really didn't either.

"But you're going to be pretty when you grow up," she said. "You could get married or even be an actress."

"You've gotta be kidding," I said simply. "I'd be scared to death to get up in front of people and wear a costume. Besides, memorizing all those lines would be pretty boring."

"Well, you could marry someone like Gregory Peck with a sexy deep voice, and when you're married, you get to make love *every day* if you want to."

"Yuck!"

"Yuck? I can't *wait* to lose my virginity."

"Page!" I said, horrified.

"But it's got to be to the right person. He's got to be an older man—I mean, not old like Dillon, I mean, like in his twenties, with experience."

"I wouldn't want to sleep with a man who had made love to lots of loose women. I think there are diseases you can get from doing that."

"No, he would have been . . . like, married before, and his wife . . . well, he couldn't be divorced. I don't think I'd want to lose my virginity to a divorced man, but his wife could have tragically died, and he could turn to me for comfort."

"You're out of your gourd" was all I could say.

One week it rained for three solid days. Kahaluu rain is the kind of rain they have in movies like *Singin' in the Rain,* but which you never see in real life—sheets of it. Pouring water, the kind that if you even take a dash to the car, you're soaked. Other waterfalls came flowing over the pleated cliffs, and the S-shaped stream through Dillon's banana farm rose about two feet, tossing muddy water over its banks, so that it trickled around the limp and unfertile banana trees. The rain pounded on the wide banana leaves, and it was kind of interesting—after coming from cloudless-sky southern California.

One night, when Dillon was reading some Paul Tillich book, Sally was reading the *Reader's Digest,*

I was reading *Wonder Woman,* and Page was listening to *My Fair Lady* on the stereo for the hundredth time, there was a pounding knock at the back door. Outside stood Mia—drenched—with Bob and Chrissie dressed in the same jeans and T-shirts they'd worn for the last four days. "Come in," said Dillon, a little confused.

Mia pushed Bob and Chrissie into the kitchen, where they stood with puddles of muddy water around their feet, looking just as confused as Dillon. Mia stayed outside in the rain and mumbled something about how she had to go, and drove off in their old clunking Studebaker.

"What's up?" Dillon asked Bob.

"Dunno."

"Was your house getting flooded by the stream?" he asked.

"I don't think so. . . . I mean, the water was up, but it wasn't near the house like last time."

"Perhaps," Sally cut in, "Mia was afraid it would rise during the night." She smiled one of her vacant smiles. "How does hot chocolate sound to everyone?"

Bob and Chrissie sort of shrugged and looked as though they really didn't give a shit, and I probably looked a little pissed off because only a half-hour before I had asked Sally for some, and she had said it wasn't good for me and that I should have some apple juice.

They slept the night in sleeping bags on the Jesus-with-the-little-lambs rug, and the next morning Mia Hammond's body was found floating face down in the stream. The autopsy showed her to be stuffed full of Seconal and King George IV scotch.

"Poor woman. Poor woman," Sally kept saying over and over until I was ready to smack her one. Dillon managed to reach their father at Hawaiian Electric, and he came in a black Ford and took the kids away. They didn't wave. They also had not cried. They took the news emotionlessly. They shrugged the same way they had shrugged at the hot chocolate suggestion.

For the first time in my life I had a strange feeling. I envied Mia Hammond because she'd had the guts to jump into a roaring, cold, muddy stream. Dillon called her a coward because she wouldn't face life, but secretly I thought she was strong. It takes more guts to end your life than it does to sit and drink King George IV and watch *The Price Is Right*. I sat very quietly, suddenly knowing I had power. I had always wondered what I would do if suddenly I woke up and found out I was a Pakistani with no food, or if I was maimed for life, or if I suddenly found myself with six kids in a house with no plumbing. Suddenly I was not afraid anymore. I didn't have to worry about things getting horrible, because if things got horrible, I could always kill myself. Simple. I'd thought a lot about death, but until I was ten and Mia Hammond ended her life in the Kahaluu stream, I had never looked at suicide that way. Lola Bloom would probably be a nothing while Page was out losing her virginity to Gregory Peck and becoming a movie star. Lola would do okay. Lola would take one day at a time, but Lola didn't need to be afraid of ANY-

THING anymore, because she had found a secret power . . . power over her own life that no one knew about and no one could take away from her.

I wanted to talk to Chrissie about the suicide, but she and Bob were in Honolulu with their father, and we didn't have the number.

Chapter

7

It's amazing the things you think about while you're lying in a hospital bed. I was trying to re-create sex with Grant in my mind. That POSSIBLY could be something worth living for, because we didn't just fuck, we actually made love. Some-times, he would enter me, not move, and talk sweetly to me. Then he would start to move slowly. He'd hold me as tightly as he could, and pick me up with my legs still wrapped around him. He al-ways wanted me to let him know when I thought I was ready to come, so he could either come with me or say, "Slowly, Lola, slowly." "Slowly, Lola, slowly," were about the sexiest words I could think of. Sometimes, when I masturbated, I didn't con-jure up erotic images but just remembered Grant's voice . . . kind . . . soft . . . sexy, saying, "Slowly, Lola, slowly," and then I would start to climb each step . . . move up each level to or-gasm. If I was dead, there would be no more lovemaking with Grant—unless there really WERE some very weird and kinky supernatural forces at work in the world. On the other hand, I had no idea how many times Grant and I had made love.

Three . . . no, four times a week for one year is fifty-two times four, but let's make it easier and say fifty times four is two hundred, and two hundred times ten years is . . . my God . . . two thousand. We'd probably made love over TWO THOUSAND times—and that doesn't count the first few weeks when we were making love three or four times a DAY. We had joked about how—in those first few weeks—we had made love more times than some MARRIED people do in a year. I lay there looking at the roses Grant had sent, and thought that I'd have to find something else to make me want to live. I mean, living for something you've already done more than two thousand times seems a bit pointless.

Grace Takamoto came in and grinned and said that Dr. O'Shea would be in to see me.

"Who's that?"

"A psychiatrist."

"I don't want to see a psychiatrist."

"I'm afraid," said a deep voice at the door, "that there's a law that says someone who attempts to take her own life must see a psychiatrist."

"I need to figure out things for *myself.*"

"Look, I talked to your husband, and from the way he described your behavior, I would think you are—I hate to just come out and say this—a certified manic-depressive. Of course, I'll have to observe, and—"

"I know," I said simply. "I'm not stupid. I've also read that, like diabetics, we don't get better."

"Do you want to get better?"

"Not if it is so simple that everything I ever was is changed by a pill."

"It's not like that."

"I'd bore myself. I don't want to teach high school English and have to go to bed sober so I can get up and teach *Huckleberry Finn* and *The Scarlet Letter* to a bunch of kids at Nanakuli High School who don't even read their assignments anyway."

"What about Grant?"

"I've asked him to leave. I think I want to try to put my life together, but I don't want it put together with drugs. Drugs are for *fun* not for salvation."

"If we get the dosage right, you don't feel like you're 'on' anything. And also, Lola, lithium solves nothing. It makes it possible for you to solve things yourself. You'll still have highs and lows, but you'll be able to control them better."

"I don't have anything . . . anything I want to do."

"Nothing? Even in your wildest imagination?"

"I already know how to ride a motorcycle, and I got to meet John Wayne before he died."

"What does that have to do with anything?"

"I've done everything I want to do," I said soberly. "I don't even want to meet Robert Redford."

I rolled over and put my face in the pillow. "It doesn't matter. I don't want to talk to you anymore."

"Well, you don't have to talk to me, but you've got to talk to someone. Somebody has to monitor your medication."

"I don't want medication."

"Do you want to be hospitalized?"

"I *am* hospitalized."

"I'm talking about the funny farm."

"God, no . . . but . . ."

"No one is going to let you kill yourself. I can make you stay in a hospital if I feel you are a danger to either yourself or others."

"I'm a danger to others only if I'm alive, and you shouldn't worry about me. I don't. No one would miss me." The tears started to come again, so I just let them. I knew what kind of tears these were. They weren't the ones that come when you cut yourself with a knife; they were the dark, frightening, uncontrollable tears—tears that could go on all night. Grant knew about these tears. He knew they wouldn't stop, so he'd hold me and look out at the stars and stroke my hair and wait for me to pass out from drink and exhaustion.

Apparently Jake O'Shea had seen a few like me, for he seemed to know that saying something like "The sun will come up in the morning" only makes the depressive lash out, cry harder, and sometimes scream. When Grant and I were first together, he had tried—at times like these—to say things that would make me feel better, but my sobs had escalated into screams, and I had put my head between my knees and screamed as if I were being repeatedly stabbed with an ice pick. Grant shook me, slapped me, but I couldn't stop. The neighbors called the police but, fortunately, by the time they arrived the screams had subsided into crying. I'm sure Grant was wondering exactly what he was getting himself into, but the next morning the euphoria returned, and we had champagne for breakfast, took the motorcycle down to Kapiolani Park, drank champagne, and flew kites—or rather,

ran around with the kites; I don't think we ever
got one up.

Jake O'Shea said nothing. He got up, walked
across the room, and glanced at the roses. He must
have seen the card that said, "For Lola Bloom, the
beautiful and amazing one. I'll love you always (all
ways), Grant." He walked back to his chair. "Your
husband loves you a lot," he said. "If you agree
to try the lithium, and he agrees to make sure you
take it, you may go home with him."

"I *told* you we were splitting up!"

"I see. Okay. Think about it. I'll come back tomorrow, and we'll see what we can figure out. But
remember, Lola, you *can* do it yourself. Lithium
isn't going to make you a brain surgeon or a tap
dancer. It will make you the self you were meant
to be, so you can become who and what you want
to be."

"I'll think," I sniffed.

That night Grant snuck into the hospital after
visiting hours and crawled into the narrow bed
beside me. I was still crying quietly from my conversation with Jake O'Shea. The ancient Samoan
woman was still in a coma. He held me, and because I was crying, I didn't notice he was crying
too. He was changed. My old Grant would have
snuck in, yes, but he would have brought a flask
and Dunhills, and we'd have laughed about how
we really put one over on the hospital this time.
Now there was no silver flask and no champagne.
He simply crawled into my bed to cry. We held,
cried, and lay there for an hour.

Finally, he asked, "It's really over, Lola?"

"For now it has to be."

"We're dangerous for each other *now*," he choked, "but maybe not for always."

"You'd love me if I was straight?"

"You'll *never* be straight. I'm ten years older than I was when I met you, and no, babe, I wouldn't . . . please believe me . . . I *wouldn't* miss the seesaw."

He clung to me, reached around, untied my hospital gown, and took my breast in his mouth. I didn't say anything. He took my gown off and laid his wet cheek on my stomach, and we lay like that—still—for about half an hour. Then slowly he moved his hand down between my legs . . . stroking my pubic hair, moving his hand to part my legs. His face still wet with tears, he moved his head down between my legs. I put my knees up, and his tears mixed with the wetness that was beginning to start in my cunt. Slowly, he got up and pulled the curtain around the bed, and I watched, by the dim light from the city that came through the window, while he took off his clothes. He came into the bed again. Both of us still quietly crying, he sucked on my breast for a long time. I gently—just barely touching—stroked his penis . . . feeling it get hard under my fingers. Then I kissed his chest, his stomach, his inner thighs. Before he entered me, we gently touched each part— each square inch—of the other's body.

Then we just fucked. We both stopped crying as he thrust his penis in again and again and again. "I'm going to start," I said, and he said, "Slowly, Lola, slowly," and the sound of his voice saying the familiar . . . the tender . . . made me come— quietly but shaking—even before he did. Without a word or even his post-coital cigarette, he held me for about an hour. I was wide awake, staring at the ceiling, knowing this was going to have to be the last time I'd see Grant for a long time. It was amazing, because I did have a flicker of a desire to live, but—as I've said before—I knew I had to want to live without him before I could live with him. If I could somehow figure out who Lola Bloom really was, I might set eyes on his face again, feel those hands again, hear that laugh again.

Grant quietly got up and put on his clothes. He reached into his pocket and took out the Dunhill cigarette lighter I'd given him for our fifth wedding anniversary. He knelt by the bed and whispered, "Someday, you will meet someone you *really* love, and then I want you to give this to him."

For the first time, I smiled. "What if he doesn't smoke?"

Grant stroked my hair. "If you love someone who doesn't smoke, he can use it to light the candles. You wouldn't love someone who didn't love candles." He paused. "Maybe you can give it back to me," he said. Then he put on his jacket, and when he leaned over to kiss me, I took his face in my hands and knew he was crying again. "I love you, Lola Bloom," he said, and was gone.

I stared out the window until the sky turned gray, then pale blue.

After Grace Takamoto had checked on me, and after the man with the food cart had served me what they called breakfast, I brushed my hair for the first time. No WONDER on all the soap operas the doctors make jokes about hospital food: it really IS terrible.

Then came the hard part: talking to Jake O'Shea about "options." I agreed to the lithium, but he didn't agree to just let me walk out of the hospital alone. He cleared his throat. "What about your father? Your mother?"

The thought of staying with either one of them while I supposedly "put my life together" was rather horrifying.

"I have a sister," I said. "She lives in L.A."

"How old?"

"Thirty-six. She's a television actress. My husband could take me to her . . ." Then, knowing that I shouldn't see Grant again and couldn't handle the pain if I did, I said, "Or *someone* could."

"Bloom? I don't watch much television."

"Page Bloom. She's the star of *Classified Ads*. She's been on the cover of *People* and *TV Guide*."

"Name sounds familiar. How do you feel about her?"

"I love her. Her show is going on hiatus next week, and—"

"Hiatus?"

"That's when they take a vacation from shooting."

Then we had this long discussion about the pros and cons of being part of Page's "Hollywood world," and Jake O'Shea decided I could stay with Page until her show started up again, PROVIDED she agreed to see to it that I stayed on the lithium, and by then, if all went well, I'd have some idea of what I wanted to do with myself.

I was actually rather interested to learn that so many people wanted me to save my life. Of course, I knew Grant did, but all of our friends came to visit, and Grant wasn't even with me. It was the first time in ten years that someone had come just to visit ME. I'd always felt they were visiting Grant, as I had no friends in Hawaii before I met him, so our friends were HIS friends, but now HIS friends were visiting ME, wanting me to live. They knew we had split up, but they came anyway. Amazing.

Page was not exactly thrilled about "baby-sitting" with me, but on the other hand, sweet Page, for reasons unknown to me, loved me and actually said (although I'm sure she didn't mean it) that it might be "entertaining" to have me around, and most certainly "interesting."

"Page?" I asked.

"What?"

"You really don't mind, do you? I mean . . ."

"It's just for hiatus."

It was agreed that Dillon would go up to our house, get my things, and take them to his house in Mililani Town. After becoming a clown minister, Dillon felt that Kahaluu didn't provide too many laughs, so he sold the banana farm, and with what was left of Helen's money bought a tract house in Mililani Town, which was a subdivision surrounded by sugarcane fields. In fact, Mililani Town had been a cane field when I first visited Hawaii in 1959. It had four models of houses, and Dillon and Sally had Model C in turquoise and white. They left most of their Jesus relics behind them, and were now into happy faces and "Have a nice day" bumper stickers. Sally always wore a pink enameled pendant around her neck that said "I'm Third" on it, and of course everyone would ask what "I'm Third" meant, and she would smile and proudly say, "God first, others second, myself last." You can see why I wanted to go directly from the hospital to Page without a stopover in Mililani Town.

There was a big discussion as to how I would get to the airport, and of course I really wanted Grant to take me, but the last thing Dillon wanted for me was for Grant to take me (Dillon was actually relieved to hear that Grant and I were splitting the sheets). So I called Grant, and we had our first conversation since the night in the hospital.

"Hi," I said slowly, "this is—"

"I know who it is."

"I . . . I . . ." I was determined not to cry again, so I cleared my throat. "I need a ride to the airport."

"Can't Dillon take you?" His voice faltered a little. "It's going to be hard to see you. You've no idea . . ."

"You have no idea how hard it is going to be for me to ride with Dillon. He *might* even wear the clown suit to cheer me up."

"I see your point," said Grant. "It's not just seeing you I mind. . . . It is seeing you go. Airports are so final. All movies with sad endings end in airports."

"I'm not going for good."

"We may be finished for good."

"Then see me looking pretty . . . not with greasy hair like I was in the hospital."

"Okay, babe," he said softly.

I washed my hair that night, and called Sally and asked her to bring over my Victorian lace

— 138 —

blouse. In the morning I brushed my hair until it was all fluffy, and put it up on top of my head in a knot. I carefully put on makeup. I wasn't very good at it as I rarely wore it, but one of the nurses helped me, and when Sally arrived with the blouse (and, unfortunately, wearing the "I'm Third" necklace), she even admitted that I looked "unrecognizably" good. I felt she really didn't need to add the "unrecognizably," but that's Sally for you.

I put on the blouse with my jeans and hoped to hell that Sally would leave before Grant came. Finally I just TOLD her to leave, but she said, "I have to give Grant instructions."

"*Instructions?*"

"He is not just to drop you off at the check-in. He is to tell the stewardess you are to have no alcoholic beverages, and he is to *stay at the gate* until the plane takes off."

"No alcoholic beverages? I mean, I can see why no Seconal, but . . ."

"Well, Lola, you *do* tend to drink a—"

"Dillon wouldn't be a minister now if you hadn't let him drink and lose four days."

"Dillon was not a suicidal."

"Airline *food* will kill you before airline cocktails will."

"I'm sorry, Lola. We've got to make you get well."

Then I remembered that I really shouldn't worry about that. Grant could NEVER bring himself to tell some stewardess that I couldn't drink on the plane. What else did people DO on planes?

In a minute, Grant came into the room. No matter what the mood, his walk made him seem happy; however, he looked less than thrilled to see Sally.

"Hi, Sally," he said, doing his best to sound glad she was in the room.

"Grant"—she got right to the point—"I have some instructions for—"

"Yeah, yeah," he said quickly. "Watch her at the airport, don't let her go into the ladies' room with a razor blade in her hand, no booze on the plane." He paused and took out a pack of Dunhill cigarettes and handed one to me. "Dillon didn't say no smoking, too, did he?"

"I'm afraid he did."

"The woman is thirty-four years old. . . ." Grant paused. "Oh," he finally said rather ironically, while carefully taking the cigarette away from me. "I see; she could set herself on fire. As a matter of fact, they should outlaw smoking on planes. Someone could hijack the thing by threatening to burn the pilot and copilot's eyes out. Yeah, good idea, no smoking."

"Come on, Grant," said Sally, a little icily. "You may not be staying *married* to Lola, but you certainly don't want her to . . ." Her voice trailed off. She was one of those people who actually believe that if you mention suicide in front of suicidals, it "puts ideas into their heads." If you're a true suicidal, the idea is ALWAYS there—even at the very back of your mind—no matter what.

Since we were most likely going to be divorced, Grant didn't try to pick a fight with her as he usually had in the past. He just said sincerely, "I want her to get better as much as you do. We have always had a difference of opinion as to what 'better' really means. I know now it means 'not dead,' and on that point we agree. I'll keep her safe."

Sally had also expressed her doubts about Page, because she somehow blamed Page personally for collecting thirty thousand dollars an episode for *Classified Ads* when children in Kahaluu were going hungry. One of the great things about Page was that although she was a compassionate person, she didn't let Sally lay guilt trips on her. She had said ironically to Sally, "Okay, I'll quit the show and solve the world hunger problem."

Sally finally left the room, looking nervously over her shoulder. When the door finally shut, Grant handed me the Dunhill and lit it. He looked nervously around the hospital room.

"Being in here for more than an hour would drive *anyone* to suicide," he commented. Then he picked up my suitcase, looked disgusted, set it down, and proceeded to peel off the happy face sticker that said "This belongs to Lola" on it. "Jesus," he said. He looked around the room and found the marker pen Dillon had left, and where the sticker had been, he wrote on Sally's green Samsonite, "Lola Bloom, the amazing one."

"Uh . . . thank you," I said almost shyly.

"You look so pretty," he said. I could tell he was resisting the impulse to kiss me. For ten years, he had been kissing me after complimenting me, so it was a natural habit.

"Thank you," I said. "I worked pretty hard at it." I paused while Grant looked around the room for anything else I might have left. "Do you *really* think I'm amazing?"

"If you weren't amazing, what was I doing with you for ten years?"

I smiled, but my lip must have been quivering or some shit like that because he quickly said, "Don't cry. You worked too hard at that makeup to fuck it up now." He ushered me out the door. "Come, you lovely one," he said in a hearty voice. "The 'fifty-seven Chevy awaits you."

When we got down to the car, I saw that the whole back seat was filled with roses and baby's breath. I sighed. This wasn't the way couples were supposed to break up, but then, Grant and I had always prided ourselves on NOT being a regular couple.

"Did you get me a lei?" I asked. "This is Hawaii, you know."

"You get that just before you get on the plane," he said.

I gathered up as many roses as I could hold, and as we drove along Nimitz Highway past the oil tanks and incomplete cement freeways, I buried my face in the roses, breathed the scent, and (I know you're pretty tired of hearing about crying, but . . .) I cried.

Grant got me all checked in, and—as was our usual pattern at the Honolulu International Airport—we checked out the souvenir shops and laughed at the plastic hula girls. Our favorite that day was a plastic Don Ho that you could fill with soap, wind up, and he'd blow bubbles and play "Tiny Bubbles."

Still carrying the roses while Grant carried my hand luggage, we walked down the long, windy concourse to the United Airlines terminal. The

Honolulu airport is truly the WORST airport in the world. Either you have to walk miles to get from your plane to your baggage or vice versa, or you have to get on one of those dumb little buses, which they endearingly call wiki-wiki buses (*wiki-wiki* means "quick" in Hawaiian). That's almost as funny as the bus system being called Honolulu Rapid Transit. It was hardly even a "transit," let alone "rapid." Grant and I made jokes about the airport all the way to the gate.

When we got to the gate, the passengers were starting to board, so fortunately we didn't have that awkward waiting time. Grant handed me my hand luggage, and I couldn't hold that and the roses too, so I took one last breath of them and handed them to Grant. He smiled, turned around, and gave them to the beautiful Chinese woman who was calling out the boarding rows for United Airlines. He kissed her on the cheek. She laughed right into the microphone. Grant walked me to the door of the jet-way and put a single strand of pikake over my head. He kissed me on the mouth and said, "Goodbye, Lola Bloom."

"I love you," I said, knowing this was our first parting where he didn't say, "I love you, Lola Bloom."

Instead he said, "I believe you." He kissed me gently, and walked quickly away.

Even if you don't smoke, you should always sit in the smoking section of the plane. Since smokers are now regarded as just this side of lepers, there are usually more empty seats in the smoking section, and usually more interesting people. In today's "thank you for not smoking" world, it takes a real rebel, individualist, or a take-death-when-it-comes kind of person to smoke.

I picked up *Cosmopolitan* magazine and marveled at it. I wondered if there were REALLY people who took the quizzes that told you how secure you were or if your marriage was in trouble. That was this month's quiz. I took it, and Grant and I came out an ideal couple. Of course they didn't have the question, "Has your spouse attempted suicide within the last three months?" *Cosmopolitan* is my favorite magazine. I love to see how people think they should dress, and how they should decorate their apartments, and how they should improve their orgasms. I wondered if everyone read it like I did, filtering it through my mind and coming up with amazement, or whether there really WERE people out there who rushed out and painted their walls this month's color, or really DID stay home on the fifteenth because their horoscope said it was going to be a bad day. Marveling at it, I bought it every month, so I guess it didn't matter to *Cosmopolitan* WHY I bought it, just so long as I and millions of other people bought it too.

The airline food on flights to Hawaii is the same as on flights to anywhere else, except they serve it on a wooden tray shaped like a leaf, and the salad always has a stick of pineapple in it. The pilot kept interrupting my *Cosmopolitan* to point out the other islands, to give us our altitude, to say he was enjoying serving us today, to announce the contest to see who could guess the halfway point, to describe the weather in California, to read a few basketball scores, and finally, to leave us alone.

Fortunately, Grant hadn't followed Sally's instructions to tell them about the booze, but unfortunately, Sally figured that Grant would "conveniently" forget to or pretend to forget, so she had called United Airlines, and the stewardess, in her navy-blue muumuu uniform, said, when I ordered a double vodka on the rocks, that she "didn't think it was a good idea," but since I was an adult, she couldn't PREVENT me from drinking; unless I "appeared drunk" or did anything obnoxious, she had to give it to me.

Funny, Grant ALWAYS appeared obnoxious on planes, and the stewardesses always loved him, and if there was the SLIGHTEST doubt that they loved him, he simply told them he wrote *Mr. Macho*, and they usually gave us a free bottle of champagne. But that was Grant. Grant, who looked like Tom Selleck, who was funny, warm, sweet (a "sweet shit," as he once described himself), bawdy, brilliant, and . . . well . . . here was Lola Bloom. Suddenly, just as the movie, *Annie*, was starting on the little screen—four vodkas later—I remembered the "Lola Bloom, the amazing one," he had written on my suitcase, and what he had said. If I really HAD been nothing, Grant wouldn't have stayed with me for ten years. Maybe it was only because I was amazing, but then, why should I feel I hadn't accomplished anything? The only goal Lola Bloom ever had was to be "amazing."

Somehow, airplanes make you feel very lightheaded. With the help of the vodka and the altitude, I was beginning to feel a little better. *I was amazing*, and not just because I was with Grant. I wasn't sure I wanted to go that route, but if I put all the energy I used up being crazy into . . . into . . . what?

Maybe Page would have some career ideas, although Page was truly the LAST person I'd hire as a vocational counselor. She always used to say to me (knowing I had no talent for acting whatsoever), "Why don't you be a model? You're tall, you have high cheekbones, and I know the best photographers in the business." That was the extent of Page's career advice to me, and now that I was thirty-four, she couldn't even give THAT advice.

Page had always wanted to be an actress, and unlike most of those people who justify the saying, "For every light on Broadway, there's a broken heart," Page always knew she was the granddaughter of Irving Adrian, and with an ounce of talent she could get started, and with the talent she believed she had, she could "make it big." She always did well in school, not to get into college or anything, but simply because Page, when she was not acting, was the sort of person whose idea of fun was to go out and LEARN something. Nothing bores Page, so learning calculus was as interesting as learning needlepoint or as interesting as her yoga class. When her schedule would allow, she'd take bizarre courses at U.C.L.A. simply because she "didn't know anything about" whatever it was she had decided to take: anthropology; how to repair your own VW (and she didn't even OWN a VW; she just thought it would be "interesting"); gymnastics. I truly believed that when she had the time, she simply opened the U.C.L.A. catalog, closed her eyes, and chose a course at random. Page would never kill herself. She probably would regard living in a flop house or even living to see the bomb dropped as potentially "interesting." Sweet Page, maybe she could help me.

Page didn't come to the gate because if you are Page Bloom you don't want your reunion with your suicidal sister to be complicated by autograph seekers. She did send a celeb greeter in a sort of little golf-cart-looking thing (for celebrities and the handicapped, she explained to me, and I wondered if I was handicapped or a celeb and decided that since I had a death wish and since I was Page Bloom's sister, I was a little of both). We drove down the aisle between two pedestrian conveyor belts to the top of the escalator to the baggage claim. Some airline official came, took my baggage stubs, and said that Page was waiting outside the baggage-claim area, and he would bring the bags. That alone seemed worth being a celeb for. Watching the suitcases thump down on the carousel was not my favorite thing.

Wearing sunglasses, Page was waiting in a BMW. I had to hand it to her for driving a BMW when I knew damn well she could afford a Mercedes or a Porsche. A BMW is a status car, but doesn't reek with wealth like the others do. She didn't get out, but reached across the seat and opened the door.

"Lola," she said, stroking my hair and looking into my eyes. "Little Lola."

Sweet Page. The smell of Joy perfume filled the car. Page was wearing a black parachute jumpsuit with lots of silver zippers all over it, a silver chain, and a pair of black high-heeled boots. Her hair—

which was sort of Farrah Fawcett on *Classified Ads*—was frizzy, and the late afternoon sun shone through it. No WONDER Page was such a popular actress. She looked rather flawless and not thirty-six at all. I felt rather beat-up, looking at her through my round glasses. Page had flawless skin that looked like "milk and honey," beautiful breasts, and she seemed not even to be aware of them. She wore no makeup (I guess when your whole work week is spent having someone dab at your makeup, it is the last thing you want to wear in "real life").

I filled the awkward silence while we waited for my bags by asking her what courses she was taking during this hiatus, and she said she was taking Lamaze Natural Childbirth and Intro to Computer Language. Computers, well, yes of course. Computers are where it's at, aren't they? But LAMAZE? "You're not . . . uh . . ."

"Pregnant?" she asked, finishing my sentence. "No, I just thought it would be interesting."

"But doesn't it get boring lying on the floor and learning how to breathe?"

"It's rather relaxing, and besides, it's better to take Lamaze *before* you decide to get pregnant, because then you'll have a better idea what you're in for."

"Have you seen Helen?"

Page sighed. "Our dear mother came up to watch the filming of the last episode this season. She told me she wished I would hurry up and get into films because television disgusts her."

"*Movies* disgusted her. That's why she married Dillon," I said. Helen often came up to L.A. to see Page, and to be made much of by the old guard in Hollywood who all, of course, remembered Irving Adrian "fondly" even though we personally knew he screwed over at least half of them.

By then they had put the bags in the car, and Page sped off down the Harbor Freeway.

"Where are we going?" I asked.

"To Lamaze class," she said simply. "They're showing the movie."

Seeing a movie about childbirth wasn't exactly what I had in mind for my first evening with my sister, but she said we could go to dinner afterward ("If we feel like eating after watching the umbilical cord being cut," she had said). I liked the way Page wasn't embarrassed to take me to eat in Beverly Hills, and how she did not suggest—as Helen would have—that we stop off at home so I could put on something decent.

We arrived at a house in South Pasadena, and Page parked the BMW, and we went in. There were eight couples in there. The men were sitting beside the women, who were all lying on the floor, their heads on pillows. I looked at their pregnant stomachs all rising up. The row of them looked like a series of rolling hills. Boy, I can tell you that if I was pregnant and in a Lamaze class, I sure wouldn't want Page Bloom—not pregnant—in it. Every eye—both male and female—went to Page's twenty-four-inch waist. "This is my sister, Lola," she said.

"Is she your labor coach?" joked one man. I noticed that one couple had two women instead of a woman and a man, and the pregnant one looked about sixteen years old. Page and I went into the bedroom to put our jackets away.

"Who's the teenager?" I asked.

"Oh, she's an unwed mother who thought they didn't *allow* you to have a baby in California if you didn't have Lamaze training. I mean, the first day we were here, we all had to stand up and tell why we were taking Lamaze . . ."

"And I bet you said it was because you thought it would be 'interesting,' " I said.

"Of course."

"Someone should write a musical like *Chorus Line* and call it *Lamaze!* and instead of all the actors standing up one at a time and telling their personal stories of how they got into dance, you could have this cross section of humanity tell their personal stories of how they got into painless childbirth. The first number could be 'We Weren't Allowed to Have a Baby without Lamaze.' "

Page laughed. "You and Grant," she sighed, "always another get-rich-quick scheme. You should act on one sometime."

Then we went back into the living room where the teacher—also with a twenty-four-inch waist like Page—was unrolling a movie screen. Page looked fascinated. Everyone made a special effort to talk to Page, and in a way it was kind of poignant to think that probably—after actually HAVING the baby—the fact that Page Bloom was in their class and that they actually KNEW her was the biggest thing in their lives. It was time for the movie.

The movie was called *The Story Of Eric*, and it was about a young couple who have a son named

Eric by the Lamaze method, and it traces the last month of the woman's pregnancy and shows the actual delivery. During the credits, Page started to giggle. "Look who wrote and directed this," she said.

Not recognizing the name, I asked her who.

"The same guy who wrote *The Omen!*" We both burst out laughing. Page had to quickly explain why she had been laughing, and no one thought it was particularly funny, but they all sort of laughed because it was Page Bloom and not just some "Nickname: none" like Lola saying it.

The film was narrated by the wife, who said they were a "typical young working couple in California who raised Labrador retrievers." Yeah, real typical. We watched Mr. and Mrs. Johnson (I think that was their name) decide to name their kid Eric, watch Labrador retriever puppies being born, walk on the beach, have "the blues," go faithfully to their Lamaze classes, and be "closer to each other than they had ever been since they'd met." Of course everyone in the class was waiting eagerly for The Birth. Finally, Mrs. Johnson got into the hospital, and since Mr. Johnson had been Lamaze trained he, of course, was VERY helpful and timed her contractions and mopped the sweat off her face. Mrs. Johnson lay on her side and panted while her voice-over said, "My uterus is working very hard, and my body is working harder than it ever worked before, but I feel no pain."(?)

Because I had started my period on the plane and had CRAMPS that were killing me, I whispered to Page, "They've got to be kidding!"

The doctor in the film came in and listened to

the baby's heart and told the calm, Lamaze-trained Johnsons that they were probably going to have a boy; he could tell by the heartbeat. (?) Then Mrs. Johnson was wheeled into the delivery room. She had a slight complication called back labor, which I didn't know anything about because I hadn't been taking the class, but of course, Mrs. Johnson handled it very well because she was Lamaze trained, and she was very calm when she was told to push the baby out. "Oh, it feels *so good* to push," she said. (?)

"I'm never having children," I whispered to Page.

"I think it would be—"

"Interesting, yes, interesting," I interrupted.

Then we got to see the baby's bloody head start to come out, and we got to hear Mrs. Johnson grunt.

"Oh, my God!" I said out loud as little Eric Johnson's mashed-up, squished bloody head pushed its way through the grotesquely gaping hole between the calm and happy Mrs. Johnson's legs.

"Is it a boy?" asked Mrs. Johnson.

"I can't tell by its ears," said the calm and witty doctor.

"Hey," said Page. "That's what the doctor said when Gloria Bunker had her kid on *All in the Family.*"

By this time, little Eric had his shoulders out, and the doctor told Mrs. Johnson to give one more great big push, and little wax-covered, wrinkled, bloody Eric fell into a bloody towel. I thought I was going to throw up.

Page just looked terribly interested, and after the film she took me to the Ginger Man in Beverly Hills, where everyone recognized her, though they were too cool to admit it, and instead just kept sneaking glances at Page with her unfamiliar frizzy hair, and the tall, skinny woman sitting with her in a Victorian lace blouse and jeans.

Page couldn't understand why I wasn't too hungry, but after seeing little Eric, I just didn't exactly feel like scarfing food down. Birth, I thought . . . the miracle of birth. Going through all that, having your child grow up, learn to brush her teeth, hoping she will make a "valuable contribution" to the world, and . . . everyone dying in the end anyway. Even though I was having fun with Page, that dark piece of lead in my middle stayed put, making my throat tighten as I saw the light shine through Page's blonde hair. I stirred my spinach salad, and felt panicky again.

Chapter

Kerrybrook Academy for Girls in San Diego was what Helen called "real posh." It didn't believe in giving scholarships, and the tuition was so high, it outpriced almost everyone. For a while in the fifties it had been a boarding school to give rich girls from all over the country the chance to go to Kerrybrook, but they found out they were getting too many girls from Texas, so they stopped the boarding policy.

When Irving Adrian died, I was just starting school, and Page was in the fourth grade. Helen instantly plucked her out of public school in Coronado, and she zipped us right into Kerrybrook where they were more than happy to take us—especially since Helen donated a hundred thousand dollars toward a new gym.

I always wished I went to a school that had uniforms, because I never knew how to dress. Page was just enough older than I was so that I was too young to wear whatever she was wearing, and I couldn't even copy her.

I lost my virginity in a madras wrap-around skirt in 1964, less than a year after people stopped wearing madras. Page had a boyfriend, and they were "doing it," and he wore rubbers and EVERY-THING. I figured they were probably doing it when I noticed that Page was carefully marking her periods on the calendar, and since she was the type who never got cramps, periods were not a terrible concern of hers.

I went into her room and sat on her bed while she got ready for the Valentine dance. Her date was in the navy, which gave her status because not only was she dating an older man of twenty-six, but he was a midshipman and not just a sailor. Only "fast" girls dated sailors, and there were sure a hell of a lot of sailors in San Diego and Coronado.

Every day we were driven onto the ferry (and then later over the stupid bridge) by Helen's driver and deposited in front of Kerrybrook. The year Page was a senior, Helen grudgingly allowed Alan, the midshipman, to drive her to school. I not only didn't have a boyfriend but didn't even have any idea how to get one. Everyone really looked up to Page because most other girls dated the sons of friends of their parents, but Page had a real boyfriend she got on her own, a boyfriend who had seen Page's hair blow on the ferry, and he had come up and had given her a Winston cigarette, and THAT VERY DAY by the end of the ferry ride, he had kissed her. But then, she was Page Bloom. Now every man in the COUNTRY wanted to kiss her.

For the Valentine dance, Page didn't wear the empire-waisted, scooped-neck chiffon gown that everyone else was wearing. No, not Page. She wore a long red velvet skirt and a SEE-THROUGH white blouse. At first Helen had objected, but Page promised to wear a beige bra, so everyone wouldn't know exactly what her bra looked like, and Helen—preoccupied—had said a vague okay.

Page also had her first pair of pantyhose. Up until the Valentine dance, she wore stockings, but pantyhose were becoming a big thing, so she bought some for herself and some for me. That was what she was like, not only beautiful, but a goddamn good person too. (Shit, who was I?)

When I came into the room to confront her about the calendar, she was putting on her bra.

"Are you and Alan doing it?" I asked incredulously.

Page hooked her bra. "Kind of," she said.

"How do you 'kind of' do it? Are you going all the way or not?"

"Yes," she said nervously, and then quickly added, "But we don't do it in the car. We don't do it in sleazy places. We do it in motels."

"Aren't motels supposed to be sleazy? Aren't motels the place where married men go with their mistresses?"

"I mean, we go to *nice* motels and don't do it in the car like most high school girls."

"God," I said, genuinely impressed. Neither of us said anything until she finished dressing. "What's it like?" I finally asked.

"You read *The Group*," she said. "You know."

"Is it really like in *The Group*"

"I'd say she was pretty accurate. I'm going to go on the pill soon, so I won't be nervous."

"The *pill?*" I was amazed at her casualness. "How are you going to get that?"

"I'm going to find a doctor who doesn't know Helen."

I was impressed. "You're a goddamn minor," I said.

"And there are some doctors who don't think minors should have babies, so they'll give you the pill."

I watched Page take the rollers out of her hair and bend over and brush out a blonde fluffiness. I took a deep breath. "Could you get some for me?" I asked.

Page dropped her hairbrush. *"What?"* she asked, even more "incredulized" by my question than I was at the fact she was doing it.

"I'd like to have some," I said.

"Why?"

"In case I want to do it sometime."

"Who would you do it with? You hated Larson that Helen brought to the cocktail party for you."

"I don't know, but when he comes around, I want to be ready."

Page looked a little worried. "I read that if you don't get checked by a doctor, you could get cancer or something from them," she said.

"Do you think they'd give a virgin the pill?" I asked.

Page looked a little worried. "I'm not even sure they'll give it to *me*."

"But if you could give me just one month, I could use them when I found someone okay enough to do it with, and then I wouldn't be a virgin, and I could get some of my own."

Page put on her lipstick. "Uh . . . I guess," she said.

Now came the major chore of finding someone to do it with. If I had gone to a coed school, I probably could have offered myself to the football team or something, but the only men I saw were teachers. I mentioned my desire to "get rid of the cherry" to a couple of girls in my class, and they just stared at me as if I had said I wanted to spend the rest of my life in a dentist's chair. "Doing it" was apparently something you had to do in order to hang on to your boyfriend, not something you were supposed to WANT to do, but I had seen the touring company of *Camelot,* and I had heard Elizabeth Taylor in *Cleopatra* say to Rex Harrison without one BIT of repulsion, "I have wide hips, and I can give you many sons." I saw her look into Richard Burton's eyes. I knew that doing it was pretty hot stuff. Page treated it casually. I intended to treat it romantically, but with WHO?

Mr. Charles Schaftner was the only male teacher I had at Kerrybrook, and I didn't think about him until one day we were studying "To His Coy Mistress" in English class, when it struck me that I might be of some interest to Mr. Schaftner because he always called me Legs. Since I wasn't the only one in the class who had long legs, it suddenly hit me that he might regard me as a sex object.

Now, Mr. Schaftner wasn't exactly Richard Burton, but neither was he hideous. He had very fair skin (which is a sin in southern California, so I felt we had sort of a common bond: we were too smart to waste hours "touching up our tans") and very dark hair. He wasn't very tall and was a Harvard grad who had to teach high school because his wife got a job at U.C. San Diego, and he got a job in some junior college in the middle of Kansas, so she took the better job, and the only one he could get was teaching a bunch of rich high school girls at Kerrybrook. In fact, one of the attractive things about him was that he seemed rather bored with us. When I had had my conference with him and we were discussing *The Glass Menagerie*, I had said, "So when the unicorn's horn breaks off, and he's 'just like the other horses,' it is symbolic of . . ." Mr. Schaftner interrupted me a little too quickly and said, "Yeah . . . yeah," and made me feel like a real el-stupido as he had done when I had had the amazing revelation about *Oedipus Rex* that it was ironical that the BLIND prophet was the only one who could actually "see." Mr. Schaftner had said, "Oh, that's *very* good," in this condescending voice. Somehow that made him attractive because he was probably pretty smart.

I mentioned this to Page who seemed to think it was pretty dangerous to fuck a teacher, and that he probably wouldn't want to because he could get fired and all. HOWEVER, she did point out that because he had to teach high school while his wife taught at U.C. San Diego, that he had sort of had his balls busted and might want to do it with me to get back at her for getting a better job than he did. But all in all, Page thought I would do better if Alan, her midshipman, found some navy guy. "All the navy guys want to do it," she said with authority.

Since I was more romantic than Page was, I

didn't want to do it with just some navy guy. Hearing Mr. Schaftner's deep voice read "To His Coy Mistress" seemed pretty sexy. He didn't mind talking about sex, because when we were doing *The Scarlet Letter*, the class had had a long discussion about different cultures' views on adultery. It was pretty titillating to hear a teacher talk so casually about sex. I had him for first period, so I always studied him carefully, wondering if he had done it with his wife that morning. It seemed truly weird to think that maybe just two hours ago he had been naked in bed fucking his wife, and now he was standing up in front of us reading "To His Coy Mistress."

I decided I would "stay after class" and "ask him a question." I tried to think of something that might be suggestive, but that wouldn't be embarrassing in case he had just screwed his wife that morning and was paranoid about displeasing the administration.

I took a long time gathering up my books to make sure everyone was out of the classroom. Of course there were a couple of girls who had legitimate questions about their semester projects. I didn't have a single question about my project— which was on Tennessee Williams's use of the South in his writing—but Tennessee Williams was a pretty sexy writer, so maybe I could come up with something. Finally Joanne Zerko and Valerie Fendors finished asking him about the various ways the word "ambitious" could be interpreted in Mark Antony's "Friends, Romans, Countrymen" speech, and picked up their three-ring binders and trudged out of the classroom

I stayed seated at my desk as I didn't want the podium to be between us as a reminder that he was yes indeed the teacher, and I was fifteen years old.

"Lola?" he sounded surprised because I rarely had questions.

"Uh, you know I'm doing my semester project on Tennessee Williams's South, and . . ."

"And?"

"Well . . . I kind of had a question about . . . uh . . . *Night of the Iguana* . . . uh . . . about why Shannon was fired from his church."

"*Night of the Iguana* is one of Williams's plays that *doesn't* take place in the South."

"Mexico is pretty south," I said. "I was just wondering . . ."

Mr. Schaftner raised his eyebrows. "It's very clear," he said in that same condescending voice. "He . . . made love to . . ." He stopped.

"I know," I said simply.

Mr. Schaftner looked totally confused. "You know." he stated.

"I chose Tennessee Williams because out of all the stuff we've studied, he has the most sex in his plays." Mr. Schaftner didn't say anything. "I think sex is pretty interesting," I said.

"Oh, it is," he said. He sat at the desk next to mine and looked even more confused.

"Yeah," I said. "It really is . . . like junk dirty books have a good chance of selling, but a terrible CLEAN book is doomed from the very beginning."

Mr. Schaftner still looked as if I were talking in some foreign tongue.

"Like *Candy*," I continued. "What would that book be without the sex?"

"About two pages long," said Mr. Schaftner, sort of smiling.

"You've read *Candy?*" I asked, amazed.

"Someone told me I'd think it was funny." He shrugged.

"I thought it was dirty . . . but it was funnier than *Peyton Place.*"

"I didn't read *Peyton Place.* I didn't think it would provide too many laughs. I take it you did."

"Yeah. It was pretty dirty." I paused. I didn't think he was getting the message, but on the other hand, why would I be discussing dirty books with him? I crossed my legs. "Why do you call me Legs?" I asked.

"Uh . . . because you've got them. You've got nice legs, and you wear short skirts, so they are . . . uh . . . well, noticeable."

I could sort of feel myself blushing. I decided I had better get straight to the point and end the agony one way or another. Mr. Schaftner didn't say anything, but he didn't get up. He fingered his tie clip. He no longer looked confused.

"I have P.E. this period," I said. "Would you . . . uh . . . walk with me up to the gym?"

Suddenly Mr. Schaftner looked VERY nervous. He was definitely not one bit confused, and obviously he was getting two different sets of messages from his brain. Finally, I guess he decided that there was no law against walking with me up to the gym, so he shoved some things into his briefcase and mumbled, "Sure."

Figuring it was not good to talk about fucking in the building that might be bugged so Mr. Schaftner could get fired (I didn't think they'd expel me because of the hundred thousand dollars Helen had given them for the new gym fund, but Mr. Schaftners are a dime a dozen to Kerrybrook), I decided the least I could do was wait until we got outside. As we walked up the wooded path toward the gym, I took a deep breath and asked, "Do you ever sleep with anyone who isn't your wife?"

"I should say that's none of your business," he said, but he was smiling.

"Well, do you?"

"Why do you want to know?"

"Uh . . . uh . . . if you *do,* I . . . uh . . . thought maybe you'd like to sleep with me . . . uh . . . only you'd probably be afraid to ask in case I got offended and then got you fired."

He put his hand on the back of my neck. "What if I got offended and had you expelled."

"My mother just gave another hundred thousand dollars to the gym fund."

He laughed. "Oh, I see."

We were right at the curve in the path that sort of snaked its way through Kerrybrook. On our left was a sloping green lawn that went up to some classroom buildings in the distance. On our right were woods and tangled bushes that grew on the hill that sloped down for about a quarter mile to the road that led up to Kerrybrook. Mr. Schaftner stopped before going around the curve that would have put us in sight of the gym. He didn't say anything, but his hand moved from my neck to my shoulder. I was wearing a V-necked blouse and a flower-printed bra. His hand moved down over my breast, and almost as if he were doing it in his sleep, he started to unbutton my blouse. He must have been pretty experienced. I'd heard horror stories from some of the girls about buttons being ripped off by clumsy teenage boys.

Suddenly, I guess he remembered where he was, and that even though the next period had already started, someone could come around the curve in the path, so much to my disappointment, but very deftly, he buttoned my blouse again.

"Wait here," he said softly. Then looking pretty sheepish, he took out an out-of-class excuse form and scribbled something on it. Jesus, he was writing out an excuse for me in case someone came along and wondered what I was doing standing on the path. He hurried toward the parking lot.

In a few minutes he returned from his car with a large red-printed Indian bedspread. He took my hand and led me into the woods on our right. We walked about halfway down the hill to where we could see neither the school nor the road. He spread out the blanket in some soft bushes, and this time he slowly unbuttoned my blouse. he looked a little surprised at the floral print bra (guess his wife hadn't caught on to that fad yet), but he had no trouble unhooking it.

Then he gave me a major adult tongue-down-the-throat kiss, and I shivered, and began to know what Elizabeth Taylor felt when she kissed Richard Burton. I was dying to have him take off his clothes. I had never seen a naked man before except like pictures of the statue of David. I don't think I ever saw Dillon naked. I did remember he walked by an open bathroom door once, but all I saw was his ass, so I was intensely curious and excited about Mr. Schaftner taking off his clothes.

He kissed me more, and then he kissed each of my breasts. I couldn't remember exactly whether or not the guy in *The Group* kissed her breasts, but as his tongue slowly circled each of my nipples, I had that same feeling between my legs that I'd had in certain parts of *Peyton Place,* and I felt my underwear get a little damp. Mr. Schaftner reached up under my skirt and took off my panties. Their dampness REALLY excited him, because he started kissing my mouth and my neck almost violently. THEN he did something that they sort of HINTED about in *The Group.* He pulled up my skirt and parted my legs, and then he put his tongue between them. "Good God!" I managed to say. Now, I did know that people did that, but I thought it was in, well, cases where people had been lovers a really long time, or prostitutes, or something, but he was just my English teacher. However, it didn't feel too bad, but it was kind of embarrassing. I closed my eyes, put my head back, and felt his tongue slop around and around my crotch. Then he pulled off his pants and sort of moved around on the blanket, and I opened my eyes just in time to see his cock right there in front of my eyes. I'm telling you, it wasn't like the statue of David at ALL. I wasn't stupid. I mean, I knew that they got long and hard, but all I could think of was How is THAT going to fit in ME? Then I sort of got the idea he wanted me to take it in my mouth, but I just COULDN'T, so I moaned a little so he would think I was really carried away with being eaten out.

Then the most amazing thing of all happened—his tongue started to feel good. Not the thrill of the climax ("the Big O," as Page called it), but the rhythm of his tongue felt nice. I tentatively licked the length of his penis, and he got excited as hell all of a sudden and turned around on the blanket and started kissing my neck and sucking my breasts and blowing in my ears. My body felt excited, and I guess I automatically put my knees up, because when I opened my eyes again, he was between them trying to push his penis into me. It DID hurt, but if I bled—as I thought all virgins did—it didn't show up on the India Imports bedspread.

Then everything started to feel kind of good. He moved in and out, faster and faster, then collapsed on top of me, and that was it. That was it. And he didn't even know I was a virgin.

I really wished I had come, as I was dying to know what that felt like, but I had also read that the first time you don't usually come. I made a mental note to check it out with Page to see how long it took her before she popped off.

Mr. Schaftner rolled off me and lay back looking at the sky and the eucalyptus trees. I thought he should say SOMETHING. . . . Of course he didn't know I was a virgin. He probably thought I did it all the time, but I thought he should say SOMETHING. He stroked my hair, took a breath, and said, "What time is it?"

"I don't know. I don't think second period is over yet."

"This didn't happen," he said, sitting up and fumbling in his pockets for a cigarette.

"Are you sorry that—"

"I'm not sorry about anything. Nothing happened. That's my story."

"But I—"

"You're a nice girl, Legs, but nothing happened. Nothing at all."

I knew he wanted to get up and leave, but I was sitting on his Indian bedspread. I wanted SOME kind of tenderness. "Do you want me to help you fold the bedspread?" I asked.

Not being a total bastard, he kissed me gently. "That would be nice, Legs, real nice."

I stood up and awkwardly put my panties back on, and looking a little embarrassed, I hunted around for my bra.

"Why do you have roses on your bra?" he asked, genuinely interested.

"It makes it prettier," I said.

"Oh," He looked a little surprised and came over and hooked it for me. Then he gently buttoned my blouse. I took one end of the bedspread and he took the other, and we folded it lengthwise, then walked toward one another. As we met with our corners, I gently kissed him. He carefully took the bedspread away from me, finished folding it, tucked it under his arm, and repeated, "This never happened."

He walked up the hill without me. I was startled. I mean, I didn't expect him to instantly offer to leave his wife or even say he loved me. It was like he didn't even enjoy it that much. I sat down on the grass and hugged my knees and stared at the bay in the distance with navy ships sliding across it full of sailors with penises. Then I opened my purse and took out my compact to see—as I guess everyone does—if I looked any different. The only difference was that my makeup was smudged. "You're now a woman of the world, Lola Bloom," I said to myself. I carefully got up, put on my shoes, and struggled up the hill. As I walked down the path to the end of my P.E. class, I was really sad. I was the one who wanted it to be romantic, and not just in the back seat of someone's father's car. I had thought under the blue sky and eucalyptus trees with an experienced married man would be more romantic, but at that moment I longed for some high school jock in a letter sweater to drive me off for a hamburger and say, "Will you go to the prom with me?" and then as we danced to "Moon River" at the Coronado Officers' Club, he would whisper in my ear the words I had always wished for: "I love you, Lola Bloom."

In Tinsel Town Page didn't live in Beverly Hills, but in the same house she had lived in in Hancock Park that she had bought when she was still doing guest star roles and didn't have her own series yet. After the Lamaze class, we drove there and were greeted by her sheep dog named—you're not going to believe this—Lola. Page had actually thought she was paying me a great compliment by naming her dog after me, and no one had told her otherwise. She had a cat named Mary Tyler Moore because that was the first show she was a guest star on. I really wished I was the Bloom daughter who had turned out to be interestingly crazy instead of dangerously crazy.

Page knew I liked soap operas, so she had taped that day's episode of *All My Children* on the Betamax for me. I hunted around the kitchen for some booze—Page didn't drink. I remembered when Page had visited Grant and me, Grant had said incredulously, "Jesus, Page, you don't drink, smoke, or take drugs, and you're *happy!*"

Even though Page never got on my case about my drinking, I still didn't like her to think that the first thing I was interested in—even more than *All My Children*—was a drink, but seeing nothing around I figured I had better make a liquor store run. I was sure Sally had told Page to stick the booze under lock and key along with all the razors and sleeping pills. Sally probably felt pretty safe about the pills, because Page was one of those people who, except for birth control pills, HAD NEVER HAD A PRESCRIPTION DRUG. I had never thought about it much until she came to visit, asked for an aspirin, and Grant had said, "Let's see, we have aspirin, codeine, Motrin, Percodan, and . . . well, no morphine but just about everything else," and Page had sort of looked amused and amazed and let the cat out of the bag that she had never had a prescription drug. Grant looked at her like she was Jesus Christ, and my jaw dropped a couple of feet.

"Uh . . . Page," I asked. "Do you have anything to drink?"

"You mean like booze?"

"Yeah, that's exactly what I mean."

"Sally told—"

"Sally is *not* my mother, my doctor, or my keeper. I'm thirty-four years old with no police record."

"I know," she signed. "I can't stop you. Please don't get too drunk."

"I'm not going to get *drunk.* I just want a drink."

"There's some scotch in a glass cookie jar in the kitchen," she said as if that was where everyone kept their scotch.

"In a *cookie jar?*"

"Yeah. We were rehearsing a scene, and needed a bottle of scotch, so I went out and bought one and emptied the scotch into the cookie jar so we could fill the scotch bottle with iced tea for the scene. I didn't want to just pour it down the sink."

Page was amazing. If you're just running through a scene at HOME, you can use a MILK bottle, but Page was the kind of actress who would say she could "relate better to the real thing." She might even have been a really good actress. It was hard to tell with a show like *Classified Ads*.

Page's kitchen looked like a more expensive version of the style of kitchen Grant and I had, but the similarity stopped there. The cupboard doors were glass like ours, but instead of a built-in diner table, Page had a little breakfast nook. Page kept daisies on the table "at all times." On one of the counters (along with her Cuisinart, her microwave oven, her toaster oven, her coffee grinder, her espresso machine, her electric pasta maker, her blender, and her electric can opener—all in the kitchen of someone who "hardly ever cooks at all") was a set of glass canisters: flour, sugar, etc. The largest said "Cookies" on it, and in the bottom, like some oversized urine sample, was about two inches of scotch. I felt pretty dumb lifting this huge cookie jar and dribbling scotch into one of Page's Waterford crystal glasses.

By this time Page had changed into Arabian pants made of light blue sweat-shirt material, and a pale yellow cashmere turtleneck sweater, with— she did have some sense of humor—an enameled pendant like Sally's around her neck that said, "I'm First," on it.

Page always wore different outfits for every-thing, and this was apparently her watching-the-soaps outfit. Her hair was pinned up on top of her head, and she had literally gone through an entire transformation just to watch television. So I picked up my scotch, she picked up Mary Tyler Moore, the cat, and a Tab, and she called, "Here, Lola!" (to the dog), and we all sat in her den and watched Greg break up with Jenny—even though he loved her more than the Duke of Windsor loved Wallis Simpson—because he didn't want her to waste her life taking care of him now that he was paralyzed from the waist down. Page sat on the floor, and I looked at her classic profile, her misty eyes, and Aunt Phoebe and Brook on the television screen, and I felt a little bit safe . . . not a life lover, but safe.

The next day was a typical Page-on-hiatus day. She got up at eight for the sole purpose of watch-ing a rerun of *Leave It to Beaver* (which she could have taped, but I guess didn't think of it) while she drank her coffee, which was always ready because her espresso machine had a timer on it that her maid, Lydia, always set before she left in the afternoon. After coffee and *Leave It to Beaver*, Page put on striped jogging shorts and a muscle-sleeved T-shirt that said "Women hold up half the sky" on it, and jogged on her jogging trampoline for half an hour while watching a rerun of *I Love Lucy* on the television in her exercise room. After that, she casually tossed off her jogging clothes and took a bath while listening to *Jacques Brel Is Alive and Well and Living in Paris* with the stereo speakers set so the ones in the bathroom played. She asked me if

I wanted to listen to it too, and I said no, I thought it was shitty music, and she said that if I changed my mind, all the stereo knobs were labeled, so I could turn it on in my room if I wanted to. Then, while she blow-dried her hair in a peach-colored teddy, which she took off later (apparently she just wore it to blow-dry her hair), she watched a rerun of *The Mary Tyler Moore Show*, which she didn't really need to watch because she had seen them all so many times that she knew what was going on. Then she turned off the television in the bathroom, and while her hair cooked in electric rollers, she read a chapter of *I'm Dancing as Fast as I Can*, which she recommended to me because the woman was driven to drugs by too much pressure, and I pointed out to her that I was driven to drugs by too LITTLE pressure. I knew she didn't get it, but she kissed me on the cheek and told me she loved me anyway.

Then she announced that she was going to cook dinner for me that night, and so "our day" would be to go shopping for groceries. If I ever write something someday, I may write a short story and call it "Shopping with Page in West Hollywood."

Page announced that we were going to have some kind of pasta thing, and I didn't pay too much attention, as whenever Page cooked it always came out a little strange. She had taken a few cooking classes, but didn't believe in recipes.

Then she put on her going-shopping clothes, which consisted of long, sort of khaki Bermuda shorts with huge patch pockets, white net knee socks, khaki jazz oxfords, a red and beige checked preppy shirt, three gold chains, two gold bracelets, and a beige sweater tied by its sleeves around her shoulders. She put on large tinted glasses but said that people didn't recognize her when her hair was not the way she wore it on the show. "Kind of like if Tom Selleck shaved off his mustache, he could go shopping like a normal person," she said. When I pointed out to her that she wasn't exactly dressed like a normal person, she stared at me and said simply, "Lola, this is L.A." Of course, why hadn't I thought of it?

Because the day was nice, we took her restored Mustang convertible instead of the BMW. She explained to me that restored Mustangs were a real hot status item now. "Like Grant's Chevy," she said. I hadn't thought of Grant's restored '57 Chevy as a STATUS item. I thought Grant just had it because it was fun. In fact I'm SURE he did.

When you shop with Page, you don't just hop down to the nearest Safeway and grab a basket. Oh, no. First we had to go to the pasta store, where Page put one of their little wicker baskets over her arm and spent about fifteen minutes eyeing the pasta and asking very learned-sounding pasta questions.

"I didn't know there was that much to know about pasta," I said. (How come she had to go to a pasta store when she had an electric pasta maker on her counter?)

"Oh, I read two books on pasta last month," she said.

"Why?"

"Because I thought they would be—"

"Interesting," I interrupted her.

"Yeah," she said, as she always did when people were astonished at whatever she thought was interesting at the moment. "In fact, when I read that Marco Polo brought it from China, I read a book on Chinese cooking, and that got me interested in China, so I read *The Woman Warrior*, and that got me interested in the Chinese in America, so I read a book on San Francisco's Chinatown, and that made me realize I knew nothing about San Francisco's history, so I read two books on that, and now I'm reading about earthquakes. Did you know that at this very second, you are standing on one of the earthquake hotbeds of the *world?*"

"Yeah. I heard all of L.A. is going to be destroyed in one."

"Isn't that interesting?" asked Page absentmindedly.

Finally she selected asparagus pasta, which looked exactly like the spinach pasta next to it, but Page definitely felt the asparagus would go with what she was cooking.

Then we had to get back in the car and drive another mile or so to a croissant ship, where Page took a long time selecting some that were filled with spinach and cheese, and some that were filled with lemon. Then we went to a fresh fruit and vegetable market, and Page, with another wicker basket over her arm, selected snow peas, carrots, cauliflower, and green beans. After that we drove about two miles to another bakery, and Page took a long time selecting the French bread. Then we went to a special shop to get some special purified cooking oil. Then we went to a deli and bought some farm-fresh butter and a carton of oily-looking pasta salad, and then Page asked, "Is there anything you want?"

"A liquor store," I said.

Page smiled. "Oh, you," she laughed. At least Page wasn't a judgmental person, and had seen last night that, yes, I had drunk her scotch, but without Grant there to cheer me on, I had not got drunk at ALL. She also knew that so far today I hadn't acted crazy. It was probably too soon, but the lithium was doing its thing.

If only we hadn't gone to the liquor store. I mean, my sadness about it has nothing to do with the booze. In all our wanderings that day, no one had recognized Page, or if they had, the kind of people who shop in the kind of stores we were in know it's tacky to rush up and talk to a television personality.

I saw a neon sign ahead that said Rocky's Liquors, and told Page to stop because this looked like my kind of place. Page acted a little strange—like she was going into a porn store or something. She studied the collection of champagne. Although she didn't drink, she had taken a wine-tasting class a couple of years ago because she—yes, you got it— thought it would be interesting.

Suddenly I heard this raspy female voice behind me. "Hey, are you Page Bloom?" Page had once explained to me that you had to be either a VERY big star or very stupid to just tell someone to fuck off. After all, fans are what make the star, and you could get a very "bad rep" if you were rude.

"Yes, I am," said Page. Then it was just like out of a bad movie. The woman yelled to her husband to come over because "this lady here is Page Bloom," and of course the other six people in the store walked over to her, and Rocky himself came around the counter and asked for her autograph. He even wanted her to send him a picture to put in the window of his store saying she'd been there. I don't think Page had been planning to buy any champagne, but I guess she thought it would be good for her image, so she picked up a couple of bottles of Moët & Chandon. She carried them over and put them down beside my Johnnie Walker Red. Rocky kept asking for her autograph, and so did the couple who first spotted her. Some hard hat told her *Classified Ads* was his favorite show. Two more people came in off the street, wanting autographs. Then it all happened. Rocky turned to me and said, "Who are you? Are you anybody?"

I stared straight ahead. I found I couldn't open my mouth.

"Well, are you anybody?" he asked again.

I started to shake. "Hey," he said to Page, "she's crying."

I hadn't realized it, but my cheeks were wet, and I could hardly hold my wallet because my hand was shaking. I took a deep breath. "No," I said simply. "No, I'm not anybody at all."

Page instantly saw the situation for what it was and, pushing Rocky aside, walked over to me. "Yes," she said. "Yes, she's somebody. She's Lola Bloom."

"Related to you?" Rocky asked.

"She's my sister," she said.

"Hey, how about that? Page Bloom has a sister."

I have no idea what made me do it, but I started to scream. I couldn't understand why no one was moving. They just stood there staring at me in horrid fascination, and the more their eyes pierced my skin, the more I screamed.

"She's wrong! I'm nobody! No! No! I'm not fucking anybody. I'm sick, and I'm not anybody! Get the fuck away! Fuck off!"

"Hey," Rocky start to say, "let's not have that smut in—"

"Shut up!" hissed Page icily to him. I burst into sobs. The feeling was coming back into my stomach. The lead balloon was expanding, pushing at my heart . . . breaking my heart. Page put a twenty dollar bill on the counter and picked up the Johnnie Walker Red and left the champagne. She carefully led me, still sobbing, out to the Mustang, where she held my head and, like you'd feed a baby, slowly fed me some scotch until I quieted down.

"Please try, Lola," she said. *"Please!* You can control a lot of this. I know not all of it, but I'm not Grant; I don't have the patience to hold you all night. You scare me, and I don't have the strength to deal with it."

"But you don't encourage me. You don't—"

"You scare me, okay?" she said, and then quietly, "I'm sorry."

I didn't say anything. We drove home past Taco Bells, used car lots, billboards, through the City of the Angels back to sedate Hancock Park.

Mary Tyler Moore the cat was waiting by the door. The crying had somehow made me feel less worried about hurting Page's feelings. "Why in the blazing fuck," I asked, "did you name the god-damned dog Lola?"

"I told you. I named her after you."

"Did you think I'd be flattered?"

"Yes," she said, looking at me rather strangely. Well, I guess she had the right to, after I had freaked out in Rocky's liquor store. I remembered when we were little, Page got a kitten for Christmas and wanted to name it Little Lord Jesus, and Helen suggested she name it after the SECOND most wonderful thing she could think of, so the cat lived for fifteen years named Bacon.

"Are you okay now?" asked Page tentatively.

"Now that we're home," I said.

Page went to change her clothes before fixing the dinner. While she changed, she listened to Judy Collins's "Hard Times for Lovers," which made me wonder who Page's current lover was. Page was always monogamous, but she grew tired of men quickly. I walked into her bedroom, and she had put on a pair of evenly faded Sasson jeans and a pale green sweat shirt. She put her hair on top of her head and added a pair of gold hoop earrings.

"Are you sleeping with anyone?" I asked. "I mean, you don't have to baby-sit with me . . . that's not what they meant. They—"

"Christ, Lola, you've only been here a couple of days. Don't you think I would want to spend some time with you, even if—"

"You're not?"

"I'm trying celibacy."

"Why in the blazing fuck would you—"

"Will you stop saying 'Why in the blazing fuck'?"

"Why are you trying celibacy?"

"It's a new thing. . . . You know the sexual revolution didn't help us."

"I'm tired of hearing about the sexual revolution."

"I read somewhere that it began with the pill and ended when *Time* magazine discovered herpes . . . and I've had too many broken hearts."

"You *have?*" I was surprised. I couldn't imagine being a man and wanting to break up with Page. On the other hand, if I had to listen to Jacques Brel and watch reruns of *Leave It to Beaver*, well . . . but I couldn't imagine Page with a broken heart.

"They usually start to like me because they've never met anyone like me, then they start to think I'm strange, and then they . . ."

"Did you tell them you had a sister who is *worse?*"

Page smiled. "I was jealous of you."

"Of *me? Why?*"

"You had Grant."

"But you always stayed as short a time as possible. You disapproved of living life on the third level of irony."

"A Grant was all I ever wanted . . . someone who would love me for what I was. . . ."

I was shocked. "But you would have to—"

"That's the *point*. I wouldn't wear a wedding gown from the window of the Ritz or drink champagne at bowling alleys. I wouldn't do that, and Grant wanted someone who would."

"Why did you want him, then . . . I mean, if he did all those things that are offensive to you?"

"He accepted people. He was sweet. He was handsome. He was funny. . . . He was so caring." She paused and tied a matching sweat band around her forehead. "Don't you think I know you'd be dead now if Grant hadn't . . . well, been so caring."

"You're probably right," I said. "On the other hand, if Grant had been here last night, I would have polished off your scotch, and Grant would have encouraged me to wear an evening gown to a pool hall in Venice."

Page went into the kitchen and put on some water for the pasta. She poured a little of the special imported oil into a pan and stir-fried the vegetables and mixed them up with the pasta when it was done. No seasoning. Just that. We buttered the bread and each had a spinach croissant, and that was it. Four hours of shopping, and I had cooked up better meals from the 7-11 store down the hill from our house on St. Louis Drive.

After dinner, I put the dishes in the dishwasher and Page changed into a lounging gown with Garfield on it. Very uncharacteristically, she poured herself a drink.

I came into the living room and sat by her. "You know I love you," she said.

I had learned in my thirty-four years that when someone starts out a conversation with "You know I love you," there's about a ninety percent chance that whatever they are going to say next is something you aren't going to want to hear. "You've always loved me," I stated.

"You can't stay here for hiatus."

"I figured you'd say that."

— 181 —

"You really scared me this afternoon. . . . Not that I thought something awful would happen, but to see you lose control in a second . . . literally, one second you were making liquor store jokes, and the next you were screaming."

"It was the 'Are you anybody?' that set me off."

"I know, but I have no way of knowing what *else* might set you off. . . . Neither do you, and I know you can't promise it won't happen again. And I can't promise the 'Are you anybody' won't happen again. Every time I'm with *anyone*—even Helen—if someone recognizes me, they ask if the other person is anybody."

"Even Helen?"

"Yeah, and she always says, 'I'm the daughter of the late Irving Adrian,' and if they know shit about movies, they're impressed by that. No one has asked her for an autograph yet, thank God. You know how she feels about the movie business."

Neither of us said anything. Mary Tyler Moore jumped up on the back of the couch and rubbed her tail first on Page's neck and then on mine.

"I'm not going to Helen's, if that's what you're getting at."

Page looked very compassionate. "Oh, no. Helen . . . well, I love her because she's my mother, but she'd drive you straight to the bottom of the bay if you went back down there. I'm sorry." The booze was beginning to get to her. "I'm sorry, you're a scary person, Lola . . . make me feel helpless."

"Well, what are you saying?"

"Go back to Dillon."

"*To Dillon!* He puts on a fucking *clown suit* and juggles for Christ and subscribes to the newsletters of the Order of the Red Rubber Noses and Clowns for Christ, and brings balloons to cancer patients, and . . . well . . ."

"We're all going to be terrible for you, but maybe living with Dillon will be an incentive for you to get your shit together." She paused. "Grant would encourage you to be crazy, Helen would send you to your death, and I . . . well, you might send *me* to my death, but Dillon, he's so into 'I'm okay, you're okay' that at least you won't push *him* over the edge. You'll be in Hawaii where you have friends. Here you'd just sit around the house. At least *there* there are more people who care about you."

"But Dillon . . ."

"The only way you're going to get better is by yourself. And Dillon is so into his own trip, you won't fuck him up in the process. . . . He's already fucked up."

"I can't . . ."

"Well, *I* can't," she said, putting her arms around me.

Chapter

Around 1967, Dillon became a hippie. He just decided one day that that was what he was supposed to be, just like one day he woke up and decided that he and Sally should become Clowns for
Christ. His new concepts packed the little church
in Kahaluu. During the summer of 1967, when I
was eighteen and Page was twenty-one, we spent
our last official summer with Dillon and Sally. His
church no longer sang "Holy, Holy, Holy" every
Sunday. Oh, no, occasionally there would be some
kind of Christian-type folk song like "Lord of the
Dance" or Peter, Paul and Mary's "Hymn," or an
occasional spiritual, but usually there were songs
like "Blowin' in the Wind," "What Have They Done
to the Rain," "The Great Mandella," "Clouds," etc.
Two guys who lived in one of the houses that used
to have no plumbing but now did—Erick Kobiashi
and Steve Hanoula—played the guitar. All the pews
were removed, and everyone sat on pillows on the
floor (which I always reminded Dillon of later on
when he would object to the fact that Grant and I
had no furniture).

One day Dillon literally threw away all his aloha shirts and started wearing jeans, robes, and sandals ("Jesus boots," Page said when she first saw them). He had rushed down to India Imports and bought Indian gauze shirts, and Sally patiently strung love beads. They removed a lot of the tacky Jesus shit from their house. Indian bedspreads replaced the corduroy ones, a water pipe sat on the coffee table, "McCarthy: Peace" stickers shaped like daisies were all over their car, *Sergeant Pepper's Lonely Hearts Club Band* replaced the sound track from *Exodus* on their stereo. Page and I were actually pretty pleased about all this when we arrived in OUR Indian gauze, and both of us wore our hair long, straight, and parted in the middle.

Lots of changes had taken place in Kahaluu. Suddenly the whole world wanted to "do good" for the third worst poverty area in the nation—which I doubt it still was in 1967, as it was the hotbed of the Pacific drug traffic, but OFFICIALLY, Kahaluu was in great need of being saved.

The do-gooders from all religions and all parts of the country were there. The feds had sent in two VISTA volunteers, both carrying Kennedy's torch and saving the poor in our own country. Also Kahaluu Ecumenical Youth (KEY) was there. We were never exactly sure what they did except start a teen canteen in a dilapidated shack where they got grant money from the government to buy a Ping-Pong table, to hire about five people from the community who needed jobs, to buy potato chips for the picnics, and to rent movies.

Then there was the Community Action Program, which started a Summer Fun for the little kids and imported two Catholic nuns to run the whole thing.

Page got a job with KEY, and I got a job helping the nuns with the Community Action Program, and we both felt slightly guilty because the jobs were supposed to benefit the community and the poor, and we had a mother who had ten million dollars. Page justified HER job by saying that they needed SOMEONE who knew what she was doing, but I couldn't even do that, because—as I believe I've established—Lola Bloom NEVER knew what she was doing.

I actually kind of liked Sister Mary and Sister Ann, and often, after the Summer Fun ended at noon, I'd go sit in their kitchen with them and have a sandwich and wonder if they could guess that I wasn't a virgin. Sister Mary was kind of a typical *Sound of Music*–type nun with wire-rimmed glasses and was of an indeterminate age, but Sister Ann was definitely pretty. She looked like Audrey Hepburn in *The Nun's Story*. She was also rather open about talking about what it was REALLY like to be a nun.

"Do you have to shave your head?" I asked her—just to get rid of that common myth.

She smiled. "No, we just keep our hair short, as it would be pretty hot under the veil."

My job was to supervise the art classes at the Summer Fun. The kids were all noisy, dirty, and— it seemed to me—hyperactive. My knowledge of children's art was limited to coloring, cut-and-paste, and drawing, but no one seemed to care that I wasn't fresh out of elementary ed classes with wonderful fresh new ideas. The kids just screamed and ran around, and I passed out the construction paper.

That was the summer I discovered drinking and drugs. It began when I started sleeping with Moses Kamahana and Adam Swartz. Moses Kamahana was part Chinese and part Hawaiian, and occasionally dropped by Summer Fun or church for no reason at all. Finally, I got the message that he thought I was "one cute buggah" (a compliment), and I was fascinated with the Pidgin English he spoke, his good looks, and the fact that he was definitely a member of a minority group. He drove a ratty old jeep, and one day drove me to a cocktail dive in Kaneohe called Honey's that claimed to be the place where Don Ho got his start. We sat in the dingy darkness, and he kept ordering straight vodka for me, and after about three, I didn't feel as much like the famous female cockroach I assumed I was.

After Honey's he took me to the shack he rented on Kaneohe Bay. He pounded on the door, it opened a crack, and a RIFLE stuck out. "Who dat?" came a voice from inside.

"Eh, eets Moses!" he called.

I was getting a tad bit nervous. "How come the rifle?" I asked when the rifle was pulled in. We were in a bare room, with a complicated stereo system and about five hundred rock records.

Moses simply, casually, announced that he was a drug dealer ("like H and grass de most").

I guess I should have heeded Helen's advice and left that second, but because I was a recent grad of the Kerrybrook Academy for Girls, I was lured by anything that had the ring of the thrilling or decadent, and face it, drugs and guns do have that sweet, seductive scent of the thrilling and decadent.

I wasn't stupid enough to do heroin, and even if I had been, my fear of needles would have kept me away. Grass always made me a little sick, but Moses had cocaine and Dexedrine, and after a Dexedrine, a few snorts of cocaine, and more vodka, Lola Bloom could conquer the world. Lola was no longer "Page's little sister." Lola was suddenly lovely, and everything I did or said seemed astounding.

Moses kissed me, and I joyously ripped off all my clothes, and we kissed some more, and I poured the rest of the vodka all over us, and we licked it off. We turned on The Doors full blast on the stereo, and athletically fucked for three hours.

Finally, I figured I should be getting back to our now mellow and laid-back little banana farm, because even though Dillon had become suddenly liberal, he just MIGHT slip back into his former self if I spent the night with Moses.

We zigzagged up the road, and as we approached the dirt road that led to the farm, I realized that I didn't have ONE THING to say to Moses. It wasn't Moses I loved; it was the drinking and the drugs. I asked him if I could buy some of the speed from him, and poor Moses, not knowing that I had money and that I really didn't want to see him again, said I could HAVE some and handed me an envelope full of the tiny tablets. As I got out of the jeep, he kissed me and told me that I was "one crazy chick . . . one, like, super chick."

Adam Swartz was a VISTA volunteer from New York, and he was my first love. During that summer the depressions started, only I didn't recognize them because I simply assumed that passing out crayons for four hours a day to screaming kids would naturally bum me out, and I thanked the Dexedrine and vodka for cheering me up. One day I woke, frightened . . . terrified, and I knew I just couldn't face little Sterling Nakaguchi and little Peter Halahau, so I called Adam Swartz, who lived in a rented Hicks house across from Kahaluu School where the Summer Fun program was, and asked him if he'd go across the street and give Sister Ann the bad news.

Sally kept asking me if I was sick. I sat on my bed and hugged my knees, waiting for the terror to go away. I had long ago run out of drugs, and even old decadent Lola Bloom didn't drink before 5:00 P.M.

Page finished getting ready for her difficult job of supervising the Ping-Pong games over at the teen canteen and came over and stroked my hair. I jumped as if she had snuck up behind me and set off a firecracker in my ear.

"Lola, what the hell is *wrong!*"

"I'm scared . . . I'm scared."

She sat down on the bed and carefully touched my arm. I started to tremble. "What are you so scared of?" she asked.

"The rest of the summer, I guess . . . college . . . I don't want to go to college next year. I just want to be someplace where it's . . . I don't know . . . safe, I guess."

"Where do you think that would be?" she asked.

—- 189 —

I started to almost whimper. "Just leave me alone. I don't want to talk to anyone."

I spent the whole morning huddled under the covers. Goddamn good-intentioned Sally kept coming in (wearing an inexpensive Indian sari and long earrings) to offer me shit like chicken soup. Finally, she got the message that there was something wrong with the head and the heart and not the body, so she assumed I was on drugs and went to work in her gift shop.

I wasn't on drugs. This was for real.

Alone in the house, I stared at the ceiling. I tried to think of ANYTHING I wanted besides learning to ride a motorcycle and getting to meet John Wayne. For the first time in my life I lost track of time. I had no idea whether ten minutes or three hours went by. I don't believe I slept, but I might have. I vaguely made out a knocking on the door. It was strange. I hadn't taken any drugs or anything, but my legs didn't seem to work. Slowly, and with great effort, I managed to get to the front door. Adam Swartz was standing there with a bunch of the gardenias that grew so well in the lush, humid, wet greenness of Kahaluu Valley.

"For the patient," he said.

I stood there for a few seconds, and FINALLY managed to ask him if he'd like to come in.

"What's wrong with you?" he asked.

"I . . . I don't know."

"The flu?"

"No, I'm not sick."

"You *said* you were sick, and, well . . . you *look* sort of sick, but . . ."

"No, first I was frightened, then I was sad, and now I can't move."

He looked concerned and efficiently went to the kitchen and found a jar to put the gardenias in. He was a medium-sized man with curly hair and horn-rimmed glasses (in 1968 to be considered "neat" you were supposed to have straight hair and wear wire-rimmed glasses). Since I always seemed attracted to the offbeat, I liked the fact that he didn't rush out and buy wire-rimmed glasses the second John Lennon did.

"What I think you have," he said, "is a sem-iserious case of the blues."

I hadn't thought of it before, but that sounded at least in the right ball park. "Maybe."

"Anything happen?" he asked, genuinely concerned.

"No. It just happened. I mean, it's happened before, but not this bad."

"What happend before?"

"It went away."

"Well," he said simply, "let's just wait for this to go away." He smiled. "Do you think Sister Mary and Sister Ann can manage without you?"

"They'll probably be sorry when I come back. The kids take one look at me and instantly misbehave. I think they know I don't know what I'm doing."

"What are you doing that job for? I know a lot . . ."

"Yeah," I interrupted, "I know a lot of people who want and need it, too. Dillon is trying to build my character."

He smiled. I felt a little better. Not like moving or dancing, but a little less scared.

"You want a beer or something?" I managed to ask.

"Sure."

Adam was very patient. For three days in a row he came over with flowers and mild wit. On the fourth morning I woke up joyous. It was the beginning of a life-long pattern.

The only thing that made me sad was the fact that I would have to go back and teach little Sterling Nakaguchi and Peter Halahau, and say, "I'm so sorry," every time Sister Ann came into the room and saw the kids throwing papers around and screaming . . . also sad that I might not see as much of Adam.

I felt so euphoric that morning that Sally seemed funny rather than annoying. I sang "Michael from Mountains" while I did the dishes, and smirked as I watched Sally in her yoga positions. Usually I despised her. Today she was amusing.

Dillon came in in a flowing white Arabian robe and his Jesus boots, and he cooked eggs (Sally and Dillon had just discovered "sharing" the work load), and he harmonized with me through the rest of "Michael from Mountains." They thought I was just feeling better, and Dillon drove Sally down to the gift store, and he drove into Honolulu to get some kites, as the next Sunday (and I'm not making this up) part of the church service would be kite flying and (really) singing "Let's Go Fly a Kite" from *Mary Poppins*. (This event was so popular with his congregation that he kept it in his bag of tricks after he became a clown minister.)

I was left alone, so I took a beer, peeled off all my clothes and ran across their squishy, green front lawn, through a grove of guava trees, to the little stream that snaked its way through the banana farm. The water was icy, but made me feel alive on this damp, humid, sunny morning. I sat so the water rushed between my legs, and rested my back against a smooth rock. I drank my Primo beer and joyously and euphorically toasted the mountains that rose like cliffs above the guava trees. I dug in the mud with my toes and scared two crawfish, which skittered in opposite directions. The guppies fled, then slowly came back to nibble at my toes. I sang the Monkees' "I saw her face / Now I'm a believer" at the top of my voice.

Just as I polished off the Primo, I looked up and there was Adam standing there staring at me, limply holding the daisies he had brought that day to help me through the depression.

"Adam!" I waved. He walked slowly over to the edge of the bank.

"You're naked."

"Get naked yourself! It's great!" I yelled.

"You're better," he said.

"I'm *wonderful!*"

Adam smiled, climbed up the bank, and one at a time dropped the daisies into the water upstream for me. Soon I was surrounded by floating flowers.

"Is anyone else here?" he asked.

"Only the cats and the crawfish."

"There are crawfish in the stream?" He looked a little worried.

"They're scared of us." I stopped. "Scared of me," I said.

Adam slowly unbuttoned his shirt and tossed it onto the grass, and then quickly unzipped his pants, took them off, and I saw he had a hard-on.

He slipped into the stream facing me. "It's *freezing!*" he yelled—used to the salty, still warmth of Kaneohe Bay in summertime.

"The water comes from way up in the mountains."

Most of the daisies had floated away, but he picked one up and put it behind my ear.

"You're beautiful, Lola Bloom," he said.

"You're not scared of me?"

"Why should I be scared of you?"

"Everyone in high school was, except my sister, and now *she's* a little scared of me, and . . ."

He took my face in his hands. "You'll never be boring," he said.

"For the last three days, I was the most boring thing *alive.*"

"You were just in a cocoon, and now look at the butterfly that came soaring out." He kissed me . . . a sweet, warm kiss. "And even cocoons aren't boring. People watch them . . . waiting for, well . . . this." He came closer to me and wrapped his legs around my body. The icy water had put a slight damper on his erection, but we kissed and clung, knowing the warmth of the day and my dry bed would restore it.

During the summer of 1967, I loved Adam. He was a lot like Grant would be later. He didn't want me better. If I hadn't gone away to college in Santa Cruz, it might have been Adam I would have had to get away from.

Chapter

The last three days in L.A., after Page told me she couldn't "handle" me, were pretty grim. Page was trying to go out of her way for me simply because she felt sad and guilty about her inability to cope. I was trying very hard—with some success—to act normal and cheerful, so she MIGHT change her mind. I didn't want to go back to Dillon, Sally, Free, and their gleaming waxed kitchen, but Page was right: Dillon wasn't the perfect answer, but I did have friends in Honolulu, none in Coronado or L.A., and if Page couldn't watch over me, it was either Dillon or the funny farm.

Page, of course, didn't wear the same thing twice the whole five days I was with her, and usually she managed at least five different clothes changes during any given day. She frantically took me to the Farmers' Market, to Universal Studios where *Classified Ads* was taped to show me the lot and the sound stages, to the La Brea Tar Pits, etc., to keep me busy and talking about things other than "the situation."

Finally, she got around to asking me what I wanted to see, which was—of course—the houses where the Manson murders were committed and the house that *The Beverly Hillbillies* supposedly lived in. Page sighed. I could tell she really wanted to understand me, but if she somehow DID move up to the third level of irony, she wouldn't be able to take Hollywood at all.

Suddenly it struck me that Page—thirty-thousand-dollars-an-episode Page—without Hollywood would be just as unequipped to deal with life as I was. She didn't even have a goddamn degree from the University of California, Santa Cruz. I looked over at her in her huge sunglasses, shifting the BMW in her Gloria Vanderbilt pants and a T-shirt that said "Memo from June: 'Ward, I'm worried about the Beaver' on it and realized that she couldn't even be a high school English teacher. Take *Classified Ads* away from her and all you'd have would be a closet full of clothes that would be out of style the next year.

Of course without *Classified Ads*, Page could probably get another series, a bunch of guest star things, or be a game show celeb, but it really was true in theory that without Hollywood, Page would be just like me. The only difference was that I was sick and Page was not; I was on the third level and Page was on the second. I realized that it's hard to be on the third level in a world that is mostly made up of second- and first-level people. When I was with Grant, it was easier because he got the joke too. No wonder I was sad. What's the fun of having a joke when there's no one to laugh at it. That thought made me a little (but not much) sympathetic toward Dillon. I don't think I ever laughed at anything funny he tried to do.

Finally, it came to be the time when Page was going to mail me off to Dillon and Sally on the plane. We had agreed not to tell Dillon that Page "didn't know how to cope," and let him think I'd thought things over and WANTED to come back. My plan, although I didn't tell Page, was to pay Dillon only a token visit and then try to figure out some way to move out. Basically, this could be one of three ways: (a) Maryanne, (b) Grant, (c) a job. Plan (a) of course could only be temporary, might ruin a friendship, and would lead eventually to plan (c). Plan (b) was what I wanted, but knew if I ever wanted to achieve (c), I should just forget it, and plan (c) was . . . interesting. Since I had had the realization that Page was nothing without Hollywood, the thought that the only job I could get would be a humiliating kind of job maybe wasn't true.

Page came to the gate with me in disguise: faded jeans, a U.C.L.A. T-shirt, her hair completely covered up with a scarf, and huge sunglasses. No one even gave her a second glance.

"You call me," she ordered rather than said.

"I will."

She frowned. "If it gets too horrible living there, and if you haven't had anymore freak-outs, I'll send you some money so you can get an apartment."

"Thanks . . . uh, but I think I should get it myself. I think that's part of the cure."

"You're right. I read *Passages*," she said seriously (second level for sure). Then she said almost formally, "I'm glad you believe that." Then she smiled, hugged me, and said, "I love you, Lola babe," and I soberly walked down the jet-way to the plane. I'm not at all afraid of flying, but I always tend to glance at the other passengers and think to myself, These may be the people I'll die with—or worse, be stuck with on a life raft for weeks in the Pacific Ocean.

This would be an especially grim flight. there would be no Grant with flowers, a lei, and champagne at the end of the flight. There would be no drunken night of lovemaking. On the other hand, there would be no morning wondering why I was alive. Boring. Safe, but boring.

One of the worst things about living in Hawaii is going home on the plane. You've finished your vacation, and everyone else is just starting theirs, whooping it up with mai tais and dreams of the Sheraton Waikiki Hotel.

I sat soberly next to a midwestern couple, and we had a token conversation about which brand of suntan lotion was the best. When I broke the news to them that I LIVED in Hawaii and rarely went to the beach unless it was for a picnic supper, they were amazed.

"What do you *do*, then?" they asked.

"Uh, read, cook, look out the window." They looked totally confused. "I have—or rather *had*—a nice view. I looked right down into Diamond Head." I said.

"What line of work are you in?" asked the man, who looked like the type whose first purchase would be an aloha shirt.

"I . . . I . . . ." I was going to lie, but what was the point? "I'm what they call a displaced homemaker."

"Oh, I'm so sorry," said the woman.

"Maybe she's not at all sorry, Gladys," said the man.

"I'm sorry," I said. "I don't like feeling displaced." I quickly ended the conversation by picking up the airline magazine and soberly reading it from cover to cover without looking up or speaking.

The movie was *Annie* AGAIN! Even though I didn't buy the earphones, just having to look at it occasionally kind of made me sick. I got up, went to the back of the plane, and was the only woman standing around the bar cart. The flight attendant, in his blue and yellow aloha shirt (to remind anyone who had forgotten that we were on our way to paradise), poured me a scotch on the rocks. I leaned against the emergency exit and soberly sipped.

"May I join you?" said a voice with a heavy midwestern accent. I looked up and saw a reasonably good-looking man with a strange look in his eyes. He, for some reason, made me nervous, but I just chalked it up to the fact that he was wearing a white belt and white shoes, polyester double-knit pants, and a Qiana nylon body shirt. You could tell he thought he looked real sharp.

Mainly because of the white belt, I didn't say that sure, I'd love to join him, but also because of the white belt, I didn't discourage it. Conversations with people who wore white belts sometimes were, as Page would put it, "interesting." Imagine getting into the mind of someone who actually went into Thom McAn and actually selected a pair of white shoes with gold buckles and a white belt to match. I smiled, thinking that this morning while Page was selecting her U.C.L.A. T-shirt, he was carefully selecting yellow socks, a yellow print stretch body shirt, and a white belt.

"Whatcha drinking?" he asked. I looked at his eyes. There was something weird about them, nothing I could put my finger on, but weird . . . slightly shifty.

"Johnnie Walker Red on the rocks," I stated. He walked back over to the bar cart and bought another one of their miniature liquor bottles, and poured the scotch into my glass.

"My name's Pete," he said. "Short for Peter," he added.

"Oh," I said, amused. "My name is Lola." I didn't add Bloom because I didn't want this guy in a white belt to call me Lola Bloom the way Grant did.

"You going to Hawaii on vacation?"

"No. I live there."

"Son of a gun. So do I."

Realizing that "getting into his mind" probably wouldn't be as fascinating as I had thought a few minutes ago, I said, "Lucky you," rather glumly.

"You're damn right," he said. "Where do you live?"

"Uh . . ." I almost automatically said St. Louis Heights, but then I remembered that I no longer lived up with the clouds and the stars at the top of our heights. "Mililani Town," I said with almost the same disdain in my voice as if I had said Harlem or Orange County.

"Son of a gun," he said. "My ex lives there.

She got the house. I'm living in a condo in Wai-kiki. Better for meeting fine women like yourself."

"How do you know I'm a fine woman?" I asked, genuinely curious.

"Well . . ." He pause. "I can just tell."

I decided to throw him a quick one, "I'm a manic-depressive," I said simply.

"Beg pardon?"

"I'm a manic-depressive," I said again.

"But you're not doing anything manic or de-pressive."

"I'm depressed as hell."

"Oh, jeez, I'm sorry. How come?"

"Because I'm going back to Mililani town."

He shifted around, and then (I'm not making this up) he ACTUALLY SAID, "Some of my best friends are manic-depressives. A person like your-self shouldn't worry about it."

"I don't," I lied.

"Whereabouts in Mililani Town do you live?" he asked.

Making probably the biggest mistake of my life, I said, "Next to the school."

"Which model?"

"I'm not sure . . . I think model C in tur-quoise."

"Son of a gun."

"Huh?"

"Me and my ex had a model C too."

At this point I thought that maybe watching *Annie* without the sound might not be such a bad idea after all. "Getting into his head" was becom-ing a drag. I sort of lamely smiled, and he zipped over to the bar cart before I could say anything and dumped another miniature bottle of Johnnie Walker into my glass, so I had to stay for a few more minutes.

"You married?" he asked.

"No." I mean, what was the point of going into a long explanation about how I had to "get my life together" to a man wearing a white belt?

"Your ex leave you the house?"

"Huh?"

"Well, like, swinging single girls like yourself don't usually live in Mililani Town unless they got the house from their exes. Kind of far from the action, ya know?"

I didn't want to go into a long explanation about Dillon, so I just shrugged and said, "I do. And I don't swing."

"Son of a gun. A single gal like yourself living in a three-bedroom house. You must have a lot of money."

I thought about dropping the bombshell that my mother was worth ten million dollars, but I decided against it. Either he would hijack me or not believe me.

"If I had a lot of money, I wouldn't live in Mililani town," I said.

"Huh?"

"I have two terribly strong male roommates who work out on a Nautilus."

"Geez! You live with *two guys!*"

"They're just roommates . . . platonic," I said. I was in deeper than I cared to be. I could just picture Grant, my sweet Grant, leaning against the other side of the emergency exit shaking his head and smiling.

"You know what I think would be real fun?" he asked. I shrugged. "If when I drive out there to see my ex and the kids, I could take you out and we could grab a cork and a fork and have a few laughs."

"A cork and a fork?"

"Yeah," he grinned. I couldn't bring myself to say anything. "Aw, gee," he said digging the toe of one white shoe into the rug. "I gotta fess up . . . uh . . . I saw who brought you to the plane. I'd know her in a minute, even with her hair in that scarf."

"Page," I stated rather glumly.

"*Classified Ads* is my favorite show. How the heck did you get to know *Page Bloom*?"

"She's my sister."

"You're spoofing me. Page Bloom has a sister who lives in *Hawaii*?"

"That's me."

"God, what's she *really* like?"

"Uh . . . nice . . . very nice."

I slowly backed away from him, moving toward my seat. I had the same horrible pain inside me that I had had in Rocky's liquor store when someone had asked if I was anyone, but I wasn't freaking out. I just held the backs of the seats and carefully walked—backwards—to my seat. I didn't scream. I didn't cry. I was going to make it. Even though I'd probably be "the amazing one" only to Grant, and I'd never be one of your major celebrities, even though the Man in the White Belt probably wouldn't have bought me two drinks if I hadn't been Page's sister, I was still Lola Bloom. I remembered Grant. Grant, who could have any woman in the world, had wanted and loved Lola Bloom for ten years. Maybe there was something there.

As I sat down, I was shaking. Fortunately the midwestern couple were intently watching Annie, Daddy Warbucks, and President Roosevelt singing "Tomorrow," so I didn't have to say anything to them. The ice cubes shook in my drink, not from air turbulence, but from the turbulence in my brain. I took a deep breath.

Suddenly, a hand attached to a polyester sleeve poured another Johnnie Walker miniature into my plastic cup. I took a very deep breath and said as calmly as softly as I could, "You get the fuck away from me."

The Man in the White Belt squatted by my seat. "The F-word, huh?"

"Yes, the fucking F-word," I stated icily. "Don't ever come near me again." He sort of looked astonished, and then backed off.

Even though it was a small thing, I felt I had a little power in the real world, when before I had felt that my only power was to live or die, and I had had trouble doing either one. I couldn't believe it. I had actually calmly told a man in a white plastic belt—who had looked right through Lola and seen Page—to get the fuck away. I noticed the ice in my drink had stopped shaking.

As I sipped the drink, I tried not to remember the homecomings of the last ten years, but it sure as hell was hard to wipe out the sight of Grant galloping across the passenger waiting area, grabbing my hand luggage, and tossing it aside. Then he would hold me so tightly I couldn't breathe. He would just stand there for five minutes holding me—even if I'd been away only a few days—and make all the other passengers in their tropical lightweight pantsuits walk around us. He'd say over and over again, "I love you, Lola Bloom."

Every time I get off a plane in Hawaii I am always surprised at how humid it is. As I walked down the jet-way, I could already feel myself beginning to sweat. Out of the corner of my eye, I saw the Man in the White Belt hurrying up to me.

"You aren't going to just go off without, you know, exchanging numbers or something, are you?"

I was totally amazed. "Didn't I just tell you to get the fuck away from me?" I was pleased with myself for being so calm. Maybe it was that look in his eyes . . . something strange, something I'd seen in my own eyes in the mirror too often. With normal people, I felt weak. I'm strange, sure, but I don't wear white plastic belts on the first level of irony, and even though I did get married in a window-of-the-Ritz wedding dress, even sitting gloriously on the third level of irony, I would never wear a white plastic belt (snob?). I was the stronger, and I liked it.

He looked confused. "Gosh, I didn't think ya meant it. I thought it was just a little fight."

"A little *fight?* I haven't *known* you long enough to have a little fight' with you. I don't *want* to know you."

He looked like a little kid whose mother had forgotten to put the tooth fairy money under his pillow. "But you gotta have a drink with me. You didn't get a chance to see what a swell guy I am." We reached the end of the jet-way, and I scanned the crowd and didn't see anyone there to meet me. Just then, I heard the paging system: "United passenger Lola Bloom, please pick up the white courtesy phone. United passenger Lola Bloom." The Man in the White Belt followed me to the phone. The message was that Sally had been late and had also had a flat tire and wouldn't be at the airport for another half-hour.

"Bad news?" he asked.

"None of your business." (God it's great to tell someone to fuck off sometimes.)

"I have a real good sense of humor too," he said. "One drink? Please?"

"My ride won't be here for another half-hour," I said. "I'll have *one* drink at the bar, but I won't talk about Page. She doesn't like to have her privacy invaded." Secretly I was afraid if we got on the subject of Page, this new rush of strength I had would evaporate.

He looked like someone had just given him a new Pontiac. "That's *great!*" he said. "Then you can find out that I'm a real fine person." He walked next to me after we got off the minibus that had taken us to the main terminal.

"Ya know," he said. "I didn't do anything to make you use that F-word and tell me to get away. I was just a regular guy buying you a drink."

"I got the feeling you were buying *Page* the drink."

We got to the bar and were seated next to a huge carved tiki god. The cocktail waitress, in a bikini top with a sarong around her hips, took our orders.

"You must be divorced," he said. "You look too old to be on your first roll around."

I didn't bother to make a sarcastic comment, and by the time I'd finished three-fourths of my drink, I had learned he was pro-nuke, anti-E.R.A., pro-Reagan, pro-U.S. involvement in El Salvador, anti-abortion (a true-blue right-to-lifer), and anti-Semitic. I told him that Bloom wasn't my married name, but that I had kept it because it was pretty, and he wanted to know what my husband's name was, so I said, with only a slight tremor in my voice, "Grant Rosenberg."

"Isn't that one of those Jew names?" he asked.

"Uh . . . yes."

"You were married to a *Jew*? You don't look like the sort of gal who would marry one of those Jews."

"I married him because I *loved* him," I said more than just a little bit coldly.

"Did you split up 'cause . . . uh . . . like, culturally you couldn't get along, like he was too attached to his mother or something?"

"I can't believe I'm hearing this."

"Well, why did you split up?"

How was I going to explain to a man in a white plastic belt the whole thing I've been trying to explain for two hundred pages? I wish I had been smart and had just said he tried to beat me up or he left me for another woman, but instead I said, "Remember on the plane I told you I was crazy, and you said "—I paused so I could say this without laughing——"that some of your best friends were manic-depressives?"

"Well, they are."

"That's why I left. I made things too hard for him, and because I love him . . . well, I didn't want . . . and he wasn't good for me either. He—"

"I don't get it."

"He left me for another woman," I said, realizing that it would be so simple—especially with someone you weren't going to see again in your life.

"God, that's terrible. I admire a person like yourself who can just come out and admit that her husband ran out on her."

"It's over. I don't think about it anymore." I finished my drink and realized he was only about halfway through his, so I decided to get the conversation going, drink up, and rush to the safety of baggage claim. Well, at least this would be the first time I wouldn't be bummed out by having to go to the baggage claim, and at least this drink had allowed my suitcase to already be there.

The luck of Lola Bloom: her suitcase is always spit out onto the baggage carousel last. No matter WHEN Lola Bloom checks in on the other end of the trip, her suitcase is always last, and when other travelers bring back rare glass antiques, they arrive completely intact, and Lola Bloom's bottle of Johnnie Walker Red has been smashed in the suitcase, and all her clothes smell like a singles bar.

"So," I said, "Uh . . . why did you split up with your wife?"

Now, I'm not making this up. It sounds like I am. That's the trouble with real life: you can't put it in a novel unless you tone it down or people will think you're making it up. (For example, one thing I didn't tell you about Page is that she believes in the left brain–right brain theory, and that her right brain is a panther named Lilah who smokes Benson & Hedges 100s in a jade cigarette holder, and all Lilah likes to do is sit around and smoke, and Page's left brain is a carrot named Duffy who wants to work twenty-four hours a day, and Duffy and Lilah have constant discussions and fights. Page also has a THIRD brain, which is a bunny rabbit named Gary who just sits around and laughs at Duffy and Lilah, who are arguing, and Lilah keeps trying to convince Gary, the bunny, to eat Duffy the carrot, but Gary won't because the bunny knows that without some left brain thinking, you die. Try putting that in a novel . . . you'd think it was just bad fiction.)

Anyway, I asked the Man in the White Belt (who had already told me he had been married to his "ex" for fifteen years, and that they had two teenage sons) why he split up with his wife, he looked a little pensive, put his elbows on our little monkey-pod table, and said with a dead-serious expression on his face, "Well, it was . . . uh . . . I don't want you to get the wrong idea, but we really *had* to split up because, well, my penis was too big for her."

My jaw dropped. I really HAD met someone crazier than I was. WHY would someone say that? I guess he thought that might get me all turned on or something. I don't know, but I'm not stupid and

knew in an instant that he was bad news altogether. I calmly put two dollars on the table (so I
wouldn't even have to admit that someone like that
had bought me a drink) and said that I really had
to rush to baggage claim.

As I stood on the escalator, I thought about
Grant. God, he'd love that story. We'd have not
only one but TWO new characters we could joke
about: the Man in the White Belt and also the
Woman with the Small Vagina. God, Grant . . .

Sally was at the baggage claim, full of apologies. I felt stronger. Even though it was just about
a dumb flat tire, SHE was still saying, "I'm so sorry,
Lola," instead of the perpetual "I'm sorry, Sallys"
I always found myself saying for things I wasn't
really a bit sorry about.

"I'm sorry, Sally," "I'm sorry, Dillon," "I'm
sorry, Helen," "I'm sorry, Page," "I'm sorry,
Grant." I am sorry.

"Did you have a nice trip?" was the first thing
Sally asked me (DID YOU HAVE A NICE TRIP? I mean,
really.)

"Page was great, and I got to see the La Brea
Tar Pits. I thought they were way out in the de-
sert like where Charles Manson had his dune buggy
brigade, but they turned out to be just right on
Wilshire Boulevard."

"What I meant was: Are you feeling better?"

"Yes," I could honestly say. (But "feeling better" is so boring . . . but on the other hand, being
in tears in Grant's arms forever is probably pretty
boring too . . . well, not BORING, but not right.)

Sally and I spent a few minutes trying to fit my
suitcase in the trunk of the Pinto, but Dillon's clown

makeup kit and bag of balloons took up too much space, so we wedged it into the back seat.

"Dillon's lawyers have the divorce papers all ready to sign," Sally said cheerfully as she started the Pinto.

"Great," I said glumly. I really didn't want to talk about Grant—especially with a woman driving to Mililani Town—a place she ELECTED to live—with an "I'm Third" pendant around her neck.

"You and Grant really should have taken our advice and bought a house instead of renting. You could stick him for half the appreciated value of the house."

"The house we wanted to live in wasn't for sale," I stated.

"Oh, you," said Sally. "At least there's only one of you. We don't have to worry about Page."

"Gee, thanks," I said sarcastically. "What happens if *Classified Ads* is canceled?"

"Lola, is it possible for *once* in your life to make an attempt to be polite to me?"

"Why couldn't you once in my marriage have made an attempt to be polite to Grant?"

"Grant is just an overgrown hippie. For all I know, he probably takes drugs."

"Did he sign the divorce papers?" I asked shakily.

"He is *generously* giving you a quarter of *Mr. Macho* for three years."

"That's a lot of money," I said, genuinely surprised. I honestly didn't expect anything. I hadn't done anything. I hadn't been a "supportive loving spouse." Grant had been the supportive loving spouse.

We pulled into the driveway of the turquoise model C tract house in Mililani Town. I mean, I didn't mind when Dillon was a hippie minister because we were all into the Indian bedspread trip then, but NOW! A "complete one-eighty." They had lime green shag carpet, and their furniture all matched and was sort of lime green plaid: sofa, love seat, easy chair, recliner, etc., and (worse) the DRAPES matched the furniture. And these were the same people who didn't get the joke when Grant said we got our cat to match our rug (beige cat, beige rug), so we had to be very careful not to accidentally step on her.

Sally's kitchen was spotless, with avocado green appliances and happy face pot holders, a happy face toaster cover, a happy face blender cover, a happy face food processor cover, happy face place mats for the avocado green Formica-top kitchen table, and (if you can believe it) happy face magnets for the icebox. Before I left Grant, I once (in jest) asked her if she'd like Grant to come over sometime and paint a happy face on the ceiling, and she SERIOUSLY considered it for a few minutes. Nothing had changed in the kitchen except there was a poster with a unicorn under a rainbow on it pinned to the bulletin board with a happy face thumbtack.

Dillon was off somewhere, so Sally just left my suitcase in the Pinto for him to bring in when he came back. She looked at me as if I were a stranger. I looked down at the scars on my wrists that got fainter every day, and I felt really bummed out, especially with all those little happy smiles staring at me.

Suddenly the most cheerful thought I'd had in a year hit me. With one-quarter of *Mr. Macho*, I didn't have to sleep in their guest room with a blow-up photo of a teddy bear wearing a red T-shirt that said "I [heart] you" on it, hanging over the bed. A quarter of *Mr. Macho* could get me an apartment that didn't look so sterile that you could do brain surgery in the kitchen.

"Do you have the morning paper?" I asked Sally.

"Well, I've cut out the Reverend Paul Osumi's 'Thought for the Day,' because I'm of the mind that your attitude was the thing that caused all your, well . . . shall we say 'problems'? And I thought he put it in a nutshell this morning."

She took the little rectangular "Thought for the Day" off the icebox and replaced the happy face magnet.

"I really wanted to see the classified ads," I said.

"Well, read this first, and I'll go get the rest of the paper. What do you want the classified for?"

"An apartment."

"You can't manage by yourself."

"I'm going to try," I said.

"Well," she said cheerfully as she left the room, "if you're going to dream, you might as well dream in Technicolor."

Now, personally I thought the Reverend Paul Osumi was at times amusing. Grant and I had occasionally read him aloud to each other. Our favorite had been the one where he said that we had liver transplants, heart transplants, and kidney transplants, but had we ever thought of TONGUE

— 213 —

transplants? The gist was that you shouldn't say "fuck" and "shit" and stuff like that, and Grant had decided he should open a tongue transplant bank and get nice clean-living Christians who didn't even say "damn" to donate their tongues when they died, so when kids got to be about twelve and started saying "fuck" and "shit," their parents could go to the tongue transplant bank and get them a different tongue. The old reverend wasn't ALWAYS that original. Usually he just had spiritually uplifting thoughts. One of Grant's get-rich-quick schemes was to make the Reverend Paul Osumi "Bigger than Sun Moon" and get him nationally syndicated, have Paul Osumi tote bags and T-shirts, get him a television show, and collect huge donations. We agreed he needed editors (us) for his "Thought for the Day" to make sure he had lots of tongue-transplant and wrinkled-hearts-are-worse-than-wrinkled-faces type columns, a few spiritually uplifiting ones, and definitely NONE of the one that condemned lust, drinking, smoking, and premarital sex. All he needed was a little guidance, and the three of us could be millionaires. Grant even looked him up in the phone book, and he was actually LISTED. We debated about whether or not he'd get too swelled a head if we called him and told him we were fans, and then we decided to respect his privacy. When we mentioned him to Sally and Dillon, they were pleased and surprised that we devotedly read Rev. Paul Osumi's "Thought for the Day."

I somehow had the feeling that the "thought" Sally had cut out wasn't going to be another tongue-transplant thought, and I was right. It said,

"Some people keep on living by the sensual until they are satiated and not satisfied. Some people keep on mistrusting others until finally they trust themselves least of all. Some people keep on hating others until they themselves become physically and mentally ill."

"Bring me the classified ads *quickly!*" I yelled to Sally.

Sally returned with that hopeless look on her face she had whenever she had to "deal" with me.

"You know," she said, "you're going to need that *Mr. Macho* money for therapy. You can't afford to move. You can't go to your mother or your sister because I will instantly fill them in on your exact condition, and they wouldn't *dream* of letting you live alone."

"I'll get a job," I said simply.

Sally put a hand on my shoulder and said sadly, "But you can't *do* anything."

"That's what I've been telling myself too long," I said. "The fact is, I believe that is part of the goddamn problem." I wanted to explain to her that at LEAST I wasn't as badly off as the Man in the White Belt. He'd probably never try to kill himself, but on the other hand, he would have to walk around in this world wearing his plastic belt for the rest of his life and wishing everyone knew he had a big penis. Sally wouldn't understand that.

She shook her head and looked at me the way parents do when kids say—in all seriousness—that they want to be an astronaut or a movie star when they grow up. Fuck, I was over twenty-one, and I could do damned well what I pleased.

Unfortunately in the "Help Wanted" section

there weren't exactly any jobs that said, "Wanted: former mental patient; B.A. from Santa Cruz; type 30 words a minute; must be on the third level of irony." However, there was an ad in "Apartments, Furnished" that said, "Quiet studio apartment. St. Louis Heights. View of Diamond Head. Great fixer-upper, $350 mo." St. Louis was my (our) heights. Diamond Head was my view. My hand shook as I dialed the phone number. I was ALMOST going home.

Chapter

12

In the fall of 1967, with my guitar, I took a cab from the Greyhound bus station to spend four years at University of California, Santa Cruz, which didn't give grades and would insulate me from "real life." Life had become more and more terrifying for me every day. I didn't understand the depressions yet, hadn't even figured out that each one would be followed by a high. The one thing that kept me going was that secret power I thought I had: I could ALWAYS kill myself.

The cab driver had the radio on, and Joni Mitchell was singing "Both Sides Now"—all about how SHE didn't really know life at all either.

"So you going to old Santa Cruz," said the cab driver. "Ya know, that place sure the hell is beautiful. Probably one of the damned most beautiful campuses in the country . . . kind of like a country club. You don't even need to go to Miami Beach—got your resort right there."

"Yeah, and they don't believe in grades."

"Ha, ha, ha! Plan to do any studying?"

"Well, I'm actually going there because Simon Rothman teaches there."

"Never heard of him. Does he coach something?"

"Well, he's a very famous American poet! He even won a Pulitzer Prize in 1960."

"Never heard of him," he repeated. "You gonna learn to write poetry?"

"Well, I'm an English major."

"What for?"

"Uh . . . I don't know. I might be a high school teacher or something . . . I think . . . ."

"A teacher. Hmm," he said thoughtfully. We drove through the gates of U.C. Santa Cruz, and he deposited me in front of my dorm. "Have a nice time," he laughed.

Well, in a way he was right. Nothing can match the experience of being in college in the late sixties.

Some Sig Ep boys were stationed outside the girls' dorm to help us take our going-away-to-college luggage in. One of the fraternities had an annual project where they got a mailing list of the in-coming freshmen, sent letters out, and got us all to send in our high school graduation pictures ahead of time. They put together a little book called "Sneak Peek," so everyone could get a good look at the new freshmen (especially the freshmen girls) coming in. They were even kind enough to send it to all the freshmen, so we could see who all the other nerds in the class were going to be. Since almost everyone—except maybe Robert Redford—looks like a wimp in a cap and gown, the freshman class of 1967-1968 at Santa Cruz really looked like a bunch of jerks. At least my roommate didn't look too bad . . . kind of like Barbra Streisand. I

had a queasy feeling in my stomach that everything "real" was going on at Berkeley and that we
were just "playing college" the way you "play
house" and totally forget about things like electric
bills and leaky plumbing. "Real" however, was too
fucking scary for me.

When I first walked into my room at the dorm,
Hannah Fine, my roommate, was sitting on one of
the twin beds. She had already put a line of masking tape down the center of the room and her first
words to me were that she was sort of a slob and
the only way things could remotely work out for
us was to "keep to our own sides." In other words,
I wasn't supposed to pay any attention to anything on her side of the masking tape.

She was mixing some pale orange paint in a
large can, and I hoped she wasn't planning to paint
her half of the room. Since my side was kind of
institutional vomit green, and I had neither the
energy nor the desire to paint, I could picture my
whole freshman year in a half pale orange, half institutional green room. Jesus, I thought.

"I'm not really so bad," she said. "When I
looked you up in the goddamned 'Sneak Peek' and
I saw you'd graduated from *Kerrybrook* and were
an *English* major, I just figured that you wouldn't
really want to go along with my decoration ideas."
She paused.

I was wearing the same poor-boy sweater and
the same Yardley slicker lipstick I'd worn in the
Kerrybrook yearbook.

"Lola Marie Bloom," she stated.

"Nickname: none," I stated. "Everyone else had
a nickname."

" 'Nickname: none.' " She paused and then grinned. "That's great!"

"Great?"

"I wouldn't want to have to share a room with someone called Muffy or Kitten or something. 'Nickname: none.'"

"I was the only one with no nickname."

"That's even better!"

I was amazed.

"Watch this," she said and took a Tampax out of the drawer, wet it in the basin, and tossed it up very hard to the ceiling where it stuck with the string hanging down. *White rat!* she yelled as it hit.

"You're strange," I said with extreme interest. I was terribly relieved that I didn't have a "normal" (if there is such a thing as "normal") roommate. Somehow (like Grant) I got the instant feeling she would tolerate, accept, maybe even enjoy my ups and downs. Of course then, and later when I met Grant, I didn't see the danger in the encouragement.

Hannah did look a little like Barbra Streisand when she used to wear those sailor dresses. She described her breasts as "African-grandmother-centerfold-of-the-*National-Geographic* tits," and we laughed and remembered when, as kids, our only sources of dirty pictures were the *National Geographic* and the underwear section of the Sears catalog.

She was wearing cords and a T-shirt that said "Staff Infection" on it. I set down my makeup case. "Uh . . . that's a really different T-shirt," I said. I was pretty sure she was insane enough to accept me. I still thought if I surrounded myself with insane people, I'd "fit in" rather than be dragged into the gutter with them.

"Oh, I got it from the P.E. department," she said. "They had the 'Staff' already on it, and I just added the 'Infection' with those little iron-on letters. You like it?"

"Yeah," I said, smiling. Maybe I really did have a friend. Except for Page, I had never had a friend before. I just didn't know how to do it.

By this time, she was pasting up squares of Hallmark wrapping paper around her side of the window and offered no explanation. When I asked why in the hell she was doing that, she simply said, "Oh, I get off on wrapping paper."

"Oh" was all I could say.

She frowned, studied me, and glanced at my guitar. "Are you a fucking folksinger or something?"

"No, I just play protest songs."

"Protesting what?" she asked with great lack of interest.

"Oh, you know, the war, the bomb . . ."

"Well, I'm not really into popular causes," she said. "Jesus, if I wanted to hear any more about the goddamned war, I'd be at Berkeley in People's Park or something." She studied my Twiggy haircut and added, "At least you're not into clogs and ponchos."

I was beginning to be a little uncertain about her. "Being against the war in Vietnam isn't *really* a popular cause. I mean, it's pretty popular to be *for* the war. You know, like all those people in Orange County who want to get the commies and believe in the domino theory."

"Shit," said Hannah. "Anything they don't like in Orange County *automatically* becomes a popular cause for me."

She offered me a cigarette. I laughed a little. She was okay.

"Do you have a stereo?" she asked.

"Uh . . . yeah," I said. "It's coming with my trunk."

"Oh, good. You see, I have a couple of thousand forty-five-rpm records all the way back from when I was in the sixth grade. I mean, I even have the colors of the labels memorized. Name a song, and I'll tell you the color of the label!"

"Johnny Angel."

"Red!" she shouted.

"Johnnie Walker!" I laughed

"Red!" she shouted, wet another Tampax, tossed it to the ceiling, and yelled, *"White Rat!"* Yeah, she was okay.

Her father was a five-foot-two-inch professional gambler who always got his hotel tab picked up by the management in Vegas because he was such a high roller. Hannah said she suspected he had something to do with the Jewish Mafia because he owned a company called Bull Brand Fertilizer, and they sold very little fertilizer and made quite a lot of money. She also told me how her great ambition was NOT to be a concert pianist.

"A concert pianist?"

"I was a child prodigy. It's really horrible to be gifted at something you don't want to do."

"What do you want to do."

"I want to work as a blackjack dealer in Las Vegas, but I'll probably have to start out in Reno, since they don't allow women to deal in Vegas, but I figure Vegas will open up soon because of all this women's lib shit."

"How come you're in college, then?"

"Same fucking reason you are: I'm waiting to be an adult."

"Huh?"

"Well, you can't deal—or do much of *anything* except get married or get drafted—until you're twenty-one, so this is a rather pleasant place to wait it out. You see, I'm only seventeen; I finished high school a year early."

"I never thought of college quite that way."

"Well not *all* college. I mean, if you're actually learning to *do* something, like in pre-med or pre-law, that's different, but you're an *English* major, and we're not at Harvard by a long shot.

"Well, Simon Rothman teaches here."

"Who the hell is he?"

"He won a Pulitzer Prize in 1960."

"For what?"

"Poetry."

"Oh, you've read one poem, you've read them all."

"What's your major?"

"Theater."

"Oh," I said. "You want to be an actress, too? My sister's an actress, but she didn't study it in college. She does lots of commercials."

"Which ones?"

"Well, in one she's the tense and harassed

mother who escapes to the warm bath with those bath oil beads."

"Yeah, I've seen her."

"If you really want to be an actress, I'm sure she'd introduce you to her agent. She's an awfully nice person."

"I don't want to be an *actress*," said Hannah with an almost disdainful tone of voice. "The only thing I've ever played was one of the girls in the restaurant in our high school production of *Death of a Salesman.* I got some laughs, though."

"How come you're a theater major? Do you like to build sets or something?"

"No, because the chairman of the department is Rod Brewster."

"Isn't that the name of some football player?"

"Not just *some* football player," she said, "but *the* football player—used to be the goddamn star quarterback for the L.A. Rams. You see, I got to fuck him a couple of times when my high school in Pasadena elected me homecoming queen for a joke, and all the L.A. area homecoming queens got tickets for the Rams, got to meet the team and kiss the quarterback. He thought I was the funniest-looking homecoming queen he'd ever seen, and he invited me to his apartment after the game, and I beat the hell out of him at blackjack, and . . . well . . . then we fucked. I wouldn't call it a real meaningful relationship. He's just a good fuck."

"Why the hell is he chairman of the drama department?"

"Well, during his last year in football, he hurt his knee—*all* those football jerks seem to get those knee injuries. Anyway, he'd taken courses in Kabuki theater and business administration at Notre Dame. His ex-wife was this opera singer, and she was always hanging around with actors and stuff, and the former drama department chairman was into opera, so he knew her, and when he retired last year and Rod got this knee injury, they hired him as chairman 'cause he was famous and no one in the department wanted the hassle of being chairman. The retiring chairman recommended him or something."

"How come he didn't get a job coaching somewhere?" I asked. "I thought all those football players with knee injuries went into coaching."

"Search me," she laughed. "But, seriously, I think he really *likes* that Kabuki shit."

"So, Hannah, you're a theater major just because of *him?*"

"Oh, partly," she smiled, "but partly because it's fun! I've looked at the catalog, and if you work it right, you can get through all four years of college without having to take too many hard courses. You get to take things like acting and makeup and stuff. There are too many gay guys in the department, but I have Rod, so it's kind of fun."

"You're really strange," I said with awe and wonder. "Do you really *know* homosexual guys?"

"Is the pope Catholic?"

"Huh?"

"Of course. I've been here all summer. My parents were thrilled. *They* thought I was getting a head start on my college education."

I was mesmerized. "I don't think I've ever *met* a homosexual. The only thing I know about them is they wear bell-bottom pants."

"If we can get you a fake I.D.," she said, "I'll take you down to the Stuffed Prune and you can see all the gay guys you want to, or I'll take you to the Dakota Card Room and you can see lesbians in cowboy boots."

As you may have figured out by now, my college education was more colorful than educational, but then, I was at the point in my life where I would have given up all the educational opportunities in the world to feel even a little amazing. With Hannah's direction—as with Grant's later—I felt a little more like the unique person I wanted to be. Hannah and I became fast friends because I was thrilled to know someone so decadent (and she thought the fact that I had lost my virginity to Mr. Shaftner fascinating rather than disgusting), and she was pleased that I—alone—genuinely loved her decadence.

While she was out bouncing the springs with Rod Brewster, I dated a few frat boys who did gross things like get you drunk on rum and Coke before dances, and unzip their pants in the car and put your hand on their penises and then expect you to be thrilled out of your mind. Hannah said I should have affairs with older men because they at least got motel rooms and no one checked your I.D. when you went to bars with them.

I therefore had what Hannah called my "obligatory affair with a married professor." This was pretty easy because the English department had four married professors who liked to screw around with freshmen girls. Larry, Hannah said, was the best bet. He had an M.A. from Princeton, wore really neat suits, and had this boring, greasy-haired wife and two whining kids who pulled things off the shelves in grocery stores. Hannah told me that if I really wanted to have an affair with a married man, he was the best because his home life was so shitty that he'd jump in a minute. Because he was also good-looking, I could kid myself that I wasn't doing it JUST to have the "experience" of a major grown-up affair with a married, older (thirty-three years old) man.

It was so easy, I was amazed. I mean, I was cute, but not THAT cute (what I didn't know was that Hannah had dropped him several subtle hints like "Lola Bloom is really hot after your bod"). I just went in for a conference wearing a short skirt, told him I thought he was "extremely attractive" (Hannah had said that "extremely attractive" is kind of a code word among married men), sat on his desk, crossed my legs, and—wouldn't you know it—he nervously asked me out for a beer.

Since he was so sophisticated-looking, they didn't kick me out of the Seaside Tavern or even ask to see my fake I.D. Larry and I had a couple of beers, and I did nothing but agree with everything he said, including the statement that he felt that "death was a mysterious thing." He didn't strike me as too bright, but how can you dislike someone who keeps telling you you are "so intelligent." He reached under the little table with the old coins, starfish, and fish hooks set in clear plastic, and pressed his hand under my skirt. When I told him his Freshman Comp class was one of the most interesting courses I'd ever taken in my life and that his lectures were inspiring, he suggested that we "get some wine and go somewhere," and boy was I glad I had already lost my virginity so I didn't have to have scruples or be nervous or anything.

We went to a Motel 6 off the interstate (that still actually charged six dollars and had the TV chained to the wall that you had to put quarters in, and the "magic fingers" on the bed for another quarter), and I got the first in my collection of motel keys. We didn't even unwrap the bathroom glass or break the strip of paper around the toilet because he had to hurry because he had to get home in time to watch Johnny Carson with his wife. Larry wore white Jockey shorts, sat on one of the two double beds, and kissed me. Now, I really hated Jockey shorts because they reminded me of all the frat boys and locker rooms and guys slapping each other with towels. Because of this, I guess I didn't get too turned on. It didn't occur to me that I just didn't have any feeling for him. In 1967 you were supposed to be progressive and get off on balling without a third act, and love was something you felt for long-haired people at be-ins. I did wish that Motel 6s came with complimentary drugs and piped-in Beatle music, though.

"Are you on the pill?" he breathed in my ear.

"Oh, yes," I said, sounding pretty proud of myself. I was part of a generation who had never seen a rubber. Someday, I must think to ask someone to use one, so I can see a part of the American-fucking-in-the-back-seat-of-a-Chevy culture, but that night I was proud to be part of the free generation.

As if that were a signal, Larry whipped off his Jockey shorts, and I figured I had better look real experienced. He seemed amazed when I started to go down on him. In fact, he was so shocked that as soon as my lips touched his penis, he came all over my chin. "God, I'm sorry," I said, not knowing yet that it was also my duty as a "liberated woman" to be pissed off that he didn't satisfy me. Since I had never had an orgasm anyway, it just seemed like a quick way to get it over with. I'm glad I didn't know what I was missing, or I would have been REALLY bummed out.

"I just never had a girl do that to me unless I really begged her to," he said. At first, I was surprised, but then I remembered he was an older man of thirty-three, and maybe older women like his wife didn't do things like that.

Ironically enough, on our way home the car radio was playing Bob Dylan. Yeah, the times were changing.

The war in Vietnam went on, and I learned from some upperclassmen in the student union that we'd still be there even if Kennedy HADN'T been shot, so I shouldn't keep on looking at him as our destroyed savior. Okay, I stopped idolizing his politics, but I still wanted him right up there with Jesus in heaven waiting for me when I tried to kill myself. The Beatles came out with "Hey, Jude," and sang about how we should take sad songs and make them better, so I started to wear my "Impeach Johnson" button, not knowing that in a few years I'd be DYING to have Johnson back in the White House.

When I started sticking "McCarthy: Peace" daisies on my guitar case, Hannah sighed and said she hoped that wasn't a warning sign that soon I'd be speaking at rallies and spending energy on what was already a lost cause. When Johnson said he wouldn't go after the Democratic nomination, I stopped wearing my "Impeach Johnson" button and wore my Dove button. Hannah didn't do her usual cynical complaining. Deep down, I think she was in favor of peace—just not activists.

When I got nominated for Sig Ep Little Sister, Bobby Kennedy was wearing his hair longer. Unfortunately (or maybe fortunately) they found out that I was a best friend of Hannah Fine—not just her roommate—and they blackballed me. On a manic high—which I still didn't recognize as such—to the amazement of everyone who had only seen my remission, I crashed the gate at the Little Sister initiation dance and walked right up to the microphone and said that just because Hannah Fine was Jewish was no reason for them to hold things against her. Some guy yelled out that before I made any more speeches, I should get my information straight. "No one gives a rat's ass," he yelled out. "She's just too gross and too strange!" I got all crazy and yelled that "people were people," and then my vision began to blur.

"Shoot the piano player!" some guy yelled.

Some Sig Ep guy started dragging me off the platform. Taking deep breaths, I wrestled away from him. Terror was all I felt. With great effort, in the silence I managed to slink to the door. As I left, I heard someone say to someone else, "Something's radically wrong with her," and someone else said, "Yeah, radically."

I went back to the dorm and lay on the bed for two days. Hannah tried to joke me out of the depression; Larry didn't even notice that he hadn't seen me around. Remission had definitely ended. And Helen Bloom said I was normal until I met Grant Rosenberg four years later.

The next week I was on a good high. I even wrote a letter to *Time* magazine about how I couldn't understand when Dustin Hoffman could have had Anne Bancroft in *The Graduate,* why the hell did he want Katharine Ross. Hannah came running in to say the bookstore just got *The Love Machine* in. Since we couldn't wait for it to come out in paperback, we shoplifted it for the noble purpose of keeping a crap writer like Jacqueline Susann from making money from it. But we read it from cover to cover, of course, and couldn't put it down. I secretly loved the way her books never had a happy ending, and the characters always ended up taking two hundred Percodan and jumping into furnaces or something. "There are no happy endings," I said casually to Hannah.

"Then where did the phrase 'and they lived happily ever after' come from?" she asked.

"From someone who wrote fiction. In real life, we all die in the end anyway."

Because we felt so stupid and guilty for reading *The Love Machine* hot off the shelf, we went to see an "intellectual" movie, *Blowup,* and came back with the unintellectual report that if you looked real close during the scene with the orgy on the blue paper, you could see a little pubic hair.

Bell-bottom pants came in for EVERYONE, not just gay guys. While I was busy sewing triangles of red bandana into the bottoms of my jeans to make them bells, and listening to Simon and Garfunkel singing "The Sounds of Silence" on the radio, they interrupted the music to say that Martin Luther King had been shot. U.C. Santa Cruz had a memorial service for him, and anyone who wanted to could get up and speak, and some jerk actually got up (I'm not kidding) and said, "I have a dream. If I ever have a baby, I will name him Martin Kennedy Eugene after the three people who changed the world." Hannah looked at me and said that that was the dumbest thing she'd ever heard at a memorial service except when her grandmother died of a heart attack while playing the slot machines, and at her service they said she had died beautifully and calmly.

Since even Princess Grace was wearing her skirts above her knees, I took all my wool skirts to Joseph Magnin's alterations department to be shortened, bought frosted lipstick, and started to let my Twiggy haircut grow out so I could look like a free spirit. When I sat on the windowsill and played Peter, Paul and Mary songs on my guitar, and with conviction sang, "How many deaths will it take 'till we know / Too many people have died?" Hannah accused me of supporting the popular cause just for the drama of the whole thing and not because I cared. She said she knew because she was a theater major, and I said, "Some fucking theater major you are," and we resolved our argument by going into the lounge of the dorm and watching *Laugh-In* and *Bracken's World*.

One evening Adam Swartz, my VISTA volunteer lover from Kahaluu, called me to say he'd got his notice and had gone for his draft physical. When they marched him naked all over the place,

he told me he felt so humiliated just at the PHYSI-
CAL that he knew he couldn't stand it in the actual
army. "Not only do they get you killed," he said,
"but they make you feel subhuman in the process. If you go, you're supporting the war; if you
don't, you get arrested." He hoped the fact he had
worked for VISTA would help him, but since he
had been with them less than six months, the draft
board said no. He tried to find a psychiatrist to
write a letter suggesting that military service might
damage his mental health. No dice. Everyone was
doing that. That was the last time I spoke to him.
My very own first love was shot in the throat in a
rice field with all those anonymous soldiers. Maybe
Hannah was right. Maybe all the singing in the
world couldn't stop the death machine.

Because good old Professor Larry had to take his
wife and kids to the circus and crap like that, I had
plenty of time to help some grad students get sig-
natures on anti–Vietnam War petitions. Since
everyone at the campus coffee shop knew the death
statistics before I got my *Time* magazine, I started
subscribing to the newspaper, and Hannah knew
that Adam's death had a lot to do with it, but said
I should concentrate on something I could control
rather than a war controlled by people in Washington, D.C., who didn't give a shit about what a
bunch of students thought.

After they passed around a diseased lung in a
glass box, I started skipping Personal Health and
Hygiene class.

I started wearing tights and clogs instead of the
$1.39 pantyhose they sold in the campus book-

store. Hannah practiced shuffling cards, and I found every excuse for not studying. On depressive days, I just lay on the bed and thought that passionately caring about a cause was way ahead of learning something. On days I felt okay, I'd pick up the books again, thinking maybe education was the key to the world peace, but in the back of my mind, I felt that no matter how eloquently we said things, the people in Washington, D.C., wouldn't listen to us anyway.

Adam's death really shocked me. Suddenly the war was real. The death of one man I had known for only three months horrified me so much more than all the thousands of pictures of mutilated people I'd seen in *Time*. I suddenly realized that each of them had had parents and sisters, lovers, wives, friends. Every death wasn't just another number on the statistics list but something that affected a whole network of people. Although I was well over Adam, dead is dead. I was shocked, too, to realize that WHY he died worried me as much as the death itself. That would, of course, bring on again all those haunting thoughts I had: if *I* was dead, I wouldn't have to worry about anything ever again.

In the spring of 1968, I typed mailing lists for the McCarthy campaign, and even though Hannah was convinced he'd lose anyway and spent her spring sleeping with some guy who was into acid, she did come out and say she SORT OF admired me.

The school year ended, and even though officially I could spend the summer wherever I wanted to, out of habit I packed for Kahaluu and Dillon with his now long and flowing hair.

As Hannah stuffed things into her suitcase she asked, "Do you think your parents will let you live off campus next year?"

"I'll work on it, but I think Helen . . . . Well, you know Helen."

"All too well," she said, "and I've only talked to her on the phone *once!*"

Since Hannah had told me my Haight-Ashbury poster was "really high school," I had replaced it with a Picasso print and an artsy photo of a nude girl holding a dead chicken. I rolled them up, put them in my suitcase, and asked Hannah if she wanted all my coral-colored straw flowers because she was driving back to L.A. in her Kharmann Ghia and they wouldn't get as mashed as in a suitcase.

She said sure and then smiled. "How did Helen Keller break her hand?" she asked out the blue.

"She just *died* yesterday, did you hear that?"

"Yeah. How did she break her hand?"

"Uh . . . I don't know. She didn't break—"

"She fell into a well and tried to yell for help!"

"Hannah!" I was shocked. "She just *died!*"

"Yeah, but would it be funnier if she was alive?"

"I guess so."

"I bet after Kennedy got shot, you were one of those people who didn't play your *First Family* comedy album out of respect. I bet you went out and bought one of those records of his speeches." She stood up on the bed. " 'Ask not what your country can do for you. Ask what you can do for your country!' "

"I worked for VISTA," I said a little defensively. "And I still have my *First Family* album."

"I'll see you in the fall," she said. "It would be nice if Bobby or McCarthy got the nomination." She stuffed the rest of her dirty laundry in a duffel bag, picked up my straw flowers, started to go out the door, but turned back. "I hate to say this, but old Hubert Horatio will get it. Bobby's acting too cool and too hip for those businessmen who rig *every* nomination; and McCarthy—well, Gene wants to end the war, and then *everyone* would lose money. Yeah, Humphrey will get it. Listen, I'll write you in minute detail about the I.U.D. I'm going to get so I won't get my body all fucked up with pills."

"You're *terrible*, Hannah!" I laughed.

"But I'm *right*," she said. "Goddamn cynics usually are."

After Hannah drove off, I walked over to Larry's office. He had already finished grading his exams because he gave everyone true-false questions—even in his Freshman Comp course. I sort of figured tenure wasn't in the cards for him. He was smoking his pipe and clicking together those little metal balls on a string.

"I came to say good-bye," I said. "I'm leaving for the summer." Larry jumped as if the college president were standing there watching him screw the cheerleading squad.

"God, Lola! Hi!" he said. Larry was not one of your terribly articulate people. "I haven't seen you in ages. What's new?"

"Other than my old boyfriend getting killed in Vietnam," I said, "nothing much."

"Jesus . . . uh . . . I'm sorry to hear that," he said.

"Being sorry won't bring him back. We weren't in love anymore. It was just that he was my *first* love. . . . I mean, not the first person I slept with, but the first person who meant anything to me."

Larry looked relieved. I don't think he really wanted to be comforting or anything. He didn't care that I had never had an orgasm in my whole life. As long as he had someone to fuck in the Pine Tree Motel, all was well with him.

"Will I be seeing you again in the fall?" he asked.

"Maybe. I'm thinking of putting all my motel keys on a charm bracelet."

Larry looked nervous. Since he was a habitual adulterer, he had a permanent shifty look about him.

"But maybe," I continued, "you won't be seeing much of me. I mean, if McCarthy gets the nomination, I'll be pretty busy."

Since I was hoping he'd be pretty upset about the fact that he might not be tossing the salad with me very often before the election, I was pissed as hell when all he said was that goddamned "I'm sorry to hear that." I began to be pretty sure that if I told him I had terminal cancer, he'd say he was "sorry to hear that" too.

"Would you like to go out for some coffee?" he asked.

Because there was a full pot right there in the English department office, I knew that meant he wanted to get in a quick fuck before I left.

"There's coffee right here," I answered.

Larry smiled his vacant smile, obviously ticked off that we were going to stay in the English department office drinking our coffee rather than hit the rack at the Cozy Inn. I realized that fucking a nerd was almost as bad as being a jerk yourself. "I can do better than you, Larry," I said seriously.

And you know what that yo-yo said? "I'm sorry to hear that."

"That's what you'll probably say when Nixon's elected," I snapped.

"No, I meant I'm sorry we won't be seeing each other."

"Well, I *can* do better than you, Larry."

"Was that a put-down, Lola?" he asked innocently.

"Yes, Larry, yes, it was," I said and walked out of the office.

On the plane to Hawaii, while I was eating my toy steak with my little toy fork and knife and wondering if airline food was the real cause of cancer, the captain made an announcement: Robert Kennedy had been shot.

"Oh, well," sighed the man next to me, "maybe we'll stop hearing about those Kennedys now."

I was horrified. "A human being just *died*," I said. "Even if you didn't like him, he's *dead*. . . . A lot of people were counting on him."

The man took another sip of his canned martini. "For what?" he asked. "Campaign promises?"

I was in tears. "McCarthy probably won't get the nomination," I managed to say. "Kennedy had a chance against Humphrey, and I don't think Humphrey can beat Nixon, and—"

"Look," said the man, shaking his head, "I've been a Democrat all my life. Those guys couldn't beat Nixon: long hair, peace. Most of the country's so scared of the day you kids grow up, they'll vote out—*wipe* out—any trace of you as soon as they're given the chance. You should always go for the guy who can win for the party, but in this case . . . well, I don't think any of them can."

I was silent for a minute, then said, "That man had a wife . . . and all those kids. He just *died*. . . . I started to cry again. "The wrong people always die."

"Look, I'm sorry. I didn't mean to make you cry."

"You didn't," I sniffed. "I just wanted everything to be different."

When I got back to Kahaluu, I didn't even want to go near the VISTA headquarters, and you can imagine how many people asked me, "Have you heard what happened to Adam?" For some perverse reason I couldn't understand, everyone seemed pissed off that they weren't the first to give me the news.

Politically aware for the first time in my life, I was shocked to find out that only about half of the eligible voters in Kahaluu were registered. (Maybe that was good—who knows who some of them might have voted for just because they liked the signs or something.) The big news was that Burger King was moving in, and Mr. Nakasone of Nakasone's Drive-In had talked a couple of drunks in front of the Purity Grocery Store into halfheartedly carrying signs saying "Stop Burger King" (stopping Burger King in Kahaluu would be like trying to stop an avalanche). For a six-pack of Primo beer you could get them to do anything. I remembered, with a slight pang, last summer when Adam had given them each a six-pack to carry signs announcing community meetings.

That summer my sexual activities were limited to about five dates with Warren Ishida, whose father belonged to the local bowling club. Warren had a pretty good collection of rock albums, and his mother was either awfully understanding or awfully stupid, because she'd fix us dinner and leave us alone in the house while she and her husband went out. Warren was into nude swimming, so after dark, we'd go to the beach. We'd bring along bathing suits to wet so our parents (either naive or understanding) would think we'd worn them. When we finished swimming, we'd fuck on the sand. I'm telling you, it wasn't like *From Here to Eternity* at *all*. Warren came in about two seconds, and sand feels kind of lousy in your mouth and vagina. Also, I really wasn't crazy about him. Maybe, I thought, there is some truth to the expression we free spirits all laughed at: "Save it for the man you love."

"Do you think I'm frigid?" I asked Warren one night after spitting some sand out of my mouth.

"What's that?" he asked.

"You know—like in *The Chapman Report*— women who don't come and would rather read *Family Circle* than screw."

"God," he said, passing me a beer. "*I* like to screw more than *anything!*"

"Forget it," I said.

Sally said that I should volunteer for something to help the community, since some people were still pissed that Page and I both had paying jobs the summer before while some families were going hungry, so I became a volunteer lifeguard at the community pool. I guess no one read the sign that said "No suntan lotion," because the pool had a permanent oil slick—kind of like swimming in Honolulu Harbor. Since this was only a three-day-a-week job, on the other two days Dillon let me drive the van into Honolulu and volunteer at the McCarthy campaign headquarters. I had dramatic visions of mass suicides all over the country if Nixon was elected. Little did I know that people would just say they were "sorry to hear that" and go on doing exactly what they had been doing before.

McCarthy headquarters was located in a former gas station. I stood on the street corner and shoved leaflets into car windows, then went inside and typed address labels and stuffed envelopes to all the people who had been on Bobby Kennedy's mailing list, urging them to take the "united we stand, divided we fall" attitude.

The great thing about being a volunteer is that if your manic-depressive symptoms start getting worse and you have to spend a few days in bed or flipping out, nobody bitches at you for not showing up at work.

It was hot and humid all summer. When I felt as if I was sinking, I would do the best I could to pull myself out of it. I'd bike down to the Purity Grocery Store. I still believed my depressions were situational. I always felt that if I was someplace else, I wouldn't feel this way.

In the Purity Grocery Store, the news came from the radio over the Hostess Cupcake display. On the mainland it was the summer of the riots; in Vietnam the Vietcong struck central Saigon; in London, James Earl Ray was nabbed for shooting Martin Luther King; in Washington, D.C., fifty thousand people marched in support of the poor. In Kahaluu the big news was that Sally had actually sold her very most expensive shell mobile from her store to some fat tourist from Omaha who was driving around the island.

From the Purity Grocery Store, I looked out at the drunks asleep, the dog asleep, the kids across the street smoking dope, the Burger King construction workers taking a beer break, and I said to Connie the cashier, "This place is nowhere."

"Where you like go?" Connie asked as she bagged my beer.

"I don't know . . . where I can feel some *life!*"

"Eh, you like gone crazy?"

"You can't do anything here. No one will join you; no one will listen to you."

"Leesten," she said, gesturing to the drunks. "You geeeve dem guys one seeex-pack beer, day carry da kine sign fo you too!"

Little did she know that in a few days, I'd be naked in our stream again, toasting the guava trees with Primo beer. I hadn't learned my pattern yet. When I figured it all out, it helped some. On dark days, I could SOMETIMES look forward to a high.

At the Republican convention, Tricky Dick was of course nominated on the first ballot. All those goddamn cheering Republicans probably believed him when he said that the "long dark night for America was about to end."

I had to watch the Democratic convention on a tiny black-and-white TV set because Sally was watching *Bewitched* and the soaps on the color one.

Tom Hayden and the demonstrators were screaming; the police arrested a hundred and seventy-eight people; and the National Guard used tear gas. Goddamned Eugene McCarthy—once my hero—just sat there and took it all. If he had just walked out, simply walked out, I might have thought there could be a better America, but he sat there and took it, just like the rest of the country.

My political days were over.

Chapter

Well, the classified ad that described the apartment on St. Louis Heights as a "fixer-upper" was making an understatement. It had once been a garage, but it was on the east edge of the heights, so I could still see Diamond Head. It was lower on the heights than our (or rather Grant's) house was and hadn't been cleaned since the former tenant left. There were about ten half-empty peanut butter jars, some moldy clothes, some dirty dishes (which I could actually use), and a handgun. I toyed with the idea of keeping the gun in case I wanted to kill myself again, but I knew for sure that would not help me along the road to mental health. Not wanting to touch it, I called the landlord, who lived upstairs, and he said cheerfully, "Oh, I guess you can keep it."

"But I don't want it."

"Throw it away."

"Who lived here before I did?"

"Said his name was Bert. Paid his rent in cash."

"What if he comes back?"

"That's why I said keep the gun," he said.

I shuddered and took it to the police, and it wasn't registered to anyone. With some of Grant's money, I bought a used motorcycle and made many trips from Mililani Town, through Honolulu, and up St. Louis Heights bringing in my things, one basketful at a time. Twice I drove by my turnoff, as I was so used to driving all the way up to the top to our (Grant's) house.

Cleaning is not my exact favorite thing to do, and it's really grotesque to clean up after someone you don't even know who owns a handgun. I though about not taking the lithium, so I could wait for a manic high and happily clean for hours, but depression would probably come first, and I might look at the place and definitely kill myself. And even if I didn't kill myself, it would be horrible lying on a dirty mattress looking at half-empty peanut butter jars. I had had trouble even with Grant stroking my hair, feeding me soup, and holding me for hours. Now I was alone, and there were no roses on the ceiling. No, not a good idea. I washed out a jelly glass with Fred Flintstone on it and soberly swallowed the lithium.

Dillon and Sally both refused to help me move. They couldn't stop me, but they'd rather be tortured by Nazis than encourage me. Sally was particularly horrified when she found out my place was so close to Grant. "You might as well move back with him," she snapped. I felt a pang. I wanted to.

When the cleaning was done, the place didn't look too bad. The only major problem was that the apartment didn't have an inside bathroom. You had to go outside, around the house, and use the one in the garage on the other side (fortunately, it never gets that cold in Hawaii). The landlord assured me no one else used it. That was the ickiest part of the cleaning. I don't think that bathroom had been cleaned since the house was built in 1939. In the apartment was a mirror over the kitchen sink, so I put what little makeup I had neatly on the drain-board along with my toothbrush, so I'd only have to use the bathroom to shower and pee.

The shower was actually outside the garage under the eaves, surrounded by a high concrete wall. The thought of taking a shower while look-ing at the stars sort of intrigued me. Huge bou-gainvillaea bushes hung over the wall, and as I washed my hair for the first time, I had to keep digging the magenta blossoms out of the drain with my toe.

I had to pay a big deposit for the phone be-cause Lola Bloom—now thirty-four years old—had never had a phone in her own name. The first person I called was Page—collect.

"How can you stand living right down the hill from him?" she asked.

"It makes me feel a little safer. . . . I mean, if something *horrible* happens, he's near, and if I live this close and *don't* go running up there . . . well, it makes me feel a little more powerful, and I need all the power I can get."

"What are you going to do?"

"Get a job . . . maybe get some therapy."

"You can't say *maybe* when you're talking about therapy. Are you crazy? You've *got* to get some," she paused. "I . . . well . . . I don't know what I'd do if you ended up dead."

"Yes, you're probably right."

"Do you have enough money for it? I'll send—"

"I have enough. Grant's given me a quarter of *Mr. Macho* for three years, and besides if someone else paid for my therapy, I'd feel dependent again, and that was part of the problem. I don't even want the *Mr. Macho* money; however, I need it. Better that than to have you or Helen just shove it over."

"I really am proud of you," she said, "really."

"I love you, Page," I said quietly, then added, "What are you going to do when *Classified Ads* is canceled?"

"Oh," she said simply, "star in another series, maybe do a film" (that's what I call confidence). "I'd like to have my own series."

"You've *got* your own series."

"No, I mean like Mary Tyler Moore or Gale Storm. *The Page Bloom Show.*"

"Oh," I said quietly.

"You taking your lithium?"

"Yes."

"Good luck with the apartment. Don't watch for Grant's car too much."

"No," I lied. "I won't."

After we hung up, I felt really down. "Nickname: none," and no bathroom, to boot.

I saw Grant's '57 Chevy once as I was coming up the hill on the motorcycle, but he didn't know I lived up there and didn't recognize me with a crash helmet on. He did seem to be driving slower than before. Sally said he'd called the house once for me, but she told him I'd moved out and had no phone. I wanted to KILL her, but that was probably best. Don't you hate it when people who do things for your own good turn out to be right?

I went to Star Garden Supply and bought some plants. I remembered the Official Page Bloom Guide to Decorating: when in doubt, hang up a plant. The furniture looked like the kind you see in movies that take place in old dusty Upper West Side New York apartments inhabited by down-and-out old men—like when you call the Goodwill to come and collect it, THEY even look bummed out about taking it. I got some bright pillows, and they HELPED, but I knew I had to save as much money as I could, because in three years the *Mr. Macho* money would stop, and therapy was going to be expensive. Medical insurance and all that crap adds up too. I didn't know when (if ever) I was going to get a job. I did have to fork out to have the whole place painted white. I just COULDN'T—after cleaning for days—get up enough energy to PAINT IT, and I didn't know how to begin painting in the first place. When the painter said, "Latex or oil-base?" I had absolutely no idea what he was talking about.

After the apartment was painted white, it looked much larger, and if you looked at the plants and the view instead of the furniture, it could pass for livable. Sweet Page had a stereo sent over (not remembering, of course, that I didn't have any records), so I went down to Ala Moana Shopping Center and bought a Buffalo Springfield record and *Cleo Laine Live at Carnegie Hall,* and after I had lived there for three months, my landlord upstairs actually came down and offered to buy me some different records so he wouldn't have to listen to Buffalo Springfield and Cleo Laine ever again in his whole life.

Anyway, about the day the place stopped smelling like paint, I was listening to Cleo Laine and reading the help wanted ads when there was a knock on the door. I thought that was kind of strange as no one even knew I lived there except Sally and Dillon. Because I didn't have the guts, I hadn't called any of our (my) friends yet. They had always been "our" friends, and calling them would be almost like calling Grant. Because of this, I just ASSUMED it was either Sally or Dillon at the door. I couldn't IMAGINE why they were up here. They had told me if I moved from the gleaming waxed safety of Mililani Town, they'd never come visit me (they, of course, didn't realize that this was about the most positive thing they could say about my move), but because I was rather lonely and figured one of them had got curious, I trudged slowly to the door and opened it.

Standing there with a strange grin on his face was THE MAN IN THE WHITE BELT! He was wearing a different Qiana body shirt but the same damn belt.

"Hi, Lola Bloom!" he said through his grin.

I guess I must have stood there with my jaw hanging open for quite a while because he said, "Cat got your tongue?"

"How did you find—"

"Turquoise model C by the school, Mililani Town, Hawaii, U.S. of A.!" he said proudly.

Remembering Dillon's old van in Kahaluu, I

mumbled, "You forgot the Universe and Mind of God."

"Huh?"

"Nothing. You mean Sally and Dillon *gave* you my address?"

"They're neighbors of my ex. They sort of know who she is."

Shit, I thought, that's Sally for you: she won't give Grant my phone number but happily hands out my ADDRESS to some jerk in a white belt who says he met me on the plane. I did remember that Sally said I should "start socializing," but she COULDN'T mean socializing with Pete (short for Peter) who had to get divorced after fifteen years of marriage and two kids because his penis was too large for his wife.

"Aren't you going to ask me in?" he said in almost a whimper.

"I'd rather not."

"Shucks, I'm not going to hurt you! Why, I'm gosh darn *crazy* about you?"

"Why?" I asked, genuinely interested.

"Well, you're the kind of girl I'd like to interface with."

I wasn't exactly sure what "interface" meant. I mean, I knew it was business talk, like "maximize." Harmless, but coming from a man who would tell a perfect stranger all about his penis, it sounded kind of dirty.

"I am not going out with you," I said as definitely as I could.

"Heck, I didn't ask you to go out. I just wanna come in, shoot the breeze."

"Why?" I asked again. "I'm not going to get you a date with Page."

"I don't even wanna meet her," he probably lied.

"Well," I said weakly and lamely, "for one beer, and that's it."

"Sure as shooting," he said.

The only reason I let him in was that for days I had been completely alone. I'd called Page once again, and that was it, except for the man selling plants at Star Garden Supply. I actually had a great need to "interface," as it were, with SOMEONE—ANYONE (I mean, I opened the door when I thought it was SALLY). Yes, I was much too weak, but I was also fucking lonely.

The Man in the White Belt looked around the apartment. "I bet you really miss Mililani Town. I sure do. They kick you out?"

"No," I said. "And I don't miss Mililani Town at *all*."

"You lied to me about your roommates being guys," he said. "How come? I was just a regular guy buying you a drink."

"I . . . uh . . . always tell strangers that."

I sat rather uncomfortably and listened to him and soon learned that in addition to all his pro-nuke, anti-abortion, anti-Semitic beliefs, he really thought that President Reagan "should just go ahead and blow up the commie Russians."

"Then the Russians will blow *us* up," I put in.

"Naa," he said. "I have it figured. I bet they don't even *have* any nuclear bombs. They're just bluffing about all this superpower bunk."

When I told him I was going to vote for Mondale because I didn't want anyone blowing ANYONE up, he said I was uninformed because I was a woman and women are incapable of understanding politics.

It was rather funny. I had the same feeling that I'd had on the plane when I told him to get the fuck away from me. I had some power—not much—but the more I heard him talk, the better I felt about myself. I let him stay—big mistake—for a second beer. I thought how great it was to be the enviable person for a change and about how great it was to meet someone who would never even figure out he was crazy. He would actually walk around forever thinking he had a "real good sense of humor," but I, Lola Bloom, was going to get better. At least if you KNOW you're acting like a female cockroach, there's nowhere to go but up. He WAS worse: he was a male cockroach who didn't understand why he wasn't president of the United States and would never have a clue as to why even Lola Bloom found him repulsive.

Unfortunately, however, there was of course no way Pete (short for Peter) could POSSIBLY understand this, so "Would you like another beer?" to him was just the confirmation that he was a regular guy with "a real good sense of humor." I never did figure out why he kept telling me what a great sense of humor he had. He never said one funny thing—or rather he never said anything INTENTIONALLY funny. He didn't even try to tell any bad jokes.

But, even though I was feeling stronger, saner, and wittier than I had ever felt before, when he said that the woman who was gang-raped in Big Dan's Tavern in New Bedford was "asking for it" by going in there and "socializing," I decided it was definitely time for him to leave. I sent him on his way, making it perfectly clear that I didn't want to "interface" with him or "dialogue" with him on ANY subject.

I finally got up enough nerve to call our (my) friend Maryanne, who had been my bridesmaid. I mean, what do you SAY? "Want to come over and look at the scars on my wrists?" She was my closest friend except for Page. Hannah Fine had actually become a blackjack dealer. In fact that's how we met Maryanne. When she was a dealer, she knew Hannah, and when she moved to Hawaii, Hannah had told her to look us up. Since Hannah never wrote or called, she and I sort of drifted apart. For the first several years after college, I would occasionally call her, but since she never called me, I sort of let her go. I felt sorry, as I was closer to her than to Maryanne. I mean, I didn't feel I knew Maryanne well enough to call her up when I was lonely as hell. What if she started telling me about Grant? Since it would be impossible to have anything but a superficial conversation if we stayed off the subject of Grant and the suicide attempt, I almost didn't call her. Then I remembered that the loneliness was what had made me let in the Man in the White Belt with the Large Penis in the first place. Out of self-preservation, I called her.

Apparently, she had been leaving messages with Dillon and Sally, which I never received. Sally, yes, but Dillon—MY OWN FATHER—trying to isolate me? It was unbelievable. I can see why they wanted to keep Grant away from me, but MARYANNE? They had told a stranger in a white belt where I lived, but not Maryanne. Then I remembered that Dillon wasn't around much. The relogous clown birthday parties were getting very trendy, and also if anyone in his growing congregation was sick or in the hospital, he had to get all dressed up, blow up happy face balloons, and zip off to cheer them up. Then he had to write his sermons, and I imagine it would be pretty hard to come up with a funny sermon every week. I mean it's probably hard enough to be a writer for Johnny Carson and write funny monologues night after night, but if you work for Johnny, you can make fun of almost ANYTHING and no one has to "learn something" from it, but to write a funny sermon must be torture. MAYBE it was just Sally who didn't relay the messages. She was pretty pissed off that I had rejected their offer of salvation.

When I questioned Maryanne, I found out that it was true: Dillon had not talked to her at all, and Sally's distorted motive for keeping the messages from me was that she was POSITIVE that Maryanne would try to talk me into going back to Grant, which she felt would be "the mistake of the century."

Maryanne came right over as soon as I called. She was pretty impressed at what I'd done to the place. Although she didn't come right out and SAY it, I think she had sort of thought—along with everyone else—that Lola Bloom was totally helpless. I mean, she always liked me, but I had done nothing to demonstrate any strength at all.

Of course I instantly broke my promise to my-self and asked her if she'd seen Grant lately.

"Yeah," she said. "I saw him last night."

"Where?"

"Oh, he threw this great party. No food *at all* . . . just booze and dope, and we all got totally drunk and loaded and then sent out for gigantic pizzas from Magoo's."

"Sounds typical . . ." I paused. "How is he?"

"Well, you know Grant . . . it's hard to tell. He's got all that energy, so he always *seems* happy. You know, like when you fast-forward on a Beta-max and see all the people running around at tri-ple speed, they all look happy."

"Did you talk to him at all?"

She paused. "He asked if I'd seen you, asked where you were living, and I said I didn't know but that it wasn't with Dillon and Sally, and he said, 'Far out!' " She laughed. "Grant is the only per-son left in 1984 who can get away with saying, 'Far out.' "

"Yeah," I said quietly. Sweet Grant, with that Dunhill hanging out the side of his mouth and his Tom Selleck mustache, which (I swear) he grew YEARS before *Magnum, P.I.* and even shaved off for a year BECAUSE of *Magnum, P.I.* My husband (my former husband), my drunken lover, my love, and I had to ask Maryanne not to tell him where I was living. I HAD to. Once in his arms again, I'd be pouring vodka down my throat while he cheered, and tossing the lithium over my shoulder, quietly dying again, not knowing when or where the urge to kill myself would come.

Maryanne kind of quietly skirted the subject of

the suicide attempt, and fortunately she didn't put her hand on my shoulder, look terribly concerned, stare into my eyes, and say in a meaningful and saddened voice, "Hi, Lola."

Finally she got up enough nerve to ask me what it was like, and I told her that the DYING wasn't so bad because at that time, it was what I truly wanted, and I actually had very calm memories of taking the 7-11 Big Gulp cup full of vodka and lying under the roses, but the bummer had been waking up and finding out that I couldn't even kill myself correctly.

Meanwhile, back at the ranch, Dillon had phoned Helen, my ever-present-even-when-absent mother, and he gave her all the "deets" (as Page would say) about what I had been up to since I came back from California, and she was pissed off because neither Page nor I had bothered to contact her. So she called me and announced she was coming for a visit but didn't want to lay eyes on either Grant or Dillon.

For once I could say, "No problem" and she quickly said she had reservations at the Kahala because, wherever I was living, she was sure beyond her "wildest imagination" of its "awfulness."

I figured I'd better get therapy and get it FAST. I was going to need someone very badly while Helen was there. I wasn't too hot on the idea of calling Jake O'Shea, nor did I want to just thumb through the Yellow Pages. I tried to think of anyone I knew who was seeing a shrink, but the only one who came to mind was Page. Page saw some shrink in Beverly HIlls, not really because she

NEEDED to, but because she found therapy "interesting." When *Classified Ads* first became a smash hit, Page went to the shrink because she "couldn't handle fame," and she just stayed on. Naturally, it was a weekday, and I had to call her on the set, which sort of upset her because no one at Universal knew she was seeing a psychiatrist. She pretended that he was a regular doctor and said she'd get him to recommend someone in Hawaii.

"What's today's ad?" I asked, as I always did.

"Well, this week Sunny answers the ad asking for volunteers to work on the Save the Whales thing, and I meet this marine biologist whose other occupation is a diver at Marineland, and he teaches me to scuba dive, and lets me go down with him in the tank at Marineland, but I screw everything up, and we almost get bitten by a hammerhead shark who chases us around the tank while they play the *Jaws* theme. It's written pretty funny. There's lots of location stuff on this one, but a lot of my part in this is done by a stunt double, so I'm taking Friday off to be a guest celeb on *The $25,000 Dollar Pyramid*."

I could never understand why Page, who refused to do commercials anymore or even soaps, OFTEN was the guest celeb on game shows when she didn't need to be. "I thought," I said, "you had to be a has-been to want to do game shows, or really want to promote yourself."

"I think they're fun" was her typical-Page answer. I was sorry I'd asked her, because she had long ago stopped asking why I did things like drink Moët & Chandon in the bowling alley.

Later she called me with the name of a psychologist who was supposed to be "brilliant" but couldn't prescribe lithium. Then I talked to Jake O'Shea, and he said he would keep on prescribing the lithium as long as I was in therapy with SOME-ONE, and as long as I came in for regular blood tests. There's something too vampirish about having blood drawn, but I said okay anyway. Why is it that the safe and "right" thing to do is always so boring? Exercise: boring. Not smoking: boring. Sober: boring. Life without Grant: safe but boring.

Fortunately, my therapist was compassionate and seemed to think all the things I found boring were boring too. He actually laughed all through the story about when—during the marriage—I decided to join the Oahu Athletic Club so I could drink more without getting fat, and how I BE-LIEVED them when they said exercise was fun, and when it wasn't at all "fun" they suggested I come more often and get used to it quicker. When my ankles started to hurt, the twenty-three-year-old aerobics teacher with a twenty-three-inch waist smiled and said, "No pain, no gain!" Everyone there was wearing Jane Fonda leotards and designer sweat bands and LEG WARMERS. Do you NEED leg warmers for an aerobics class in HAWAII? I wore some sport socks over my tights, and one woman actually came up to me and said, "Where did you get your leg warmers? They're so far out"—she couldn't get away with saying "far out" the way Grant did—"they go all the way down into your shoes."

"They're socks," I said simply.

"Holy shit!" she said incredulously.

Robert, the therapist, laughed when I told him

I'd even tried hanging out at the juice bar to see if that made this horrifying experience any better, but it didn't. He seemed to understand when I said the only good thing about the class was that when it was over, I could have a beer and watch *Wheel of Fortune* on their large-screen TV.

Robert actually seemed to identify with me, or if he didn't, he did such a hell of a job of seeming to that I decided not to worry about his motives. He told me I had a lot of courage and all that crap to leave Grant, and he laughed at the end of the session when I asked him ironically if I was cured yet. He smiled and said, "You tell me after your mother leaves. It sounds like her visit might be regression time."

"That's what made me come here."

"Then it's good," he smiled.

Then I went to the Medical Group to have blood drawn, so Jake O'Shea could monitor my lithium level. Even though it HURTS more, I would rather have blood drawn from my finger. Somehow it seems less vampirish. Even when I'm looking the other way, I always faint. Just the IDEA of it kind of makes me queasy.

After recovering from the bloodsucking, I called Maryanne to see if I could use her car to pick Helen up at the airport; in my wildest imagination I just couldn't see her on the back of my motorcycle. Even if she had no luggage at all, I know if I arrived at the airport on a motorcycle, she would just jump on the next plane and go back to Coronado. Not a bad idea, but she WAS my goddamn mother after all.

After exchanging my motorcycle for Maryanne's beat-up Datsun, I drove up St. Louis Heights to put some fresh flowers around the place so Helen wouldn't be quite so repulsed by it. I saw Grant's Chevy coming around a curve. As I said, I had seen it a number of times when I was on the motorcycle with my crash helmet on, but would he recognize Maryanne's Datsun? I was glad it wasn't a distinctive color or anything—just a green Datsun. He zoomed on past without even looking my way. From the car, I had a better look at him than from the motorcycle. He was still Grant, my amazing lover (my amazing FORMER lover).

When I got home, there were FIVE letters in my mailbox. Since Page never wrote—just called—I couldn't imagine who would POSSIBLY write to me, let alone FIVE people. After opening the box, I saw they were all from the same person: Pete (short for Peter), the Man in the White Belt. I couldn't believe it: FIVE letters, all at least three pages long, typed, single-spaced. He poured out his love for me in purple prose. He said he prayed I wouldn't hang up if he called to "dialogue" with me. Then in the fourth letter he really got carried away and started talking about how he couldn't understand why I wouldn't go out with him because he was such a great "A-number-one" guy. He even wrote a poem for me (I guess referring to Grant) called "Abused by a Jew, Come into My Arms." I about died. I wanted to rush to the phone and read it to Grant, read ALL the letters to him. Like Pete's speech, his letters were full of that business jargon like "interface" and "maximize." I apparently struck him—from our two brief meetings—as a person who liked to "maximize" herself. THAT was probably the funniest thing he'd ever written. Gloria Steinem, yes, but LOLA BLOOM? He even said that if I didn't want to "have intercourse" with him, he'd just LOVE to lie in my bed and "just hug." YUCK! That would be almost WORSE than "having intercourse" with him. I mean, if you were somehow forced to fuck him (like if someone was holding your baby for ransom and the only way you could get her back was to fuck him, or something like that), you could just kind of close your eyes and lie there and try to pretend it was Robert Redford or Roy Scheider (or Grant), but to lie in bed and "just hug" . . . God, you'd actually have to participate. The man was nuts. Then I began to wonder if he might be dangerous like John Hinckley. At least John Hinckley tried to shoot REAGAN and not Jodie Foster, but STILL, I'd hate to have the Man in the White Belt try to shoot Governor George Ariyoshi just because I wouldn't "hug" him.

Twenty minutes later a bouquet of flowers arrived. The card totally blew my mind. It was so disgusting that I almost called the florist to chew them out for sending it, but then I saw it had been in a sealed envelope with his handwriting, so they probably never saw it. It said (and I'm not making this up), "This afternoon I sat alone, thought of you, of what your body would look like naked, and I played with myself until I came." YUCK! I'd met Mr. Polyester TWICE. I almost felt raped. There was no way I could keep him from fantasizing, but it was horrible to think that the Man in the White Belt was thinking about my naked body and there wasn't a single thing I could do about it. Thank God

Helen was staying at the Kahala. She'd go berserk. She didn't even like it if GRANT, my HUSBAND, gave me a kiss in front of her that was a little too passionate for her taste. I set a match to the card and dropped it in the sink. The flowers weren't even pretty: I hate huge bouquets of big feathery homecoming-game mums, but I figured they might brighten up the place for Helen, so I put them in a jar on the drainboard. I almost dumped the letters in the garbage, but I decided to save them to give Maryanne a few laughs. She'd especially like "Abused by a Jew, Come into My Arms."

Amazingly enough, I did feel stronger, not because some nut wrote me five letters in one day, but because *I* was not the nut. *I* was the sane one. I just hoped he wasn't dangerous.

Helen's hands shook as she reached for me. She took a long look and then held me very tight. I could feel her cheek was wet, but I had absolutely nothing to say to her. I just held on to her. I wondered if I'd ever have kids, and with whom? Was there another Grant walking around somewhere?

I was kind of hoping Helen would say her usual, "Take me straight to the Kahala," which she had always said since she had seen our (Grant's) house once, but I guess she was kind of curious as to what dump I was living in now. After she finished holding me, mopping her eyes, smearing her mascara, and getting her composure back, she said, "Let's go to your apartment. I want to see if there's anything I can buy to—"

"I don't want you to buy *anything!*" I snapped.

She really reminded me of the mother in *Terms of Endearment:* one minute you could think about loving her, the next minute you didn't want to be in the same room with her.

As we drove up St. Louis Heights, she ALSO noted that I "didn't live too far from Grant." Why can't people just leave you alone, especially when you're really making an effort to change. On the other hand, Helen was a mother, and mothers by nature can never quite let go.

When I opened the front door of my apartment ("my space," I should say—it hardly qualified as an apartment), I quickly said, "Look, Helen, I now have *furniture!*"

She glanced at the furniture that the Goodwill wouldn't want and said, "I never thought a positive thing about Grant's house until I saw this. How can you stand it?"

"It has my view, and besides you should have seen it *before*. I mean, I've *really* accomplished miracles."

Helen shuddered. "What is it that won't let you take money from your own mother? You know, you don't *have* to live here. I could—"

"That's the whole *point!* That's why you married Dillon. You were sick of lying around being Irving Adrian's daughter. You chose an acceptable 1940's way. I married Grant, but I couldn't live with the feeling that I couldn't live *without* him, without you, without Dillon or Page. That feeling scared me."

"You really astound me," she said. "You spent thirty-four years sitting back, living off Grant, and being proud of yourself because you wouldn't accept help from me, and God knows you needed more than one kind of help. Now suddenly Grant is out of the picture, and"—her eyes softened—"you don't need to be proud. You are better off without him. I know he was handsome . . . had that smile, but—"

"His looks and his smile were only a tiny part of why I love . . . loved Grant. I'm sick of explaining it to you."

"Yes, something about irony and plastic toys, I think . . ."

"Forget it," I said. "I'm not trying to be all feminist or anything like that. You've just never woken up when you thought you'd be dead. I had two choices—dead or get my shit together. And I'm *not* preaching! Getting my shit together is about the most boring thing I've ever done, but I'm *doing* it!"

"Please don't say 'shit,' Lola," she said softly. She looked around sadly. At least she couldn't do the old white-glove routine on my house. It was CLEAN. A dump, but CLEAN. She looked at me nervously. Her voice quivered. "Can I at least buy you some clothes? Mothers are at least allowed to do that."

Now, that seemed to me an acceptable mother-type thing to do. She was right. Even mothers who didn't have ten million dollars bought their daughters clothes (even their thirty-four-year-old daughters), and if I really was going to get that mythical job I was supposed to be getting so I could save the *Mr. Macho* money, I had to have something normal to wear. You can't wear jeans and a Victorian lace blouse to a job interview.

I took her shaking hands. Helen actually seemed sort of afraid of me, afraid now even to be generous. "Of course," I said. "What are mothers for?" She smiled and looked like I'd just given her the Brooklyn Bridge.

"We go *now!*" she smiled. "I can't stand to stay in this dump another second."

And she never did find out it didn't have a bathroom.

Going to Liberty House department store with Helen wasn't as amusing as shopping in West Hollywood with Page, but, boy, did she know how to shop. Remembering the silk panties that had to be dry-cleaned, my one rule was that whatever she bought me had to be washable, and her rules were that I couldn't get anything "weird, with fringe or bells, *Flashdance* clothes, ripped up clothes, things that looked two sizes too big, or anything that fell off one shoulder." Since it wouldn't occur to me to get any of those things, I quickly agreed, and Helen was totally amazed.

She whipped out her American Express card, and we hit the Crest Room. "Pretty" was about the only notion I had of style, so Helen zipped through the racks and occasionally held up something, and I'd nod at the "pretty" ones and shake my head at the ones that looked like something Helen would wear. Then, when we got around to trying them on, we discovered that the Crest Room at Liberty House doesn't know the meaning of the word "washable," so Helen signed, and we hit the other departments.

Finally, we came out with, I'm sure, at least a thousand dollars' worth of clothes. I felt I looked like Faye Dunaway in *Network*, which—although Grant would have been amused if he'd seen me—wasn't altogether too bad a feeling. I wondered if, through Grant's eyes, someone in the dress-for-success look could still qualify as "the amazing one," but that didn't matter much now. Helen was actually smiling, and—as I said—she never found out I didn't have a bathroom.

Chapter

14

After the summer of 1968 in Kahaluu, U.C. Santa Cruz didn't look so bad. Even though it wasn't Berkeley, it at least had people who knew there was going to be a presidential election in November. I returned to Santa Cruz hoping for two things: that by some magical (and it would TAKE magic) means, McCarthy would get on the ballot, and that maybe I'd have an orgasm. Depressed, lying on my bed, I didn't believe either was possible. I was so discouraged, I didn't even want to bother to take petitions around to get McCarthy on the ballot, and when you walk around with a—seemingly—perpetual sad look on your face, meeting the man to have an orgasm with just isn't in the cards.

When the election rolled around, it's too bad so many people didn't realize that voting for an honest Democrat—even though he wasn't our first choice—was better than not voting at all or splitting the party. If we hadn't all given up, we might have saved America from some of its "long dark night" with Richard Nixon.

Because Hannah Fine had returned to school early, she really scored a great room for us—one of the few that had its OWN BATHROOM. (In a college DORM, I had my own bathroom; when I was thirty-four, I had to go outside and walk around the house.)

Hannah had spent the summer fucking this guy who swore he was straight but wore glitter eye shadow and Sally Hansen Hard-As-Nails (in peach). Her uncle had given her a job on his avocado farm counting the avocados as they came by on a conveyer belt, but because the job was a tad bit tedious and her heart was really in Las Vegas, she quit after two weeks and went there and lived off the guy with the glitter on his eyes. She said that Rod Brewster was so jealous he was even going to give her a role in *A Funny Thing Happened on the Way to the Forum*.

"I thought he did that Kabuki stuff," I said.

"I said he studied it at Notre Dame. That doesn't mean he can direct the stuff! It would be much too hard for him."

"But I thought college theater departments were supposed to do, you know, real serious plays, like *Oedipus Rex* or *King Lear* or, well, classics."

"Ah, you read one of those Shakespearean plays, you've read them all. At least, *A Funny Thing Happened on the Way to the Forum* is about Romans."

"Shit," I said. "What are you going to play?"

"The Virgin."

"*The Virgin!* You're kidding."

"Why not?" she asked dramatically. "I was once a virgin."

"Many years ago. Can you even sing?"

"I don't sing protest songs, but I can sing good

— 268 —

enough for *this* production." She brushed her hair out of her eyes. "You going to keep screwing Larry?"

"Naa . . . I'm actually going to try to get an education."

"An *education?*"

"Yeah. You know, *learn something.*"

"What?"

"I'm going to try to get into Simon Rothman's poetry writing class."

"Is he that guy who won the Pulitzer Prize?"

"You got it."

Since Simon Rothman was the English department's star attraction, they had a separate bookcase for his five volumes of poetry in the outer office. There was a single red plastic rose in a crystal bud vase on top of it.

"Can I help you?" asked the secretary, who looked as if she'd graduated from the department a couple of years ago and couldn't get a job anywhere else. She wore wire-rimmed glasses and a poncho.

"I'd like to see the chairman," I said. "Dr. Knowlton."

She pushed her glasses on top of her head. "Regarding what?"

"I'd like permission to take Simon Rothman's poetry writing class."

"You've got to be kidding!" she said. "That class was filled two semesters ago! It's a small seminar, and only senior majors are allowed to take it. Even if you *are* a major, you're definitely not a senior."

Still hoping she didn't know what she was talking about, I said, "I'd still like to maybe talk to the chairman about it."

She sighed, got up, and disappeared down the corridor. As I turned to sit down, I saw a man standing in the doorway. He was about my height, wore a trench coat, and sort of looked like the man who works in the accounting department in all those 1950s British "terror" movies, who you know is going to turn out to be Jack the Ripper in the end. If he hadn't been wearing a tie, I would have assumed he was the janitor, because he stared at the floor with that nervous, humble look janitors have when they come into an offfice to empty the wastebaskets and something important is going on.

He had a runny nose and sniffed loudly. Because sniffing is like coughing—when you hear someone else doing it, you feel you have to too— I started sniffing as I sat down. He mumbled something unintelligible.

"What?" I asked.

He looked at the floor. "I asked why you wanted to t-t-t-take Simon Rothman's class so much."

"He won the Pulitzer Prize," I stated.

"Does that m-m-m-make it a good class t-to t-t-t-take?" he mumbled.

"Oh, I don't know, really," I said, "but all you ever hear when anyone mentions the English department is that Simon Rothman teaches here. You see, if I took his course, I could justify not transferring, and I really like going to school here. I know it isn't Berkeley or Yale, but I have my first real friend here—except for my sister, and 'no grades' comes in handy when you have to take stuff like physics, but I need a solid reason to stay on. I mean, he must know something about poetry writing and all. Then I could become a poet like Sylvia Plath and win the *Mademoiselle* college competition, and my mother would stop asking me what I was learning."

"She d-d-died . . . k-k-killed herself." He paused. "S-s-suddenly it gave her poems d-d-d-dimensions they didn't have before."

"Huh?"

"Sylvia Plath. Suicides shouldn't be c-c-can-onized."

"I've thought about killing myself," I said, wondering why I was having this conversation at all with a strange man in a trench coat who stuttered, "but if you *really* want to die, I don't think you'd even care."

"P-p-perhaps not."

"Well, I sure wouldn't do it to get my poems famous. What a stupid thing to do. You wouldn't be around to collect the royalties. No autograph parties. I think people who are real serious suicidals just want to be dead."

The man smiled. Even though his fingernails were bitten down to the quick, he had an awfully nice smile—boyish. He wore a very conservative haircut for the sixties and Buddy Holly glasses. He looked like the kind of person who was a wimp with acne in high school and still believed himself an acned person.

"What's your n-n-name?" he mumbled.

"Lola Bloom."

"Like Molly."

I laughed. "Yes. Yes. Yes. Yes," I said. I hoped he would think I thought of that comeback right on the spot. If you go through life with the last name Bloom, you'd better have a *Ulysses* comeback.

"I'm glad to know you," he said. "You're an interesting p-p-person, and you remind me of Tuesday Weld. I'm awfully fond of Tuesday Weld."

"Oh, yeah?" I had reminded people of a lot of things, but never TUESDAY WELD. Page was the Tuesday Weld in our family. I wore the round glasses.

He held out his hand to me and mumbled something else. "Huh?" I asked.

"I said I'm Simon Rothman," he mumbled. He was sweating. He quickly took a handkerchief, wiped his forehead, and said, "I'm sorry. I . . . uh . . . m-m-meant to tell you. I just couldn't fit it in. You kind of talk . . . uh . . . fast. I *am* very fond of T-T-Tuesday Weld. You look like you're from the Midwest or . . . uh . . . California. You know . . . All-American. You look like America."

Having seriously considered leaving the country that fall, I wasn't exactly sure how to take that. "Is that neat? That I look so American?" I asked, thinking about the blacks, the Indians, and all the immigrants who came through Ellis Island, and wondered why WASPs were considered all-American. No one would ever have described Martin Luther King as all-American.

"How come you're teaching here?" I asked, genuinely interested.

"It's p-p-prettier than New York, they offered me a lot of m-m-money, and I don't like giving grades." He mopped his head again, blew his nose, and nervously put his hand on my shoulder. "Was I right about you? C-C-California?"

"Well, I grew up here, and I spend my summers with my father in Hawaii."

"Oh, Hawaii," he sighed. "Uh . . . is it nice there? In Hawaii?"

"It sometimes sucks dogs."

He smiled and peered at me through his Buddy Holly glasses. "That surprises me. I've had Hawaiian fantasies, you see. . . . Well, the ocean . . . the p-p-palm trees . . . You know, as Stevenson put it, 'The loveliest fleet of islands anchored in any ocean.' "

"Mark Twain," I stated.

"I beg your p-p-pardon?"

"Mark Twain said that. Not Stevenson."

He mopped his forehead again. "Yes, yes, exactly. What's it like there?"

"Well, most of it is *pretty*, but there's lots of racial tension and poverty and stuff. And there are only about four bookstores in the *whole state!*"

"Oh," he said, looking sad—just the way I did when I heard there were a bunch of condominiums around the pyramids, "I'm . . . uh . . . sorry. You're pretty."

"I *am?*"

"Yes. I like your glasses."

As he sat down beside me, he steadied himself and almost fell over. Jesus, this just didn't seem like the man who had written *Points of Light on Black Velvet and Other Sonnets to the Stars.* "Sorry," he said. "I just had an operation on my knee."

"Oh, I'm sorry to hear that," I said automatically, just like Larry. I felt stupid. "Does it hurt you?"

"No. It just feels stiff. They replaced my knee-cap with a p-p-plastic one."

"Really? Can I feel it? Does it feel like a real knee?"

"You want to t-t-t-touch my knee?" he asked.

"The plastic one—that is, if it doesn't hurt you."

"No . . . no, not at all . . . uh . . . please go ahead.

As I touched his knee, I thought, "God, I'm touching SIMON ROTHMAN's knee."

"It feels just like a real knee," I said to him.

"Thank you. I slipped in some mud."

"While you were out contemplating the stars?"

"While I was going to my c-c-car . . . by the driveway . . . there was mud."

"God, that's interesting."

"Do you really think so?" I could tell he was actually pleased that I found the story of his knee interesting. Since I hadn't taken my hand off it yet, I moved my hand up a little bit, so that if I never saw him again, I could say I had put my hand on Simon Rothman's thigh. He jumped what seemed like four feet in the air.

"God, I'm sorry. Does that hurt?"

"No . . . n-n-no . . . I just . . ." I glanced down and saw he had a hard-on. This was almost better than if Paul Newman had been sitting there, because Paul Newman wasn't a Pulitzer Prize-winning poet like Simon Rothman. Paul Newman was just an actor.

"I want to take your poetry writing class. May I?" I asked, figuring that while I had my hand on his thigh and he had a hard-on was as good a time as any to ask him.

He had tears in his eyes. "I'm *so* sorry," he said. "It's f-f-full, but you're so pretty . . . like the girl in that cornflakes commercial." He touched my hair, which was getting long then. "Could we have some coffee together?" he whispered.

Interrupting my first beautiful moment with Simon Rothman, the secretary came back in and started to tell me that Dr. Knowlton had said AB-SOLUTELY NO about the class. When she saw Simon, she almost stood at attention. "Oh, I didn't know you were coming in today, Mr. Rothman," she said.

"I'm n-n-not," he said, taking my hand.

As we walked out into the fall (or rather Santa Cruz's version of fall), I wondered if he saw the trees the same way I did. I remembered in *Our Town* when Emily asks if people ever realize life while they're living it, and the Stage Manager says, "Saints and poets, maybe they do some." God! Saints and poets!

As we stood there among the trees, it suddenly didn't matter if Richard Nixon was going to be elected. There was absolutely nothing he could do to wipe out *Points of Light on Black Velvet and Other Sonnets to the Stars.*

"Would you put your arm around my shoulders?" I asked Simon carefully. "It's kind of . . . chilly."

He put his arm around my pea coat. "You should have some c-c-coffee to warm you up." He pulled me closer.

Because I knew I couldn't let this moment pass,

I stopped, looked into his eyes, and parted my lips just the way Grace Kelly did in *To Catch a Thief*. God, it was just like out of the movies: misty woods, and a poet kissing me right there under the trees. Looking into his eyes, I kissed him again, he sighed, and I fell in love.

We went to this restaurant near campus called Buttons, which had the worst shit food anyone ever tasted. Since it was close and had really good homemade pie, everyone went there in spite of the hamburgers caked with grease and the watery Cokes.

Not quite realizing that I was supposed to be loved for myself and that REAL LOVE (the kind of love I had for Grant) had nothing to do with whether someone had a label like "Pulitzer Prize" attached to him, I was simply thrilled to be near this man and thought nothing of the fact that he liked me only because I had neat glasses and looked like a goddamn wheat field.

"I've never d-d-done this before," said Simon, his hand shaking as he lifted his coffee cup.

"Taken a student for coffee?"

"No . . . uh . . . kissed someone . . . uh . . . like you." He added some sugar to his coffee and struck three matches trying to light my Salem cigarette. "In fact," he mumbled, "I've never kissed anyone since I've been married. . . . I mean, my wife, of course, but no one else . . . the way I kissed you." He took out his handkerchief, mopped his head again, and laughed nervously. "I c-c-can't help imagining you naked."

"You're imagining me *naked*?"

"Oh, yes."

"What do I look like . . . I mean, through a poet's eyes?"

"Like Tuesday Weld."

"Have you ever seen Tuesday Weld naked?"

"N-n-no, but you look the way I've always imagined her."

"God!" I said, and without finishing our coffee, we went straight to the Pine View Motel.

He stroked my hair, my face, and kissed each finger. I reached up and slowly loosened his tie. Removing each piece of my clothing as if it were a rare and beautiful object instead of a Bobbie Brooks special, he breathed my name over and over again, the way Grant was to do later: "Lola Bloom, Lola Bloom."

When he leaned over and kissed my neck, my breasts, and my back, I felt he was really kissing ME—Lola Bloom. For whatever reasons, Simon Rothman was kissing ME, and at that moment no other body, no other person would remotely do. As he carried me to the bed, I was wet and shaking. "Lola Bloom," he breathed.

I didn't say anything because I could feel the strangest thing happening. He hadn't even entered me, but was kissing my neck and touching my vagina in a way I'd never been touched before. After his penis was in me, as he moved in and out, he kept breathing, "Are you ready? Are you ready?" Because I wasn't exactly sure what I was supposed to be ready for, I managed to breathe back, "Yes, I think so," and he started to move faster and faster, and my God, I couldn't believe it: my body felt rigid for a second, and then full of shivers and sparkles. Simon moaned, and we fell together, wet and sticky. Jesus Christ, this was it! The Big O! I'd had it, finally an orgasm. God almighty. Okay, so Nixon would be elected. Big deal: I had had my orgasm.

I looked over at Simon, and his eyes were closing. "I love you," I whispered.

He opened his eyes and looked at me sadly. "I could love you too, Lola Bloom," he said, "but I'm going to try not to."

"Simon Rothman!" Hannah screeched. "You're hitting the rack with *Simon Rothman?*"

"Yes," I said, demurely lowering my eyes.

"Is he that nerdy-looking guy in a trench coat you were with at the student union yesterday?"

"Yes, and he's not nerdy-looking. He's got a really sweet smile."

"Face it, Lola, he makes Woody Allen look like Steve Reeves. Would you even look *twice* at him if he hadn't won a Pulitzer Prize?"

"Looks aren't important to me. Besides, I love him."

"Shit," she sighed. "You've been to bed with the genius only two times, and you're talking about *love?*"

"He cares for me, Hannah."

"He just likes to fuck you."

"Why would he bother to make sure I eat when I'm depressed? It's not too entertaining to have a lover who sometimes spends days in bed. Yesterday he called, and I said I couldn't move, and I started to cry, and he came rushing over."

"You mean you fucked in *here?*" she asked.

"We didn't do it. That would have taken more

energy than I had. He just held me so I'd feel a little safer."

"I still think he just likes to fuck you."

"You don't understand. I told him it made me feel cheap to go to motels all the time . . . kind of reminded me of Larry and his Jockey shorts and all, so Simon is going to *pay* for an apartment for me next term. Of course, I'll still get my mail here at the dorm so Helen won't find out."

"Jesus, Lola," she said. "You mustn't fall in *love* with him. Men like that don't ever leave their wives. It will only fuck you up. God, what do you *do* for entertainment together? I can't exactly picture him going out for pizza or to a Canned Heat concert."

"Well, he shows me his works in progress, and that's almost as interesting as the sex."

"Shit. What do you show him? Your book report on *The Bell Jar?*"

"No," I laughed. "I tell him what's happening on *Hope for Tomorrow*—all about Henry being killed in a car accident and how it's really hard on Amanda because little Brian died of leukemia right after the brain operation, and how little Brian's *real* father is trying to bomb the Martins' house, and—"

"I bet he just *loves* that," she said sarcastically.

"He *does!* He laughs and says I tell it so much better than it ever is on television. He makes me feel beautiful and kind of creative."

"He likes to fuck you," she stated.

I spent the next few days fantasizing about exactly what kind of apartment Simon would choose. Since he was a poet, OF COURSE it would be tasteful, but because of the wife, it wouldn't be too expensive so she wouldn't wonder what was happening to their money. Definitely small and tasteful. I visualized natural wood, hanging plants, tall trees, etc., and even entertained the thought of making a quilt for the bed.

Hannah just sort of watched me with an amused look on her face while I packed.

"You're really going ahead with this?" she asked.

"Of course. I know it's sort of like being a mistress or a kept woman, but I love him, and motels are too sleaze-bucket."

"What do you mean 'like being a kept woman'? It is being a kept woman."

"I'm paying for my own food."

"Big deal. You can buy Kraft macaroni and cheese on sale for seventeen cents."

I decided not to add that he wasn't paying for my clothes as I was sure she would have pointed out to me that Helen paid for them.

She sighed. "Well, when's the house-warming party?"

"I'm going to keep this kind of quiet."

"You're going to miss a lot."

"What? Sharing a room with you?"

"Well, for starters, yes."

"I will miss you," I said.

"Don't worry," she said. "I'll come around . . . see the genuine love nest, see the *very bed* the genius fucks on."

"Hannah!"

"Look, Lola, I do wish you the best, but don't

let the guy hurt you. They *never* leave their wives for twenty-year-old students. They never do."

"I don't care. I . . ."

"If a Pulitzer Prize can lead you to orgasm, so be it."

"Uh . . . Hannah?" I asked. "Uh . . . could we use your car to take my stuff over? Four suitcases on the bus is a little awkward."

"Why? Doesn't the genius have a car?"

"Yes, he does. I meant you and me. He can't just come over to the dorm and leave with me and four suitcases. That wouldn't even be subtle."

"Okay," she sighed. Then her face brightened a little. "At least I'll get to see the place. What's it like?"

"I don't know yet. I just have the address."

"You're moving in *sight unseen?*"

"I trust Simon's taste."

"Definitely headed for heartbreak," Hannah said to the wall.

I ignored her, and we carried the suitcases out to the Kharmann Ghia.

While I studied the map, she drove with an amused look on her face, and the Doors sang away on the radio. When we got to the address, she smiled and shook her head. The apartment building didn't exactly look like one a sensitive, artistic poet would pick out for his young mistress. The building was a sort of faded pink and had a huge silver sign on it that said "Bertha Apartments." It was two stories tall and about ten apartments long. The walkway to the manager's office was cement with those little flecks of silver in it.

The manager had her hair in curlers (OF COURSE! Don't all resident managers answer the door in curlers?), and she looked a little amused as she handed me the key. I guess she'd probably seen a number of young girls in this "living situation." What she didn't know what that this wasn't your average married man. It was Simon Rothman, and he had chosen ME, Nickname: none, above all others (except his wife, but I had already painted a mental picture of their terribly unhappy marriage).

Hannah and I lugged the suitcases up the outdoor stairs, and I opened the door of number 16. The carpet was that baby-shit yellow harvest gold stuff, and the furniture was made out of that fake wood and plastic. There was a matching couch and chair in the living room, and one of those plastic and chrome flowered dinette sets in the corner by the kitchen. In the bedroom stood a double bed, a fake wood dresser, a print of a ship with a plastic wood frame, and a fake wood nightstand with a built-in lamp with a pleated shade. To make the living room look larger, someone had stuck those mirror squares on part of one wall. On the mirror was etched yet another ship.

"Simon really does like the Motel 6 look," commented Hannah.

"Well," I said, "I really didn't exactly expect his taste to—"

"*Taste?*" she asked. "We're not talking taste here. We're talking economics. This place is probably the closest el-cheapo place he could find."

"Yeah," I said. I was slightly let down but already bursting with ideas for "fixing it up."

While I started to unpack, Hannah went out for some cigarettes, and the cloud of disappointment enveloped me. I shook it off by thinking about Simon and orgasms and Pulitzer Prizes.

When Hannah returned, she brought a bottle of André champagne and two plastic cups. I smiled, and she poured two glasses.

"To your new home," she said. "May you brighten it up with love, and," she added smiling, "may you learn to like harvest gold."

I smiled. "Thanks, Hannah."

For the next five months, I passionately loved Simon Rothman. I was insanely jealous of his wife, Ella, whom I'd seen on a couple of occasions. I think she "knew," even though Simon said she didn't. The two times I saw her at campus functions, she gave me a little smile and looked at me out of the corners of her sparkling eyes as if to say, "I'll just wait. You will pass." She taught art at the school and dressed "real sixties" and had beautiful long, dark hair. Sometimes I wondered why he even bothered with me, but even at twenty years old, I knew that NO ONE knows what goes on in a marriage except the two people involved. Simon rarely said he loved me and never mentioned leaving his wife.

"I think I know how it will end," said Hannah. "That is, if he isn't a horrible bastard and just stops calling you."

"He'd never do that."

"Okay, he'll take you out to dinner at—"

"We don't *go* out to dinner, we go out to lunch."

"Well, he'll take you someplace really expensive, and then instead of going back to the apartment, he'll give you the ax right there in the restaurant. That's how it always happens."

I started to get nervous every time we went anywhere remotely nice. Then, one day in the spring, we took a drive up 101 and stopped at a little outdoor seafood café, and just as I was beginning to dig into my mussels, he reached over and put his hand on mine and said, "Lola, we've got to talk." ("We've *got to talk*"—you'd think a Pulitzer Prize-winning poet could start off with something a little more original than "We've got to talk.")

Suddenly I wasn't a bit hungry. "You're going to dump me," I said, still holding the mussel, with the butter sauce running down my arm.

"Well, I wouldn't p-p-put it quite that way."

I could feel my throat tighten up and tears start to come. "Then you are. *Why, goddammit? Why suddenly now?*" I yelled, and the other four people in the place probably figured I was getting the ax.

"B-b-b-because . . . well . . . it should never have gone this far."

"That's what they say on *Hope for Tomorrow*. Are you going to say, 'Let's be just good friends,' too?"

"N-n-no. I was going to say we shouldn't see each other again."

I pushed my plate to the side and put my head on the table and sort of whimpered like a scared child. "Why?" I managed to say.

"The first time we made love, I had no idea you were g-g-going to love me. I had no idea of the extent . . . of the nature of your mood swings, and [long pause] . . . and Ella's going to have a b-b-baby.''

I mean, intellectually, I knew Simon and Ella were fucking, but this was the first time I was actually slapped in the face with it. "Was this sort of an accident?"

"We've been trying to have a baby for years . . . years."

"You were trying to have a baby all the time you were sleeping with *me!*"

"I d-d-didn't know I was going to keep on seeing you. Every day that you were happy, I fell a little more in love with you, and each time you were depressed . . . well, I couldn't break it off."

"Why did you sleep with me in the first place?" I managed to get it out and quickly put my napkin up to my eyes. I look so fucking horrible when I cry.

"I thought it was g-g-going to be a one-time thing. It happens often."

"Huh?" I was confused. "But you told me I was the first one."

"I lied," he said. "I thought it was going to be a one-time thing. Ever since the P-P-Pulitzer, students . . . women have often come on to me. You see, when I was g-g-growing up, girls never looked at me twice, and . . ."

His voice trailed off.

"Are you going to drive me home," I choked, "or are you just going to drop me off at the bus station?"

Do you know what that bastard said? "M-m-m-maybe the bus would be a good idea. It's a long ride home, and the bus would make it a lot less painful."

"For *you*," I tried to say, but it came out as just a gigantic sob.

I couldn't believe it. During the ride to the bus station, I cried. Every time I opened my mouth to say anything, all that would come out was a heave.

On the bus, too many goddamn people asked what was wrong. It was horrible. I wasn't well.

When I got home, there was a check from Simon on the kitchen table, giving me a month so I could have the apartment until the end of the term. I lay on the bed, and tears ran into my ears. I felt lost and scared. Hannah had been right again. As she always said, "Goddamned cynics usually are."

Chapter

Therapy. What a bummer. It's like buying tires or having the roof redone—necessary for health and safety, but expensive, and you get no immediate gratification out of it. Most of the time it is kind of like buying a new muffler or going to the Timber Town to buy a garbage can, but sometimes therapy can be a little entertaining.

At least Robert wasn't like Jake O'Shea, and after a few sessions, I honestly thought that MAYBE Robert "got the joke." When I explained the third level of irony to him, he didn't look at me as if I was insane; he actually said I'd make a brilliant sociologist. And he didn't constantly keep telling me stuff I already knew. He instantly understood WHY I loved Grant still, and why I'd had to leave him. He didn't spend a lot of time blaming Grant for feeding my madness. He said he was dealing with ME—Lola Bloom—and not with Grant. Love and fear of my disease were Grant's problems, not mine.

But, as I said, Robert didn't come cheap, and I had to save as much of the *Mr. Macho* money as I could. Get a goddamn job, Lola. What could I possibly DO? I typed a little more than twenty words a minute, and even though I'd been an English major, I couldn't spell worth shit, and I had no real transcript because U.C. Santa Cruz didn't give grades when I was there.

When I walked into Kelly Girl and told the woman this, I was AMAZED when she smiled and said, "I have just the job for you." WHAT, I thought, was "just the job" for "the amazing one"? I figured that, after what I'd told her, the amazing one was probably going to be doing a job similar to Hannah's where she had to sit all day and count the avocados going by. I wasn't too far off base: she sent me to a Xerox place near the university called Kopy Kats (real cute, just like the people who call their shops "shoppes").

My job was to simply stand all day and Xerox things. Since it was near the university, there wasn't even any time to goof off and contemplate existence. All day shoving paper into a Xerox machine for four dollars an hour.

At least Robert was making me feel a little better about myself. And the lithium—while keeping me from dancing in the rain to Jerry Lee Lewis and tossing flowers in the air—also kept me from trying to make myself believe that "dead" was the safest place to be. Damn lithium. As I said, everything that's good for you is boring.

The only entertaining thing about the job was that I got to glance at some of the things I was Xeroxing. Particularly interesting was the stuff I got from would-be fiction writers, screenwriters, and playwrights. Once I made an extra Xerox of a play just to read it. It was so horrible it was totally entertaining. It was trying to be—I guess—Shakespearean, because it had a lot of "What ho, my lords" in it, but it was about a woman with no arms. I wanted to write, ironically, "Good Luck" on the folder, but I figured that a Xeroxer's confidentiality is kind of like that of a doctor or a lawyer. I told this to a totally embarrassed woman who had written a novel, and the DIRTIEST page got stuck in the machine, but she didn't get it.

Amusing as some of it was, WHAT kind of life is it? Go to Kopy Kats, come home, go to Kopy Kats, come home, all to pay for my ninety-dollar-an-hour Saturday with Robert. He said I had "guts" and "courage," which are two things that had NEVER been in anyone's description of Lola Bloom before. Hearing that was almost worth the ninety dollars alone.

Of course there was a lot of BORING Xeroxing—themes, term papers for physics classes, etc. Some of the English term papers were amusing, but face it, Xeroxing near a university is not career heaven.

Career? I thought to myself. Shit. I'm not interested in anything. BUT . . . I hadn't called Grant. Although it was fucking hard not to, I hadn't done it. Even if I wasn't flying, at least I was standing.

After a couple of weeks at Kopy Kats, I started getting more letters from the Man in the White Belt—passionate, dirty, disgusting letters. He also sent more ugly flowers and even had the florist bring up a quart of Johnnie Walker Red. Well, sure, that was part of life's joke: the ones you don't want in a million years are always the ones who want you.

Even though the Man in the White Belt made me feel less crazy, I kept wondering if someone who would write a poem called "Abused by a Jew, Come into My Arms" just might be dangerous. I took all his letters to Robert who—bless him— laughed hysterically at them, and then said yes.

"Who's your divorce lawyer?"

"Grant's . . . I don't know. They worked it all out while I was away with Page."

"You can't do anything about him now because he hasn't hurt or threatened you, but what you can do is get the lawyer to write a letter to him saying that any further contact with you will be subject to legal action or something like that. He'll probably stop, and if he doesn't, he'll be, well, subject to legal action."

"Can I really do that?"

"Sure. All it takes is a phone call."

God! Lola Bloom was going to be the heavyweight! And I had my first good excuse to call Grant.

Then I remembered that all I had to do was look at the divorce decree; the lawyer's name would be on it. Shit.

I looked him up and was amazed when the lawyer took my call right away. I was under the impression that lawyers never took calls right away and rarely returned them.

"So you're Lola Bloom," he said with an eagerness that I thought was reserved for celebrities. "I've heard a lot about you."

"I'll bet," I said rather ironically.

"Well, I must say your divorce was the easiest and strangest I've ever handled."

"Huh?"

"Your husband spoke of you. . . . I mean, here's a guy getting *divorced* from someone he still loves. He told me you were an amazing person— so pretty and brilliant, and I must say that Grant Rosenberg was the absolutely most entertaining client I've ever had. As a matter of fact, we're going drinking together next week."

"He said I was brilliant?"

"And sexy," he laughed, "but he did say 'brilliant' before the 'sexy.' "

"That's neat . . . uh, please say hi to him for me."

"You're the weirdest couple, the first couple I've actually wanted to refuse to do their divorce. I think you should . . . well, never mind." He paused. "What can I do for you?"

I explained to him about the Man in the White Belt. He got a laugh out of "Abused by a Jew, Come into My Arms," but when I said that if *anyone* was abused in our marriage, it was *Grant*, he sobered up. He said he'd send the letter.

When I got home, there were three more letters from the Man in the White Belt, telling me what an insulting bitch I was because I hung up every time he called and then changed my phone number. One letter started out, "Dear Bitch," and I shuddered. WHAT would he do when he got such an official Dear John letter?

Just then there was a knock on the door. I jumped, and ran over to look out the window to see who it was. Fortunately it wasn't the Man in the White Belt, but a man with jeans and a beard. I opened the door.

"Hi, I'm Bert!" he said with a smile almost as winning as Grant's.

"Bert?" I asked confused.

"I used to live here. I came for my clothes and gun."

Holy shit, what was I going to do now? At least the Man in the White Belt didn't fool around with guns . . . at least not that I knew of.

"Oh, Bert!" I said as cheerfully as I could.

"Did you dump the junk?" he said, still smiling. His eyes were sparkling.

"Well, sort of," I said.

"How do you 'sort of' dump things?" he said as if he were asking me to the prom instead of trying to get a bunch of grubby clothes and a gun back. My first thought was that it was too bad there there had been a gun in the stuff, because I would have asked him in. He smiled and looked at me helplessly.

"Well," I said, "the unrecognizable things I dumped, and I washed the dishes, and—"

"Great!" he interrupted.

"*Great?* I don't think it's great at all. They're the only dishes I have."

"Oh," said Bert, looking genuinely sorry. "Uh, I guess you can have them. I was never too keen on Corelle Living Ware."

"They really don't break," I said. He smiled that winning smile again and looked a little confused. "You know all the ads say they don't break. . . . well, they really don't." I thought about my dish-smashing days and wondered if my life would have been substantially different if we'd had Corelle Living Ware.

"What about the clothes?" he asked. "You wash them too?"

"I've got one shirt. I kept the one with the embroidery on it. I . . . thought it was pretty."

He shrugged. "Does it *fit* you?" he asked, eyeing my size seven body.

"I sleep in it."

"Far out. You can keep it too." (Amazing. He got away with saying "far out" the way Grant did. Not too many people can.)

"What did you do with the rest of them?"

"I gave them to the Goodwill."

He smiled that smile again. "That's where I got them in the first place." He shrugged and laughed. "Cycle completed," he said. Cycle completed. I had said that once.

"Now," he said with a grin, "here's the big one. Where's the gun?"

"I . . . uh . . . took it to the police. I was kinda scared to have it around."

"The Goodwill didn't want it?"

Although I had been fighting it, I smiled too. "Uh . . . no, they didn't."

"Ah, win some, lose some," he said.

"You're not pissed off?"

"Naa. I can always get another one, and that one—as you probably found out—isn't registered to anyone."

"Uh, how come you had a gun?"

"Somebody gave it to me." He paused. "Someone who looked a little like you."

"Why?"

"She—shall we say—feared for my safety."

"Are you a criminal or something?"

"*Me?* I've never even been stopped for speeding."

"Are you in some kind of trouble?"

"Do I look like the kind of guy who would be in some kind of trouble?"

"Well, no," I had to admit. "Why the gun? What do you do?"

"I'm an artist. I'm restoring a painting at the Art Academy. They give me a free lunch on Fridays because they don't serve lunch on the weekends and need to get rid of the leftover food."

"I didn't know they had a restaurant."

"It's not a *real* restaurant—just sandwiches and soup and shit and no booze, but the help is *great*—all these society women with nothing to do who volunteer. I'm kind of a favorite of theirs."

"I'll bet. But how come the gun?"

"Oh," he said casually, "I'm a drug dealer."

I tried to look very sober, but I'm sure he could see the sparkle in my eyes.

"You going to tell the police?" he asked, obviously knowing I wasn't. "I'll even give you my name. My whole name is Bert Doranathal."

"Your name sounds like some kind of a drug." The thought of living dangerously again was very appealing to me.

He laughed. "Well, you going to tell them?"

"Of course not."

"I knew that the second you didn't slam the door in my face when I said I was Bert. I'm sure the landlord told you my name." He leaned forward, took me in his arms, and kissed me so passionately, I returned it without question.

Then I pulled away. What I wanted to do—even on the lithium—was to pull him into the house, break out my only bottle of champagne, and instantly take off my clothes. The idea was so very interesting, but if I did that, I would NEVER have been able to go back to my Xeroxing job. Although I didn't know him, he reminded me of Grant, and he was not the sort of person you left each morning to Xerox term papers. I suspected that with Bert, I would slowly but happily sink into the world of drugs, booze, and laughter. . . . Interesting, but—for me—life-threatening. I was going to be a tight ass and say no. Boring. Safe, though.

"I'm not going to," I said.

"Why?" he asked—curious, not pissed.

"Because . . . because I'd love to. Some people can handle it. I can't."

"Handle what?"

"Living dangerously."

"I didn't ask you to live dangerously. I just wanted to kiss you."

"And for me that would be the first step." I explained very briefly about Grant and the lithium.

He smiled, shrugged, and said, "Ah, you win some and you lose some."

"You're sweet, Bert."

"If you get bored someday—especially if it's a Friday—come by the Art Academy and see the painting I'm restoring."

"I might."

"Well, ciao . . . uh, what did you say your name was?"

"Lola Bloom."

"Well, ciao, Lola Bloom," he said and got into an old beat-up, boat-sized Cutlass and roared off.

"Courage," Robert said when I told him I'd sent away the first man who had attracted me since Grant.

"You bet," I said. "I could have loved him."

"You heard anything from the Husband of the Woman with the Small Vagina?" (Robert got the joke.)

"The lawyer wrote to the Man in the White Belt, and he wrote a note back to the lawyer, which said, 'Aw, gee, and I thought I was trying to date and court her.' "

"Poor guy."

"Yeah," I said. "He'll probably never realize what a jerk he is."

"A sick jerk."

"Yes, but I'll miss the letters."

"You'll *what?*" he asked.

"They made me feel sane, and they made me laugh, and even though it was a total jerk adoring me, it was still a *little* flattering."

"You *are* sane," he said seriously.

I laughed. "It's a little boring to admit I'm getting better."

Robert smiled. "Yeah, I understand," he said.

Working at Kopy Kats was not exactly what I would call a meaningful career. My co-worker was a nineteen-year-old boy. Although he was a very sweet kid, he was by no means "good company." I did learn a whole hell of a lot about Michael Jackson and heavy metal music, and—for lack of anything better to do—during breaks we'd play Ms. Pac-Man and Lady Bug at the game arcade that was next door to Kopy Kats. When we first played Ms. Pac-Man, he thought it was hysterical that I thought you were just supposed to keep away from the ghosts and eat dots. I didn't know about power pills and eating blue ghosts. I told him I wished I could take a power pill and eat all the blue ghosts in my life, but he didn't get it.

When he found out that I was "almost thirty-four, he was so astounded that for a couple of days he treated me with the respect usually reserved for Queen Elizabeth or the pope. He actually told me he didn't know that "old people" were "allowed" to play Ms. Pac-Man, but after a few days, the re-spect-thy-elders time was up, and he went back to using Valley-speak and telling me to fuck off every so often.

Every day: stuff the paper in the Xerox machine, pull out the copy, stuff the paper, pull out the copy. It was just this side of being a Dickensian non-union sweat shop.

Robert agreed with me that it would be no good to take money from Helen or Page, but after the stereo, Page sent me things and Helen sent me more clothes. Since the only places I went were Kopy Kats, drinks with Maryanne, the video arcade with a nineteen-year-old kid, and (yes) the Art Academy to shoot the breeze with Bert, the Laura Ashley dresses didn't get worn all that often.

Bert turned out to be a lifesaver. I purposely

rearranged my schedule at Kopy Kats so I could have Fridays off, and at about ten or so, Bert and I would meet at this restaurant called Johnny Appleseed—not because we liked it, but because it was close to the Art Academy—and have breakfast (it's pretty hard to like a place where everyone else has just finished a morning aerobic workout at the Honolulu Club, when you're just trying to wake up). Then we'd walk up to the Art Academy and talk while Bert worked on restoring the painting. At lunch, as he had promised, the society-lady volunteers gave us all the leftover food, and we'd eat lunch and take the rest home.

Bert told amazing stories. When I found out that he had ACTUALLY BEEN IN THE CIRCUS, I was hooked. The circus was always a fantasy of mine. When I was a child, I wanted to grow up and ride an elephant. I LOVED the elephants and the smell of popcorn and hot dogs. I LOVED all the sleazy-looking people in the circus. Since riding an elephant could hardly be dangerous—except in the rare event of a stampede—I felt that when I grew up, I could experience all the magic and the sleaze of the circus without having to learn how to do something "hard," like walking a tightrope. I had dreams of how I'd decorate my bunk on the train, traveling from town to town like a semi-respectable Gypsy.

Bert had only been one of the guys who put up the tent and watered the elephants, and not a performer, BUT for one season he was a substitute clown for that act where twenty clowns all come out of the little car. Even though he only got to do it once, on his taxes he always put down that his occupation was "clown." Then he graduated from art school, and no matter what odd job he would do, on his taxes his occupation was "artist."

He had some great circus stories. The big entertainment for the tent hands was to purposely leave a gap in the women's dressing tent, and then on breaks, walk by and sneak a look at the starlets taking their bucket baths. When he got tired of the circus, before he went to art school, he'd also traveled all over the country jumping trains. I asked him how he ended up in Hawaii, and he had ACTUALLY been a STOWAWAY on the *Queen Elizabeth II*. He'd simply rented a tux in L.A., bought one set of Calvin Klein casuals, and simply mingled with the passengers. I thought that was truly amazing.

Robert thought Bert was a good "transition" figure between Grant and the real world. Since I wasn't sleeping with him, the powerful sexual bond wouldn't be there, and would in time make it easier for me to let go, or if things continued as they had been going, maybe the need to let go wouldn't ever come up.

Still there was the drag of Kopy Kats. Even if the kid quit and Clark Gable (or Grant) came and took his place, it still would be only slightly better than the meat packers' jobs in *The Jungle*. Shit.

Then one day the most amazing thing happened. Usually, people can't EXACTLY pinpoint "turning points" in their lives down to the exact second, but I can. It happened at exactly 3:09 P.M. in Kopy Kats while I was Xeroxing some sheet music for a music professor from the U.H. Anyway, the little red light on the Xerox machine went on to let me know it was out of paper.

"Can you get me another pack of paper?" I called to the kid.

"Get it yourself, titless," he said. (See what I mean when I say that the respect-thy-elders time had passed?)

I sighed and pushed my sweaty hair out of my eyes, went to the supply shelf, and took down a brand-new SEALED package of copy paper, opened it automatically, and just before shoving it into the machine, I looked at it. Xeroxed on EVERY SINGLE PAGE—obviously by some unhappy Xerox employee—on EVERY SINGLE PAGE was Xeroxed "Herein lie the seeds of revolution."

"Holy shit," I said.

"Far out!" said the kid (he didn't get away with it the way Grant and Bert did).

"I'd like my music, please," said the music professor.

I calmly got some different copy paper and sweetly finished Xeroxing the music, handed it to the music professor, and walked out the door, never to return except to pick up my final check. I just HAD to find something different to do with my life, something where I could save money to go back to school—this time to actually learn something USEFUL, I hoped.

Bert suggested I go to Sarasota, Florida, the winter home of the circus, and join up, but I explained to him that that had been a CHILDHOOD fantasy, and it had sort of evaporated with age.

"Well," said Bert, shrugging as if it was the simplest thing in the world, "let the job come to you!"

"Right, Bert," I said ironically.

"No, really," he said. "That's how I got this job. I just put an ad in the paper saying, "Trained artist looking for interesting work."

I smiled. "You would have got a lot more interesting calls if you'd written, 'Trained drug dealer looking for interesting work,' " I put in.

"Right, Bloom," he said in the same tone of voice in which I had said, "Right, Bert" a few seconds earlier.

"Well, it worked." He shrugged.

"Really?"

"Goddamn really."

"Let's see. How about 'Beautiful and amazing person looking for interesting and meaningful work'?"

Bert laughed. " 'Amazing person looking for interesting work' would be cheaper."

"You really think I should do that?"

"Why not? You saw the handwriting on the wall: 'Herein lie the seeds of revolution.' "

"Okay . . ." I said slowly. "It couldn't hurt."

Chapter

"Looking for interesting work," my ad said. I honestly wondered if there was such a thing as "interesting work." Even Bert admitted he'd rather be "sitting around" or at a hockey game than restoring paintings at the Art Academy, and that was the job he had CHOSEN out of the big three answers to his ad.

I decided against saying I was an "amazing" person in my ad, because I was afraid someone might ask me to do something "amazing," and I wouldn't be able to think of a single thing. Just like every time I went to California, Page would have told SOMEONE that I was a "funny" person, and if I knew ahead of time I was expected to be "funny," I couldn't ever come up with even one witty comment.

I did put down that I was a college graduate (hoping people wouldn't exactly ask me WHERE I'd gone to school, and if they did, maybe they wouldn't ask for a transcript). Bert was still of the mind that I should just pack it all in and have "at least one season with the circus," but I told him I wanted to earn enough money so I could save some and go back to school in psychology, and that—again—the circus was a CHILDHOOD fantasy.

"You want to go to school in *Psychology?*" he asked.

"It's the only profession I know anything about. I'd hate to waste years studying something, well, like architecture and know all about structures and mechanical drawing and stuff, and then find out I didn't have any *talent*. All my houses would be just boring, and I'd get all depressed looking at the good ones in *Architectural Digest*."

"But what the hell makes you think you'd be a good psychologist? Kind of seems . . . well, you being a psychologist is kind of like getting the Boston Strangler to counsel delinquent boys."

I laughed, then said seriously, "If the Boston Strangler was totally cured, he might be the best one. He's been there . . . knows where the kids are coming from."

"But you're not cured."

"Not *now*, no, but by the time I save money for school, go to school, write the goddamn dissertation, there's a pretty good chance. I mean, you have to be mentally healthy to get your Ph.D. without losing your mind and come out of graduate school alive."

"That's why I stopped with my M.F.A. It's horrible being a graduate student," he said. "Where are you going to go to school?"

"Look, I have no idea. I don't even have a new *job* yet. I need time to *really* think about what I want to do. I mean, I just threw that out as a possibility. I know I've got to learn how to do *something*, and the *Mr. Macho* money can finance it, but I've got to save it until I'm sure. You know I just *can't* go back to Kopy Kats."

"Well, good luck, Bloom," he said, smiling.

During the next two days, the phone rang three times. The first time it was Bert wanting to know if I'd got any calls, the second time was Maryanne wanting to know if I'd got any calls yet, and the third time it was Page wanting to shoot the breeze and find out what I was up to, so I told her.

"You're *advertising* for a *job?*" she asked.

"Yeah."

"God, that must be so *interesting* to see the kinds of responses you get."

"Well, I haven't exactly got any yet."

"How long has the ad been running?"

"Two days."

"Oh," she said a little sadly. "But it *could* be pretty interesting. I'm going to mention it to Bob Goldstein . . . might be a good idea for an episode of *Classified Ads.* Sunny could advertise for a new job, and it could be . . . well, like, so horrible that she wants her old job back. It would be neat if she could find a better job, but then we'd have problems with the Screen Actors Guild, as we couldn't dump Carrie Henderson or Randolf Wood . . . well, at least not until the end of the season."

"Who are they?"

"They play the two kooks who work with Sunny at the advertising agency."

"Oh . . . I never read the credits."

"Well," she said, "good luck." She paused.

"Are you sure you don't want me to set up some meetings with agents over here?"

"No. I can't even *lie* very well, let alone *act* . . . and—again—Robert really feels that the only way I'm going to get better is to do as much as possible on my own. It's bad enough having to take the *Mr. Macho* money."

"Well," she said, "I sure hope someone answers your ad."

"So do I."

"And you be careful. Don't get lured into being a white slave or something or working with . . . uh . . . the mob or selling drugs. You know."

"I hope it's something a *little* weird, though."

"What the hell are you talking about?"

"I mean, if I wanted to do something like work in a bank, I'd just go out and learn to be a teller."

"Well, as I said, be careful. You'll meet all the weird people you want to when you're a psychologist."

"*If,*" I said.

"*When,*" she stated and hung up.

I didn't exactly "sit by the phone" for the next two days. I didn't take it off the hook when I went out for groceries, and I didn't take it into the bathroom when I took a shower, but I did stay pretty close to home.

Robert thought advertising for a job was a rather entertaining idea, but said he somehow doubted anyone would call simply because any work that is actually INTERESTING that isn't specialized is usually snapped up pretty fast. I told him I'd give it another week and then answer one of the "teller trainee" ads even though, for me, working in a bank would be just this side of checking into Auschwitz. Robert said there just HAD to be something in between working in a bank and what would qualify as "interesting." I agreed and thought and said that I wouldn't mind working as a waitress too much if the restaurant wasn't too disgusting, and I could always remind myself that this wasn't my CAREER, just something I was doing to earn extra money for school.

On the fourth day, the phone rang, and I assumed it was Page or Bert, so I ALMOST answered "Magoo's Pizza, we deliver," but remembered the ad, so I just said hello.

"Uh . . . I'm calling about your ad," said a nervous female voice.

"You saw my ad?"

"Yes, this is rather awkward. You're female, right?"

"Yeah," I said slowly. In this world full of firepersons and delivery persons and mailpersons, I was slightly surprised that my sex was the first thing of interest. Maybe they WERE looking for a white slave or a massage parlor girl. It would certainly qualify as "interesting work."

"Well," said the woman, "this is *terribly* awkward, but may I ask your age?"

(Definitely wants a white slave.) "Uh . . . thirty-four," I said, now DYING to know what this "interesting work" was going to be, even though the odds were that it would be something I didn't want to do. Maybe it WAS something highly illegal. I was the sort of person who always was looking for a good story. The sadness was that Grant was the person who appreciated (and told) "a good story" better than anyone else I knew.

"That's not *too* old . . . nowadays," she said.

"Too old for *what?*" I asked eagerly.

"I really can't discuss this on the phone, but could we meet . . . maybe tomorrow?"

"Can't you tell me *anything?*"

"It would be better for you to meet with me and my husband. Would the Willows for lunch— say one o'clock—be okay?"

(Definitely something illegal.) "Uh . . . sure," I said and then, remembering that I was going to try to avoid living dangerously, I added, "Would it be okay if I brought a friend with me?"

"Yes, of course," she said.

I hung up and called Bert at the Art Academy. He agreed that they probably wanted a white slave, but couldn't understand why they would choose the Willows. Some dark and slightly sleaze-bucket bar was called for in this case.

"Maybe they're using the Willows because it's respectable, and they're afraid if they say Danny's Den or Club Hubba-Hubba or something, I might get scared off."

"Well, I'm never one to turn down a free meal," he said.

"How do you know they'll pick up the tab?"

"If they don't, then *you'll* pay for me," he laughed. "Protection doesn't come cheap. Too bad I don't have the gun; I could stop them if they tried to carry you off."

"Okay, but be there at one, and—I hated to

sound like a mother, but this WAS kind of like a job interview—"please wear something . . uh . . . nice, okay?"

"Sure, Bloom," he said and hung up.

About half an hour later, the phone rang again. Maybe this was my lucky day. It was a different woman. Before she even asked if I was still looking for "interesting" work, she said, "You know I'll need references."

"Uh . . . my father is a minister . . . Church of the Crossroads."

"Isn't that the church where they do all that weird stuff?"

"It's still a church," I said, suddenly wondering who the hell I was going to get if I needed references. Grant could be one, because he had a different last name, and he could neglect to mention that he was my former husband. Maryanne of course would be one, but I didn't know exactly how much weight a reference from a cocktail waitress at the Torch Room would carry.

"What kind of job do you have?" I asked, thinking if it was a good one, I'd snatch it up and forget the Willows and the white slave traders.

"Working with children," she said and then quickly added, "very responsible children."

"Oh," I said. Since I had never really known a child before, I had no idea whether or not I even LIKED them. None of our friends had kids, and I avoided little Free—my half brother—not on the principle that he was a KID, but because he was obnoxious. Grant said he felt sorry for him because he had to go through life named Free, and I said it probably wouldn't be as hard for him in his generation because it was full of kids named Rainbow, Angel, and stuff like that, and Moonunit Zappa had survived, so I didn't feel too sorry for Free.

"You mean like teaching nursery school or something like that?" I asked the woman. I didn't exactly see that as "interesting" work, but some people do.

"Not exactly," she said. "I'll have to explain."

"I hope you can explain over the phone. It would save us a lot of time . . . I mean, in case it's something"—I didn't want to say BORING—"Uh . . . something I'm not qualified for."

"Well," she said, "summer is coming up, and school will be out."

"Yes," I said, waiting.

"My children will need someone to help make this summer educational as well as a fun vacation."

"Educational?"

"Well, for example, if you were to take them to the zoo, you would first go to the library with them and select books on various wild animals and teach them about them before going to see them, or before you played Ping-Pong with them, you would teach them about the history of the game."

That didn't sound like her kids were going to have all that much "fun." When I was a kid, if I had been dying to play Ping-Pong and someone took the paddle out of my hand and taught me about the history of the game, I'd have been pretty pissed off. STILL, if she offered me enough money, it might offer a little more variety than stuffing paper into a Xerox machine at Kopy Kats.

"How many kids do you have?"

"Before we get into details, does it sound interesting to you? It could be a very rewarding summer for all of you."

"Well, I'm sure it would be quite rewarding, but are you sure the kids will *like* that kind of stuff? How old are they anyway?"

"They range from fifteen to six months."

"*Range?* It sounds like you have quite a few, and I'm not sure a fifteen-year-old would like . . . uh, exactly how many kids do you have?"

"Well, ten to be exact. We're Catholics," she added rather unnecessarily.

"*Ten!* Why, that's more children than Maria Von Trapp had to take care of in *The Sound of Music.*"

"Pardon?"

"Look, I'm really sorry, but I can't—"

"People *always* say that as soon as they hear I have ten children. What they don't realize is that I have ten very nice, responsible children."

I wonder how you could tell if a kid six months old was nice or responsible, and I knew that even if I could make it a "rewarding" summer for them, I would be forced to check into a mental hospital before it was over. Also, I didn't think a good Catholic mother of ten would be all that thrilled to have a governess with scars on her wrists who had a secret desire to live dangerously and rode a used motorcycle.

"It's not the *number*," I lied. "It's . . . well . . . you wouldn't want me. I haven't worked with kids before, and I'm not very reliable."

"But I'm *desperate*," she said. (No wonder.)

"I'm sorry," I said. Well, there were still the white slave traders at the Willows the next day.

I got to the Willows before anyone else and asked if they had a table for Kaufman—the name the woman had given me—and they said that the Kaufmans had reserved a table by the water. I sat next to the railing overlooking the pond. The only other time I'd been there was when Helen was in town and Grant thought it would be a good place to take her because it had a real tropical atmosphere, it wasn't in Waikiki, and she could eat next to the water, surrounded by tropical flora and fauna. While she ate frogs' legs, it was a little unnerving to see frogs hopping in and out of the pond all around us. I checked and was glad there weren't any frogs' legs on this lunch menu.

Bert arrived in a striped button-down shirt (amazing!) and corduroy pants. He said the pants were the Calvin Klein casuals he had worn while he stowed away on the Q.E. II, and I told him that I hoped he wouldn't mention this to the Kaufmans because this WAS sort of a job interview, after all. To do what? At this point, I was prepared for ANYTHING.

Bert ordered a beer, and very uncharacteristically I ordered a mai tai, simply because it seemed like you should drink something tropical at the Willows. I stared at the carp in the pond and the red torch ginger while Bert told me about the fourth graders from Liliuokalani School who had toured the Art Academy that morning and one had almost squirted the Monet with a water pistol. He frowned when the waitress—in her muumuu—

brought my mai tai. "How come you're drinking that stuff?" he asked.

"Well, first of all," I said, "I have an excellent sense for props. I mean, if you did, you wouldn't have ordered a *Budweiser*. You should be drinking something like St. Pauli Girl or that Hinano Tahitian beer. The second reason is that I want to be a *little* looped. I mean, I know this is a job interview, but I'm rather new at that, so I need a little artificial courage. Also, when I go to a restaurant, I always like to order something I don't make at home. If you don't do that, what's the point of eating out?" I held the mai tai up to the light. "They're pretty too," I added.

Bert laughed. "You would have probably drunk that purple Kool-Aid in Guyana. Not because the Reverend Jim Jones told you to, but because it was 'pretty.' " We both laughed.

The Kaufmans arrived about five minutes later. She seemed rather affected and wore a wide-brimmed hat. Her hands shook as she lit a cigarette. I couldn't quite figure out how old she might be, but they were a good-looking couple. Either they were rich or they were the kind of couple who LOOK rich until the parking valet brings out the used Toyota.

She looked at me with one of those meaningful glances. I was glad I'd worn long sleeves, as the razor scars were still there—faint now, but there just the same. I made a note not to reach for anything because my armpits were beginning to sweat.

"So you're Lola Bloom," she said.

"Uh . . . yes. I'm glad to meet you, Mrs. Kaufman."

"Call us Jean and Roy," she said.

"Call us Lola and Bert," commented Bert, taking a swig of his beer.

Jean smiled. "Bert Bloom," she said. "What nationality is the name Bloom?"

"Oh, I'm not married to her," he said, "but it's probably English . . . ya know, back then some people called themselves Gardener and some took—as Lola would say—the 'pretty' route and called themselves Bloom."

The Kaufmans looked a little confused.

Since this WAS a job interview, I suddenly felt it necessary to quickly explain about Bert. "Oh, he's not even my *lover*," I said. "He's my friend. I brought him along in case you guys turned out to be dangerous or something."

Bert grinned, and the Kaufmans looked at each other with a little doubt in their eyes. Fuck. Lola Bloom had blown it with her first sentence.

Roy ordered a Manhattan, and Jean ordered a glass of white wine. I had figured she would. You know how there are some people who you know at first glance are the glass-of-white-wine types, just like you can tell instantly if someone has a food processor or not (I figured Jean did).

The Kaufmans and I ordered rather conventional lunchy things, and Bert ordered chicken curry with all the condiments. While he slowly and artistically sprinkled coconut, crushed peanuts, raisins, crumbled hard-boiled eggs, chutney, and guava jelly on his curry, the Kaufmans' food probably got cold, as they were the type of people who don't just dig in but wait until everyone is served. Fortunately, I'd just ordered a salad.

— 313 —

FINALLY, after what seemed like HOURS of chit-chat (Where are you from? What's your family like? Where were you born?) they finally got down to business.

"I find," said Jean, "that you may be the perfect candidate for . . . well . . . what we're looking for. You're a little old, but someone younger might be irresponsible."

"Just tell her what you want her to do!" put in Bert, who obviously was as curious about the job as I was.

"You come from a good solid family," continued Jean. "I have fond memories of all the Irving Adrian pictures I saw and, well, with a sister like *Page Bloom* . . ."

Fuck, I thought. She wants to hire me for something because I'm Page's sister. She doesn't even KNOW Page, but because Page is famous, she must be okay. For all Jean knows, Page could be a drug addict screwing half of Hollywood.

Jean continued. "And your father is a minister . . . uh, even though it is at that Church of the Crossroads . . . well, the *way* you worship really isn't as important as the fact that you worship."

Fuck, I thought. For all she knows my father could be another Jim Jones. People can be stupid sometimes.

"And your former husband. I just can't *believe* what we've stumbled into. Your ex-husband is the creator and writer of *Mr. Macho*. I had absolutely *no idea* he lived in Hawaii. Imagine that."

"Lola's a pretty swell person too," Bert put in with his mouth full of banana muffin.

"I just can't believe it," said Jean, smiling.

— 314 —

"Well, now," put in Roy. "We may be barking up the wrong tree. You see, we got the impression from your ad that you were in financial need."

"Understatement of the year," said Bert.

"Actually, I am," said.

"But what about your mother and Page and—"

"I just said Page had money and my mother had money. I didn't say *I* had money." I decided to be brutally frank. "There really isn't much I know how to do. I'm rather unskilled."

The Kaufmans looked at each other and smiled. I took a bite of salad.

"You *are* in good health?" asked Jean.

"Physically, I'm fine," I said. (Well, I was telling the truth. I was physically very healthy, and my MIND . . . well, that was doing somewhat better.)

"Well, we—of course—would have to have that confirmed by a doctor before we proceeded with . . ."

"With *what?*" I asked a little too forcefully.

Jean and Roy looked at each other, and then Roy said, "How much money do you feel you need?"

"I need enough to live on. I live pretty simply, but I need to save because I'm going to graduate school, and I don't have enough self-discipline to work *and* write dissertations and stuff. (Shit, I thought, I just put myself down again.)

"Graduate school," said Jean. She and Roy looked at each other and smiled again. Then they said they needed to go into the bar and discuss something, and then they'd clue us in on what this was all about.

"Drug running," stated Bert.

"You don't send someone to a *doctor* if you want them to deliver drugs. You check to make sure they're not narcs."

"Well, this better be good," he said. "Every hour that ticks away, I lose money."

Finally the Kaufmans came back, and while they both ordered "mile-high" banana cream pie, both of us sat on the edge of our seats. Then Jean said, "This is a very delicate subject to discuss, and chances are you won't be interested in this, but we . . . well, we've been married for fourteen years, and . . . well . . . we want a baby."

"A baby," I stated.

"Uh, yes, but we can't have one, so . . ."

"There's nothing wrong with me," Roy put in a little too quickly.

"I had cancer of the cervix," said Jean. I looked over at Bert, and his eyes were huge and he had a piece of banana muffin frozen halfway to his mouth. "We went to several adoption agencies," she continued, "and every one of them said it could take *years* before our name came up, and . . . well, I'm over forty, and"—she paused and nervously lit a cigarette—"we don't want to wait so long. It's hard in Hawaii to get a Caucasian baby . . . and—"

"You could adopt one of those Vietnamese orphans," Bert put in helpfully.

"Well," said Roy, "we want to feel that it is *really* our own, so . . ."

Jean continued. "We want to use Roy's sperm, and . . ." she stopped.

"You want me to have a baby for you," I said.

"Well, sort of."

"How do you 'sort of have a baby?" asked Bert.

"Uh . . . yes. Yes, we want you . . . or someone . . . to have a baby for us."

I looked at Roy. "Would I have to actually . . . uh . . . do it with you?" (Oh, shit, I thought. My tone of voice had indicated that doing it with good old Roy was something I definitely wouldn't enjoy.)

"Oh, no!" Jean quickly put in. "Artificial insemination."

"Of course," I said. "It's just that I saw this movie with Barbara Hershey where she had to do it with—" Bert kicked me under the table, so I stopped.

"How much?" he asked a little too directly.

"Well, if you do prove healthy," Jean said to me, "no mongoloids or anything like that in your family"—fortunately she didn't add manic-depressives, and I had already found out that you can be on lithium and be pregnant at the same time—"well, Roy and I just discussed it in the bar, and we will pay all your living expenses during the pregnancy—that is, within reason."

"She wants to live at the Kahala Hilton," Bert put in. All three of us just gave him a look.

"And," she continued, "of course we would pay all medical expenses. In addition we will give you ten thousand dollars, and we will pay your tuition for graduate school, provided it isn't something long-term like medical school."

"Oh, no, it's just psychology . . . but I do want to get a Ph.D." Things were happening a little fast here. I suddenly realized that, like Bert, I was holding my fork in midair.

"Do you already have a master's degree?"

"Well, no. I've only got a B.A."

"We'll pay for your master's, and if you want to go on," said Roy, "we will lend you the money, interest free, for your Ph.D., providing you agree never to try to contact the child."

"Uh . . . can I think about it for a couple of days? It's sort of hard to decide to have a stranger's baby in an hour at the Willows."

"I assume," said Bert, "you're going to get a lawyer to draw this all up legally."

"That's a must," said Roy. "I don't want any funny business here."

"You're thinking of doing *what?*" asked Page when I told her—as casually as I could. "You're in no position to raise—"

"I'm not going to raise it. I'm going to have it for someone else."

"For someone *else?* That's sick, Lola."

"For money . . . a lot of money."

"That's even sicker. That's what whores say when they try to justify using their bodies for money."

"These people can't have children."

"Won't it be deformed or something because you're on lithium?"

"No. I checked that out. The parents won't even know. All they'll be told is that I'm physically healthy and don't have V.D. or herpes or anything like that."

"So you're casually going to give a poor childless couple a manic-depressive baby?"

"No one has proved it's congenital. You aren't one; Helen's not one; Dillon's not one."

"*Please* if you want money so badly, just let me support you. I can understand why the thought of asking Helen for money makes you sick, but this is *Page* you're talking to. We've always helped each other . . . stuck up for each other."

"I've got to do it on my own, and to quote you, it might be *interesting* to have a baby. Then, if I ever decide to have one of my own someday, I'll know what I'm in for."

"*What* are you going to tell Dillon and Helen?"

"I'm not going to tell Helen anything unless she plans to visit, and I'm not going to tell Dillon unless he wants to see me."

"*Then* what?"

"I'll just tell them I got knocked up and didn't want an abortion, so I'm giving it up for adoption and a good home."

"You're sick."

"That's what everyone has been telling me for years."

"Lola, don't joke about this. This is *serious.*"

"I *am* serious. I've thought about it for three days. . . . Besides, it isn't like *Rosemary's Baby.* I'll know who the father is."

When I said that to Page—although I didn't admit it to her—a new wave of doubt spread over me. The thought of carrying a baby had become rather appealing to me, but when I said that at least I would know who the father was, the thought of carrying *Roy's* baby almost made me think about backing out.

"You've got to get a car," said Bert. "Can't have a pregnant woman riding around on a motorcycle."

"There'll be time before I need one."

"Maybe the Kaufmans would spring for one. Oh, yeah, ask them for a Betamax too."

"Right," I said ironically. I watched him scrape some moldly paint from the painting. Finally, I said, "You know, maybe I shouldn't go through with it."

"*What?* It's the deal of the century. If I were female I'd do it."

"I'm not sure I want to carry Roy's baby around for nine months."

"They said you didn't have to do it with him."

"No, it's not that. Even if I *did*, it would only take about fifteen minutes. . . . I'm talking nine months here."

Bert looked thoughtful for a minute. "Pregnant is pregnant," he said.

"It's just that I thought if I ever had a baby, it would be Grant's baby. I mean, I'd *love* to carry around Grant's baby."

Bert grinned. "Then do that."

"Huh?"

"Grant's the same physical type as Roy."

"I don't understand."

"Simple. Mark your calendar all wrong and keep a second one with the correct information on it. Then you zip in to be inseminated on the *wrong* dates, and go up the hill and screw Grant on the *right* days."

"But I'm scared to even *talk* to Grant, let alone sleep with him. I can't even think about the sound of his voice. Everything I've gained would be down the toilet. I'm not strong enough to see him. Besides, he might be living with someone else now. And you can't just go up to your former husband and out of the blue say, 'Let's fuck for old times' sake . . . uh . . . but it has to be on this certain day.' "

"You're stronger now, Lola," said Bert. Then he grinned again. "Scared to see Grant's face, but brave enough to have Roy's baby."

"I just said that maybe I *wasn't* brave enough to have Roy's baby."

"Chicken shit." He smiled. "You're going to be a psychologist, and these folks are going to pay for the whole shebang, and they are going to get their life-long dream: a little baby."

"It's very dishonest. What if they found out and cut me off? I'd be stuck with no money and a baby."

"Grant's baby."

I thought for a minute. IF I got up the nerve to sleep with Grant again, and IF I got pregnant right away, I could tell the Kaufmans that Grant was the father (I mean, they DID say they thought *Mr. Macho* was brilliant), and that they could still have the baby, and that Grant *was* Roy's physical type, and if they didn't want it, I could get an abortion, and if they *did* want it, I would be carrying Grant's baby, realizing a brilliant and amazing person was growing inside me. Also I wouldn't feel the guilt of dishonesty.

I ran that by Bert, who seemed to think it was a sensible plan, and I sort of felt better. The thought of Roy jacking off into a clinical cup kind of turned me off, and Jean didn't look like the type who would do it for him.

Now all I had to do was take my temperature, mark my calendars, and gather up enough courage to see Grant again. If I could get out of his bed and go home alone, I knew I would feel a little more power. I could believe a little more that someday the world wouldn't scare me so. Maybe someday I could help other people rid themselves of terror.

On THE day, I got on the motorcycle, and instead of driving down St. Louis Heights, I drove up, around the familiar curves to our (Grant's) house, which still had "natural vegetation" instead of a front lawn. I smiled. If there had been a perfectly trimmed lawn, I would have had to just turn around and be injected with Roy's sperm.

My whole body shook as I tested the doorbell, which—of course—was still broken. I opened the screen door and knocked on the glass panes of the inner door. When I heard the familiar galloping footsteps, my knees felt weak. Even when losing my virginity to Mr. Shaftner in the bushes, my heart didn't beat this fast. I felt anxious—like a mistress whose lover is hours late.

"Holy shit," said Grant as he opened the door.

I had tried to look as pretty as I could without looking like I'd worked too hard at it. Of course I hadn't worn anything Helen had brought me; Grant would probably have laughed, so I had pulled out the good old Victorian lace blouse, and I had piled my hair up on top of my head. Although I was risking laughter from Grant, I wore lipstick for the first time since Grant had put me on the plane to go to Page.

"Hi," I said, feeling shy and excited all at the same time.

"Lola Bloom!" he said, smiling, and picked me up and carried me into the house.

I didn't even need to propose that we have sex "for old times' sake," because he didn't set me down until he got to the bedroom. He gently put me down on the flowered sheets under the roses on the ceiling and kissed me.

He slowly took off all his clothes while I watched. I always loved to watch him undress. He hadn't even touched me, but I felt as if I was going to come. Suddenly I was terrified. What if I *couldn't* leave? All the shit I had gone through would have been for nothing.

Without a word, he gently unbuttoned each tiny little button on my blouse . . . all the way down the back. He slid it off and lovingly set it on top of his clothes. As he gently touched each breast, I shivered. Suddenly nothing mattered: not my supposed new strength, not Roy and Jean's baby, not the fear that I couldn't leave, not the fact that Reagan would probably be reelected, not nuclear war, not death; nothing mattered. I was in Grant's arms again. Was I self-destructive for loving a man I shouldn't live with, or were we wrong for each other? At that moment, we seemed to be one; I thought that if there was such a thing as reincarnation, we had loved passionately in another lifetime. But his amazing energy had dragged me down, because I had had none. Jesus, I thought, please let me have enough energy to leave him again.

Then it really DIDN'T matter. He turned me over, kissed my mouth, first very delicately and then passionately, forcing his tongue under and around mine. I put my head back, and he kissed me under my chin and then all the way down my neck, between my breasts, slowly over my stomach, and finally between my legs. I parted my knees, and he sat up, opened my legs farther, opened his eyes, and looked at me—first right into my eyes, then down my body, and finally long and lovingly at my vagina. I loved it when he looked at me like that . . . loved sharing my deepest privacy with him. He gently stroked my clitoris, and I shivered again. I gently touched his penis and moved my finger down the length of it . . . first just stroking it and then licking it.

"I see that sparkle in your eyes," he said, smiling. He moved around and again kissed me passionately on the mouth, entered me, and we fucked, talked, and fucked again. Then he went to the kitchen and came back with a bottle of champagne. I remembered the first night we were together and he had said, "I have two kinds: one is more expensive and the other is prettier to look at." I had chosen the pretty one, which was the same one he brought to the bedroom. He lit the obligatory post-coital cigarettes.

"Why did you come back?" he asked.

"I didn't."

"What do you mean you didn't? You're here."

I wanted to throw my arms around his neck, get blindly drunk, and stay that way forever. Interesting. "I'm going to leave after we have the champagne," I said. Boring . . . but safe.

"I don't understand," he said. "I thought when you got all your shit together, you might come back, and then I saw you at the door with your sparkling eyes, and I was pretty sure you had."

"Well, I haven't got my shit together."

He clinked his champagne glass against mine and leaned back on the pillows. "I wonder what you'd be like with your shit together."

"Safe but boring," I said. This was the first time I'd verbalized this theory to anyone but Robert.

"That's why I don't get *my* act together," he said, smiling.

"I even registered to vote," I said.

"You're worse off than I thought. Didn't you give that up in 1968?"

"Yeah, but I want to take a stab at keeping Reagan out of the White House. Can you *imagine* how dangerous he'll be when he doesn't have to worry about being reelected?"

Grant gave me one of his sideways, amused looks, usually reserved for second-level people. "Discussing politics now?" He smiled.

"I even let Helen buy me an Anne Klein suit."

He stroked my hair. "I hope you wear it to a bowling alley," he said sadly.

"I even quit smoking."

He looked seriously worried. "You just smoked a Dunhill."

"I'm with you," I said sadly this time.

"Next thing you're going to tell me is that you've joined a health club again."

"No, I didn't go *that* far. I wouldn't have had the nerve to come up here."

I wanted to cry and cling to him, but I managed to smile again. "I heard you were a good fuck," I said.

We polished off the pretty champagne, and I put on my blouse. As gently as he had unbuttoned it, he buttoned it slowly all the way up the back, the way he used to. I started to rearrange my hair.

"Don't," he said. "I always loved your hair after lovemaking . . . messy . . . and you always look so languid." He brushed a strand out of my eyes. "Lola Bloom, Lola Bloom," he said. Then he smiled and said the very seductive and very dangerous words: "Want to take some drugs?"

Using all the energy I had, I said, "Uh . . . no. I've gotta go."

"Oh, Lola, don't tell me you gave up rock 'n' roll too."

"You have all the records."

He rolled off the mattress and went into the other room. In a minute he came back with a worn Jerry Lee Lewis record and handed it to me. I put my arms around his neck and buried my face in his chest. He stood there naked holding me for a long time. Then I quickly pulled on my jeans, picked up my purse and the Jerry Lee Lewis record, and just before going out of the room, I noticed I still had a swallow of champagne in my glass. Just so Grant wouldn't be too worried about me, I clinked my glass to his and said, "To sex, drugs, and rock 'n' roll." He smiled, and we both took a sip. I managed not to cry until I was outside and had my crash helmet on. I heaved and sobbed all the way down the hill. I knew if I didn't get pregnant on this try, I would just have to forget it. I didn't think I had enough energy to leave him again.

I called the Kaufmans at a time of the month when pregnancy was practically IMPOSSIBLE to achieve, and Jean said she'd send Roy down to the Medical Group (she didn't say "to jack off," but that's what she meant). I was supposed to go to the gynecologist there who had checked my health to begin with and knew the whole story.

God, I was glad I wasn't really going to get pregnant. How could a brilliant and amazing child be created in a sterile room with its mother's feet in stirrups and its father beating his meat down the hall?

Mrs. Fukahara, the nurse, squeezed my hand. "You excited?" she asked cheerfully.

"I'd be happier with candles, roses, baroque music, and champagne," I answered, but she didn't get it. She just looked at me rather strangely. Since I had been looked at strangely so many times in my life, it didn't bother me. Also I had a secret: I might already be carrying Grant's baby.

I don't think anyone in the history of mankind has checked more often to see if her period started than I did for the next two weeks. I'd shove the Kleenex up as far as it would go. So far so good. No blood.

I knew it was POSSIBLE that I could be pregnant from just the one time with Grant, because I was the type of person who got pregnant if you LOOKED at me. During our marriage, I think I forgot the diaphragm maybe four times, and two of those four times, I got pregnant. Fortunately, we both knew we were too crazy to be parents, so I sadly had abortions—wanting to carry Grant's baby, but knowing I wasn't fit to care for it.

Artificial insemination is so disgusting. I'm sure many couples are grateful for it, but as I lay there, I thought I'd almost rather be actually DOING IT with Roy—even having a three-way so Jean wouldn't feel left out.

When a month had gone by (with Jean calling every so often "just to see if anything has happened") and there was still no period, I went out and bought the E.P. home pregnancy test. Positive. Baby. Grant's baby. I was carrying the beginning of a brilliant, amazing human being.

Now the hard part. I was going to have to break the news to the Kaufmans. Maybe they would still want the baby—after all they'd TRIED adoption agencies first—before they saw "College graduate looking for interesting work" in the newspaper. Maybe if I explained to them about Grant, they'd be delighted. Not bloody likely, but maybe . . . If not, I figured I'd have another abortion and pay them back for whatever it cost them to inseminate me. God, why had I been so stupid? Maybe Helen was right when she said that Lola could never think things through to the end. Of course, I COULD just pass this off as Roy's kid and collect the money, but that would be a dirty deal and might end up like on all the soap operas when someone somehow years later finds out that his father isn't his

REAL father. No, I just couldn't do that. I really did hope they'd accept this baby as theirs. I hated the thought of flushing yet ANOTHER of Grant's babies down the toilet.

The first sign that there was trouble brewing for *Mr. Macho* was when *Real Men Don't Eat Quiche* became a best-seller, but I didn't see it as "trouble" for *Mr. Macho*. I just saw it as an imitation, and I assumed that imitation is the sincerest form of flattery. THEN the second sign was that Grant's agent stopped mentioning that the comic strip would make a good weekly TV series. After I left him, I didn't even think about the fate of *Mr. Macho* until I was in Job Lot (bargain hunters' heaven, but noted for having last year's fad toys drastically reduced each Christmas), and right up there with the slashed-price Annie dolls was a huge pile of Mr. Macho dolls that weren't selling, even for two ninety-eight.

Then one morning while I was sitting around trying to figure out how to tell the Kaufmans they should adopt Grant's baby and not be pissed off that it wasn't Roy's baby, and they should respect me for being honest (fat chance), I casually opened the newspaper, turned to the comics, and *Mr. Macho wasn't there*. I frowned, thought about dialing Grant, but called the *Honolulu Advertiser* instead. *Mr. Macho*, they told me, had been canceled.

"Well, you should put it back. Everyone reads *Mr. Macho*. That's like canceling *Blondie* or *Hi and Lois*."

"We can't put it back, because it is no more.

We didn't want to cancel it, because Mr. Rosenberg lives in this state, but apparently Mr. Rosenberg isn't drawing it anymore."

"Well, *why not?*"

"I guess it lost popularity. We were the last paper to cancel it. For a month, he was drawing it just for us, but I guess a guy can't make a living drawing for one paper once a week."

I hung up slowly. No more *Mr. Macho* money; pregnant with a baby whose adoptive parents probably didn't want it; no skills; divorced from a man I was still in love with. The only bright side was that I wouldn't STARVE or become a bag lady or something, because I COULD borrow money from Page, but then everything I'd worked for would be down the tube.

Both Bert and Maryanne were of the mind that I should just lie to the Kaufmans. After all, Roy and Grant were similar physical types, but I was afraid the baby would be born with some weird blood type or pick up a crayon in kindergarten and start drawing Mr. Macho or something. Robert said I should level with them completely. (Well, I took that with a grain of salt, because what else was a psychologist supposed to say—'Swindle the suckers'?) I decided to do a little of both. I WOULD tell them it was Grant's baby because that was important, but I wouldn't tell them I had done it on purpose. To me, that sounded like a rather wise way to handle it, and after all, they HAD tried an adoption agency, so they weren't opposed to adopting a baby that wasn't biologically related to one of them.

I went to the Medical Group to have an "official" pregnancy test and a bunch of other tests, all of which confirmed that, yes indeed, in eight months a little bundle of joy would arrive. As I rode home, I got more and more apprehensive. I remembered going to Lamaze class with Page and seeing that "reassuring" film *The Story of Eric,* and I thought, Fuck, what have I done? Only Lola Bloom would deliberately get pregnant after seeing *The Story of Eric* and totally forgetting about it.

I called Jean Kaufman. "Test positive!" I said as cheerfully as I could. "I told you we'd probably score on the first try."

She didn't even bother to say anything to me, but I could hear her yelling, "Roy! It's positive! She's *pregnant!*"

Then I heard Roy say something that I couldn't make out, and then she said, "We'll have to meet with you and our lawyer."

"Ah . . . yeah. I sort of feel the need to meet with you."

"The Willows?" she said.

I just COULDN'T take the Willows again. I mean, it's a nice restaurant and all, but you sort of feel like a tourist, or a university professor (it's near the U.H.), or someone who is entertaining a tourist. Also, I figured I'd better suggest a place I could afford because they might just be so pissed that I'd be stuck with the check. If they didn't think of it, I was sure their lawyer would suggest it.

I almost—for irony's sake—suggested the Hee Hing Chop Suey, where Grant and I had decided to get married, but I wasn't feeling too ironical, and if the Kaufmans were going to be pissed off, at least they should be pissed off while eating something reasonably good. I suggested the Hong Kong Menu in Kaimuki.

"Why?" she asked.

"Uh . . . craving. Nice hot northern Chinese food. Pregnant woman's craving."

"Oh," she said understandingly.

I had Bert come along to give me a ride, as I figured they wouldn't be thrilled if the mother of their child arrived on a motorcycle and also to protect me in case they started throwing dishes. He told me I was stupid to tell them the truth, and I said, "But not the *whole* truth . . . if that helps," and he laughed and shook his head.

When we arrived at the Hong Kong Menu, Jean, Roy, and a lawyer type in a reverse-print aloha shirt were watching the live prawns in the tank with the kind of bored looks on their faces you see on people in elevators who are watching the numbers light up, simply for lack of anything else to watch.

"Lola!" said Jean giving me a hug and giving Bert a look. Roy shook my hand like a proud father, and I started to get that female cockroach feeling. We sat down, and they of course INSISTED that the little mother order "anything she wants" and they wouldn't "take no for an answer."

After I ordered, I figured it was time to tell them, because there would be no food to throw around, and because stomachs would be empty and there would be no food to be thrown up. Bert was giving me one of his "you owe me one" looks, but he stayed at the table because he knew I'd KILL him if he quietly excused himself and went to the men's room.

"Uh . . . there's something I need to say before we eat," I said as calmly as I could.

"Grace?" asked Bert sweetly. I was definitely going to kill him when this was over.

I smiled lamely, and the Kaufmans looked at me sympathetically, like they felt sorry for me for having such a scraggly and rude friend.

"I'm just going to come out and say it," I said noticing that the chopsticks were quivering in my hand.

"Is there something wrong? Complications?" asked Jean.

"Well, complications," I said, and then quickly added, "but not the kind you're thinking about . . . a different kind of complications."

"Well, what?" she looked at me as if I had said World War III had started. This was going to be harder than I had thought.

"Uh . . . well . . . there's some good news and some bad news: the bad news is that . . . uh . . . Roy isn't the father of the baby." Jean dropped her teacup. *"But,"* I quickly added, "the good news"— I gestured in Bert's direction—"is that *he* isn't the father either, in case you were worried, and you can still have the baby if you want it."

Everyone sat there in stunned silence. Mr. Lawyer opened his mouth to say something, but changed his mind. Finally Roy said, "Just what the hell is going on here!"

"The father of the baby is Grant Rosenberg, my former husband. . . . Uh, remember when you said how much you liked *Mr. Macho* and all? Well, Grant is a healthy, brilliant, and amazing man. He's got Roy's coloring, and you could have this baby

— 333 —

without waiting three years or more at an adoption agency. Eight months and he's yours." There was still a stunned silence. "And Grant doesn't know. I'd just check into the hospital under your name, and the birth certificate would be as if he were your own child."

Jean looked questioningly at Roy. Naturally, Roy looked more upset than she did. The lawyer just looked pissed off. Still nobody said anything.

"Could you pass the tea?" asked Bert. I did. Still no one said a thing.

"I *know* it's a boy," I went on. "I just have this feeling that this baby is going to be a boy." Silence. "Well, it'll be a healthy boy . . . brilliant. . . . He *will* be, I know. His father is . . ." And then good old Lola Bloom burst into tears.

"Just where the hell do you get off pulling a stunt like this!" yelled Roy.

"Where the hell do *you* get off," shouted Bert, "yelling at her!"

The waitress was just coming out of the kitchen with one of our dishes, and cowered by the door. Perhaps she feared food throwing.

"Be *quiet*, Roy," hissed Jean.

"It's not a stunt," I lied, "it just *happened*." I started to sob again, "and I'm trying to be as honest as I can. . . . I mean, I could have just not told you, and you'd never have known, but I didn't think that was fair, so . . ."

"We appreciate that, Lola," said Jean rather coldly.

"You don't *have* to adopt it," I said, managing to stop crying. "I could give it up to an adoption agency, and some people who've been waiting

— 334 —

three or four years—like you'll have to—could have it."

"You're damned right we don't *have* to adopt it!" said Roy angrily. The waitress scurried over, set the rice down, and scurried back to the kitchen.

For the first time, Jean was looking a little receptive to the idea.

"You *were* going to go the adoption-agency route first," I put in meekly. The waitress—still looking terrified—came out with the chicken with chili peppers, timidly set it on the table, and rushed back to the kitchen.

"You were comfortable with adoption," said Jean. "You *were*, Roy, until they told you it would take three or four years."

"She gets my goddamn hopes up," said Roy bitterly. "My own son . . . makes me think that's a reality, and then calmly tells me the father is really some jerk who writes cartoons."

"He's *not* a jerk!" I shouted for the first time.

"Then why the hell did you divorce the bastard if he wasn't a jerk?"

"Because we found it hard living together," I said quietly.

"Leave her alone," said Bert. He stood up and picked up my purse. "We'll get the money you've spent on her back to you." He dug into his pocket and pulled out a twenty dollar bill—probably his last—and put it on the table. "Enjoy your lunch," he said. "Come on, Lola."

Just as I started to get up, the lawyer in the aloha shirt spoke up. "Uh . . . wait a minute, you two." He turned to Roy and Jean. "This could be your answer. As Ms. Bloom pointed out, you have tried adoption agencies, and"—he cleared his throat—"even the black-market route. Look, here is a healthy baby you can have in less than nine months. As Ms. Bloom pointed out, she *could* have been dishonest and passed this off as Roy's child."

Roy and Jean looked at each other. Obviously Roy was the type who listened to a male lawyer more closely than he listened to his wife. I was glad I hadn't had to do it with him. I thought of Grant's head resting gently on my breasts after he came . . . thought about his face and our naked bodies under the roses on the ceiling, and I actually felt good about this unique boy I was carrying . . . someone who would grow up to make some yet unborn girl as happy as his father had once made me. Maybe Roy and Jean wouldn't even tell the baby it was adopted. That would be okay too because genetically at least half of him would be superior . . . and maybe more than half. I really wasn't such a cockroach after all. The Grants of this world don't bother to spend ten years with a cockroach.

Roy frowned. "True," he said slowly. "But I don't like the fact I know who the father is."

"Well," said Jean, "with the . . . other situation, *I* would have had to walk around knowing not only that I wasn't his mother but that Page Bloom's sister was his mother."

"Don't call her Page Bloom's sister," said Bert. "She doesn't like it. She's got a name of her own."

For the first time I didn't melt, want to throw up, or even feel strange. "That's okay," I said softly. "I'm fond of Page." Bert looked astonished and then pleased.

After exchanging glances for what seemed like the entire Ice Age, Roy finally said, "Okay. We will still pay your living and medical expenses while you are pregnant and any post-partum expenses that may occur. You will still get the ten thousand dollars, but because this isn't *my* baby, we won't pay for your graduate school."

"Roy," said Jean with a frown.

"Well, all right. We will lend you the money for school interest free, and hope to God you're a successful psychologist so we'll get it back."

I smiled and shivered. In just ten minutes I'd been given an independent future. I could start school the next semester at the University of Hawaii and then transfer to a better school after the baby was born. And every time I felt it kick, I'd feel close to a part of Grant.

Then the lawyer in the aloha shirt said he would have his office draft slightly different papers, and we'd meet next week, now that our wheeling and dealing had been done.

"Let's hope there won't be any *more* surprises," said Roy rather sternly.

"Oh, no," I said. "Don't worry."

As Bert and I drove home, he said, "What if you want to keep it?"

"I'll owe the Kaufmans a ton of money, which I don't have because *Mr. Macho* isn't worth two dimes anymore , . . even if they sell all the dolls at Job Lot."

"Would you go to Page and borrow money to pay them off?"

"That *might* be the one time I would, but then, once I'd paid them off, not only would I have a baby to raise, but I'd have no money for school. I can always have another one when I can afford to raise it . . . that is, if I ever love someone enough again to want to be the mother of his child."

As you've probably guessed, everything didn't work out as "nice and tidy" as it seemed it would in the restaurant. Besides adjusting to being a student again—which was quite hard, since I hadn't done much studying at Santa Cruz and I was competing with people ten years younger than I was who HAD studied in undergrad school and had better backgrounds in psychology—I threw up pretty regularly every morning. Waking up to a spinning room and staggering all the way around the garage to the toilet hadn't been in my scenario at all. Sometimes when I was sure I wasn't going to make it, I'd throw up in the sink. I wished I had found out a little more about the realities of pregnancy before diving head first into it. At least it was Grant's baby; I wouldn't have wanted to throw up for Roy's baby.

Another thing I hadn't counted on was the depression. Although it wasn't a dangerous manic depression like before, I would find myself on the bed quietly sobbing for hours.

Robert was proud as hell of me and again said all the stuff about courage, and when I told him about the crying, he said, "Talk to the baby. It's part of Grant." At first I thought that was a pretty dumb idea, but I didn't tell Robert because since he had so few dumb ideas, maybe this might work. And it did . . . sort of. It didn't stop the crying, but I didn't feel quite as alone and scared as before.

Bert traded me his car for my motorcycle. It was a clunker, but it got you there, and even though Bert got the better end of the deal, we both felt a little safer with me in a car—although I always waited for the whole thing to just explode every time I turned the key.

It was sure strange being a student again. Being a first-year graduate student at the age of thirty-four is kind of humiliating. With all my grand plans about going back to school, I hadn't thought about the fact that you still had to go to classes, still had to sit in a little desk, take notes from the blackboard, and raise your hand. Fortunately, in addition to my large classes, I had one SMALL seminar taught by a guy who had actually been in a mental hospital and had electric shock therapy. Somehow that made everything he said more interesting, like if you hear a movie is funny in advance, you might laugh at something you normally wouldn't laugh at, or like *The Bell Jar*—it became a much more significant piece of literature when the readers knew that she REALLY DID kill herself.

We usually just sat around in Dr. Hawkins's office and drank beer or sometimes held classes in the Manoa Gardens, which was a classy name for a simple student hangout with umbrella tables and a bank machine.

One afternoon as the others got up at the end of the seminar, Professor Hawkins put his hand on my arm. "Stay for another beer?" he asked.

"I can only have one every so often. I'm pregnant, and I've read all those books that say that smoking and drinking aren't good for babies."

"They make pregnancy sound worse every year. First it's that natural childbirth stuff where you don't get painkillers, and now no smoking or drinking. Next thing you know, they'll say no sex and rock 'n' roll. Sit down anyway and have a soda." I shrugged and sat down.

"I didn't know you were married," he said.

"I'm not."

"Oh," he looked a little embarrassed. "Well, I think it's great that you've decided to keep it."

"Well, actually I'm not keeping it. I'm having it for the money."

He laughed—people always laugh when you tell them the truth. I explained in a little more detail, and he thought that was rather fascinating. Then I mustered up some courage and said, "What was shock therapy like? I mean, if you'd rather not talk about it or something."

"Well, of course I'd *rather* not talk about it, but I don't mind."

"Oh, no. Really, that's okay. You don't—"

"I don't mind. Actually I don't remember much of it. It was the events that led up to it that sort of haunt me . . . the depression. Then I had allergic reactions to every medication they tried."

I decided I'd better tell him where I was coming from, so he'd know I understood and all, so I told him about the suicide attempts and the lithium, and a LITTLE about Grant. Strange. Grant was the hardest of all to talk about.

"You know," he said, "you look very well and very pretty now."

"Really?" I was touched. "Did it hurt?"

"What?"

"The shock therapy."

"No. You're under anesthetic. The worst part is that you lose a couple of weeks. I don't mean just that you have to stay in the hospital, but you don't remember anything. It's scary—like an alcoholic blackout."

"Oh, yeah," I said. "I know about that one."

"And the stigma. You feel rather strange when you're sitting in the solarium and someone says, 'What are you in here for?' "

"You mean this was a *regular* hospital where people go to have open-heart surgery and give birth?"

"Yup. I envied my roommate because he was only in to have a melanoma removed."

I laughed.

"How old are you anyway?" he asked.

"Thirty-four . . . uh, just thirty-four. I never like to say it here at school in case I'm older than the teacher."

"You're certainly not older than I am, and I'm glad you decided to go back to school. What did you do before?"

"I was married for ten years. You know, I'm one of those displaced homemakers who decided she now needs a meaningful career."

"What displaced you?"

"Manic-depressives are hell to live with, and I loved the man I lived with. You see, he encouraged my craziness. He even called it 'user-friendly madness.' I had to leave him to get my shit together."

He smiled and stroked his beard. "I've never gone to bed with a pregnant woman before," he said sweetly.

"I've gone to bed with a professor before. In fact, two: one with tenure and one without . . . and my high school teacher," I added.

"I'd like to try it with a pregnant woman."

I smiled. "I'm too scared. I haven't slept with anyone since I left my husband. I have a male friend, but we're not lovers, and . . ."

He smiled and stroked my arm. "I'm not talking about right now. We'll go out, maybe have a drink after class, I'll call you, and we'll get to know each other. You see, I want to wait until you really show."

"Kinky," I laughed.

"I've just always wanted to, that's all. . . . Oh, yes . . . I like you, too . . . a lot."

I smiled. "Let me buy you another beer," I said, taking his hand.

Chapter

Richard Hawkins was true to his word. He actually didn't try to fuck me until I started showing—and I mean REALLY showing to the point that I could throw away my "I'm not fat; I'm pregnant" T-shirts. I was amazed that he actually did what he had said he would do, as we all know that most men NEVER do exactly what they say they'll do. Sometimes he took me out for a drink (ONE drink—I was pregnant, after all, and didn't want the baby to be born retarded or something and have to pay the Kaufmans back all the money they were spending to support me). In the evenings he'd either call, drop by for a drink, or sometimes take me to the movies. He was a really nice man, BORDERING maybe on the third level.

There were, however, a few warning signs. Even though he'd been a mental patient—which I regarded as an enlightened past—he had pretty terrible taste in movies: he didn't laugh at the end of *Yentl*; he didn't cry in *Terms of Endearment*; he didn't laugh when Woody Allen breathed in the helium in *Broadway Danny Rose*; and worst of all, he didn't laugh when the bear leaped out of the forest and grabbed Elaine May in Walter Matthau's fantasy in *A New Leaf*. He also couldn't understand why I wanted him to rent the movie of *A Little Night Music* because it was so bad it was funny. "That was a *terrible* movie," he said to me when it was over, and I'd be in hysterics and say, "Yes, I know. It's better than a comedy!" He also didn't get it when I told him about when Grant (I didn't say "Grant"; I said "someone") told me I had a unique way of taking the realities of life or art and filtering them through my mind and having it all come out funny. But AT LEAST when I explained about the third level of irony and the cosmic joke, he understood. (But if you REALLY get the joke, no one has to explain it to you.)

At the Art Academy, while dabbing tiny bits of paint on some hideous painting, Bert said, "I don't think you should fuck him."

"Jealous?" I smiled.

"Of course, but that's not the point. The point is that if he wants to wait until you show, he's kind of kinky, and if he's kinky in one area, just *think* of the other things he might want to try. Watcha going to do when he hauls out the police handcuffs?"

"Jesus, Bert. He's a really nice guy."

"A very nice former mental patient."

"*Former*," I said. "Besides *I'm* a very nice former mental patient."

Bert was silent for a few seconds; then he smiled. "I like the way you say 'former,' and I like the way you seem to really believe now that you're a 'nice' and worthwhile person." Then he said, "Is he anything like Grant?"

I paused, then said, "He isn't as interesting as Grant, but someone as interesting as Grant might just be too interesting to live with."

Bert smiled again. "I still don't think you should fuck him. Doesn't that hurt the baby or something?"

"No. I think you're *supposed* to . . . you know, so you don't drift apart before the baby is born."

"That's with the baby's father, *if* you're going to raise the child *together*, not with your psychology professor."

"Well, I'm pretty sure the kid won't be able to tell the difference."

"Just remember to plan an escape route, in case he brings out the leather vests and puts on the Nazi uniform."

"Sit on it," I laughed and walked across the tile courtyard, waving and feeling light on my feet for the first time in a long time.

When I was about seven months pregnant, I—correctly—guessed that Richard Hawkins was about to make his move. He asked me out to the Bistro. Now, there is always a dispute about which restaurant in ANY given city is the best, but rarely is there a dispute about which is the most expensive. The Bistro could fit nicely into either of those categories. It wasn't that Richard Hawkins was cheap; he was just normal. Regular people only go to the Bistro on special occasions. We usually went to the Thai Hunt in Kaimuki near where we both lived. Richard often took me to Keo's; I never told him I didn't like it because it was too trendy and was always in the columns and always had people like Lana Turner dropping in and taking some of their hot sauce home. It's a restaurant made in heaven for second-level people. Sometimes we'd go to the good old Hong Kong Menu where I had met with Jean and Roy, but when Richard said, "Get dressed up, we're going to the Bistro," I figured this was my night to get laid.

Good food is like part of foreplay. You try to make your eyes sparkle as you look over the candle, and you try to figure out a sexy way to pull the escargots out of their shells. I broke my no-smoking-during-pregnancy rule and lit a Dunhill with the Dunhill lighter Grant had given me and spoke softly to Richard through a veil of smoke and sipped a martini in a way that looked like I wanted to be kissed. I hadn't felt so sexy since Baby Kaufman was conceived.

By the end of the meal, we had an unspoken agreement that we were going to go home and fuck. "We should go to my apartment," he said.

(That must be where he kept his police handcuffs.) "Why?" I asked. "You always said you loved my view."

"Well." He smiled rather sheepishly. "I can't make love to Jerry Lee Lewis, *Cleo Laine Live at Carnegie Hall*, or Buffalo Springfield."

"I guess I should see if the Kaufmans can cough up some money for more records. I'm so used to them that I forget I'm tired of them." I paused. "We could turn on the radio. I've got an FM one. You see . . . uh . . . it's just that I find my view rather sexy."

He touched my hand. I shivered, and we drove in his VW Rabbit up the winding road that snaked up St. Louis Heights.

When we got home I immediately started lighting my two dozen candles, and he expressed a great concern about fire and looked at me oddly when I said I'd rather be fried alive than make love without the candles. Then I remembered when Grant gave me the Dunhill lighter and said, "Give this to someone you *really* love," and I had said, "What if he doesn't smoke?" and Grant had said, "Use it to light the candles. You wouldn't love someone who didn't love the candles."

I went to the refrigerator and over my shoulder said, "I have two kinds of champagne. One is more expensive, and one is prettier to look at."

He had followed me into the kitchen, and I held one kind up to the light so he could see the slightly reddish hue . . . definitely NOT pink champagne, just pretty champagne. Then he looked at the other and said, "Oh, Moët et Chandon, that's a nice champagne." Then he started looking at my photograph album, so I couldn't turn off the lights to watch all the little sparkling cars drive around the tiny black city of Honolulu.

As he flipped through the album, he started to frown.

"What?" I asked.

"Bloom," he said. "I never thought about it."

Fearing the worst, I decided that if he made a big deal about Page I wouldn't sleep with him.

"Page Bloom is your sister or your relative or something. She's in a lot of these pictures."

"She's my sister," I said flatly.

"Oh," he said casually, as if I'd just said my sister was a dental assistant. He turned to a different subject. He was okay. Yes, he was really okay, but he didn't like the candles. . . .Richard was a sweet if not brilliant lover, but I felt strange carrying Grant's baby and making love to—well, not a STRANGER, but a man I didn't know too well. My orgasm was physical and felt great, but for ten years I had made love to a man I loved, and it is sure the hell different from making love to a man you just LIKE. Yeah, I liked Richard. I liked the sex, but after he left, I stroked my swollen belly and spoke softly to Grant's baby.

At first I thought it was a gas pain, but when I actually felt a little elbow or knee push against me, I knew the baby was moving. I wanted to rush up St. Louis Heights and place Grant's hand on my naked stomach, but maybe that would be dangerous. Next thing you know I would have half a bottle of vodka down me and be chain-smoking Dunhill cigarettes. I lay down on the floor with my hands on my stomach and—alone—felt Grant's baby do cartwheeles and tumbles. Safe. Boring, alone, but safe.

Richard called the next morning to say how WONDERFUL last night had been. Wonderful? It had been a fuck, that was all. Of course I didn't say this to Richard, but instead said, "So sleeping with a pregnant woman was a turn-on?"

"I don't know if it was you or because you were pregnant. Probably a little of both."

"That's great," I stated rather flatly.

"Can you meet me at Horatio's for lunch?"

"Uh . . . ." I was undecided. Bert had told me never to turn down a free meal, but at HORATIO'S? I'd rather have had a hot dog from the concession stand at Ala Moana Park. "Yeah . . . sure," I said.

Now there's nothing WRONG with Horatio's—I mean, the food isn't terrible or anything, but it is just too second level. It is where Sally and Dillon liked to eat. All the waiters wore pirate shit, and in the middle of the cocktail lounge was this boat that held two booths. I knew I'd die if we had to sit in the boat to drink, but then, since most of the second-level people who went there WANTED to sit in the boat, I guessed I was safe. Of course it had hanging Boston ferns, and—trying to add a touch of manufactured originality—mismatched tables and chairs. It was in a shopping complex called the Ward Warehouse, which was even worse than Ghirardelli Square in San Francisco. At least Ghirardelli Square had once been a REAL factory that a bunch of second-level people had converted into second-level chic, but the Ward Warehouse had been built NEW to look like an unfinished or gutted warehouse . . . with lots of Boston ferns, of course.

God, it would be embarasssing to go to Horatio's after Grant and I had laughed at it so much. At least I knew I definitely wouldn't run into him there.

As I was about to go out to the car, the phone rang. It was Richard, full of apologies, saying there was no reason for me to MEET him there, but that he'd pick me up. He sounded rather flustered and said he didn't know what got into his head.

This relationship wasn't going to work. Anyway, I thought, I'll probably be going away to a different school after the baby is born and dumped safely into the Kaufmans' loving arms. Suddenly I was a typical, teary pregnant woman. "Grant's baby," I thought, "and I'm never going to know him." At least I had been smart enough not to give the baby a name.

Richard picked me up, and we went down the hill and stopped at the 7-11 for some pipe tobacco (he really played the U.H. professor role to the hilt: a pipe and an aloha print safari shirt). I said I'd stay in the car, as 7-11 stores depressed me. The only time they were entertaining was about 3:30 in the morning. Grant and I used to get very drunk and loaded and go in and play Pac-Man. This was before I knew that Pac-Man could eat the blue ghosts, so we never kept score, but just watched the parade of weird people who walked in. Probably some of them had been watching us. Some people were just getting up and stopping in for coffee before the early shift. The makeup on the drag queens was often smeared, and the things people buy at four in the morning are usually amazing, and of course there was always someone running in for Pampers or Tampax. Once at four in the morning someone came in and bought ALL the cans of beets. If I ever have to work at a 7-11, it will definitely be the three A.M. shift.

As I sat in the car waiting for Richard, I casually looked to my right and saw a very familiar '57 red Chevy convertible pull up RIGHT NEXT TO ME. Well, of course he'd be there. We ALWAYS used to run down to the 7-11 for something. Grant was probably running in for beer and cigarettes. I didn't duck down, nor did I call out. I just stared. He was the same old Grant . . . hadn't shaved yet. He still had that whimsical, amused look in his eyes, and his "serious" mustache. He leaped out of the car without opening the door. Suddenly he stopped. He'd seen me. Looking dead straight into my eyes, he walked up to the car and almost had a cardiac arrest when he saw my swollen belly.

"Hi" was all he said.

"Hi" was all I said.

Just then, Richard walked out of the 7-11, stuffing some tobacco in his pipe. Grant looked amused, gave me a sideways glance, and said to Richard, "Don't you teach at the U.H.?"

"Psychology department. Hawkins," said Richard, "Richard Hawkins."

"Yeah, yeah. I met you at a costume party. You were the only one who didn't wear a costume."

"Oh, are you the one who draws the cartoon?"

"Drew," said Grant as if he wasn't the least disturbed about it. But if you get the cosmic joke, it's no problem.

Richard gave Grant the macho handshake, and Grant gave me another amused sideways glance. I wanted to die. He probably thought it was Richard's baby. I couldn't let him go wandering through life thinking that.

"Bye, Lola," Grant said quietly, and walked into the 7-11.

"So you've met him too?" asked Richard.

"He was my husband," I said sadly.

"You're *kidding?* You mean that the one you told me about was *Grant Rosenberg?*"

"I don't want to talk about it," I interrupted.

We drove off to Horatio's where Richard had reserved a booth IN THE BOAT. I hoped no third-level people were walking by and thinking how dumb we looked sitting in this little boat with life preservers on the outside that said "Welcome to Horatio's" on them.

We talked about Reaganomics and the election. Richard didn't do anything wrong. He was very nice. He said he had been for Mondale and thought Ms. Ferraro was "a breakthrough," and I smiled and smiled. He thought I was smiling at what he was saying, but it really was because it seemed so funny to be talking about "the political situation" sitting in a little boat in the middle of a restaurant.

After lunch, we walked around Ward Warehouse and Ward Center, which is like Ward Warehouse only it's air conditioned and has more expensive shops . . . still pretty second level.

Then I figured correctly that he wanted to fuck me, so we went to his house in Manoa, which had a Boston fern hanging by the door, Denby stoneware, a butcher block in the kitchen, and a stretched fabric wall hanging. He was still a nice lover . . . even bordering on a good fuck, but I don't know, there's something very unsexy for me about making love on a bed with an Interior Systems headboard with a digital clock radio on it. His sheets and comforter were a definitely "male" dark blue.

After we had had our intercourse, he served me a martini (ONE, because I was pregnant) on a sectional couch, and made gazpacho in his food processor, and I thought any other woman would probably think this was a "very nice date." The problem was that it WAS a "very nice date." If I had gone on this "very nice date" six months ago,

I would have been terrified that I didn't fit in. Now, feeling Grant's baby turn over, I was glad I didn't fit in. You didn't have to fit in to save your life. You just had to fit into yourself. You could be a third-level person and still have an amusing time on the second level . . . all the time watching from the third level. Sure, I was having a pretty good time, but I knew I could never love this man.

Even if it wasn't Grant, I was glad when at that moment I knew. I knew I had the power to know who I could love and still appreciate those I could only like. Even though I knew I could never live dangerously again, I also knew that that DIDN'T mean I had to become normal.

The next morning I woke up in my own bed to the NON-digital clock radio playing NPR's *Morning Edition*, where they were interviewing a feminist novelist who didn't believe that adults should have special privileges over children, and in my sleepy haze I wondered if she went to bed at eight and gave her kids vodka martinis. Then I remembered, and felt a little bummed out. I had had a "really nice date," and pregnant single women probably RARELY have "really nice dates." I should appreciate it more . . . maybe.

I got up and looked at myself in the mirror. I bet even Bo Derek doesn't look too hot when she first gets up; I sure didn't. Suddenly I remembered all those times when Grant stopped me from combing my hair because he liked the sleepy, languid Lola Bloom. I mean, he wasn't perverse: he loved me in my wedding dress; he loved me in my Victorian lace blouse with MAKEUP; he had loved ME, and the Grants of this world are pretty choosy—I hate to say this—but because they CAN BE. Fuck.

Without combing my hair, I put on jeans and a "real sixties" India Imports blouse, and slowly and deliberately (the same way I'd taken the sleeping pills) walked out of the house and got in Bert's car. The eight-cylinder clunker probably used an entire gallon of gas just starting up. It sort of heaved as I drove up the hill instead of down. I snaked up our road and pulled into the garage behind Grant's '57 Chevy. I walked up to the front of the garage (the only garage in Honolulu with a view) and looked out at the city trying to settle itself into Sunday morning. As I walked around to Grant's front door, my knees actually felt weak, the way you hear in all those songs.

I knocked, and there was no answer. Feeling pretty stupid and pretty sad, I started to walk back to the clunker. OF COURSE, he had another woman in there. Sunday morning? Champagne time.

Just as I reached my car, he called to me. I tried to resist the impulse to turn around and run into his arms. Tacky, yes, but what the hell? I turned around and ran down the walkway, and he took me in his arms and held me the way he used to hold me at the airport. There was no way I could leave him again, but then, perhaps there was no need anymore.

Finally, he pulled me away and looked into my eyes, and just like out of a bad romance novel said, "I love you, Lola Bloom." Then it got all awkward. He invited me in for some champagne, but I said no because I was pregnant and didn't really drink until after five.

He said that he was relieved that I hadn't stopped totally because he knew how much I'd miss the occasional moments of relaxation a good old-fashioned drink allows you.

"I'm sorry about *Mr. Macho*," I said.

"Yeah. That means I'll have to act on another of my get-rich-quick schemes."

"And that involves too much work," I added for him.

"I'm glad you're back," he said.

"I didn't say I was."

"I didn't say *forever*. I'm glad you're here. I've always missed your comments."

I smiled. "I've missed your stories."

He reached down and put his hand on my stomach. Just at that moment—as if it knew Grant was its father—the baby did another cartwheel. Grant sort of jumped, but then pressed his hand harder on my belly, and the baby moved again.

"Amazing," he said.

"Yeah."

"It's not the kid of that psychology professor in the safari shirt, is it?" he asked.

"No," I said.

"Whose is it?"

God, how I wanted to say, "Yours," but I thought he might freak out, or I might freak out, or . . . well, I just couldn't. "I don't know," I lied.

What a reversal! Usually if a woman doesn't know who the father of her child is, she wants to pin it on SOMEONE. I knew exactly who the father of mine was, and it was the man I loved, and I was actually standing right there saying I had no idea who the father was.

At first he didn't say anything; then he said, "You look pretty."

"I didn't comb my hair just for you," I laughed. He looked into my eyes, picked me (and the baby) up, and carried us to his bed under the roses.

He carefully took off my clothes, and put his head gently on my swollen stomach. "Is that your heart or the baby's I hear?"

"Most likely mine."

He parted my legs and kissed my spine. Then I turned over and took his head in my arms and violently kissed him on the mouth. Then—and I bet you're tired of hearing about this—we fucked, I cried, and we fucked again. I know other people's sex tends to sound boring, but then you just READ about it. *I* actually had the orgasm.

Grant fell asleep with me in his arms, and I lay there wondering. Even if we WERE to get back together, I didn't think we should keep the baby. I had so much to do yet to get (here comes another cliché) MY life together. PERHAPS Grant—being brilliant—could get together another way of earning a living without having to do much work, or one of his get-rich-quick schemes could possibly happen, but I knew that wasn't definite. All I knew was that I loved him. I had loved him the moment I saw him, and I would love him always (all ways).

I got up out of the bed and wandered into the kitchen. When I opened the refrigerator, I smiled. Grant was still Grant. There were three bottles of champagne (two Korbel, one Moët & Chandon), and a jar of olives. I opened the freezer and, yes, there was the Bombay gin. Nothing else.

I wandered back into the bedroom, and Grant was smoking his obligatory post-coital cigarette. I sat on the floor and rubbed one of his feet and kissed his ankle (at least I didn't kiss his FEET). "Want me to take you out to breakfast?" I asked.

He looked skeptical. "Where?" he asked.

"The Kaimuki Inn," I said.

"Yeah," he smiled. "The safari-shirt psychologist didn't change you. I was afraid you'd say the Summit or the Yum-Yum Tree."

"Grant," I said, "you've got to remember that once you're third level, there's no going back. It's like being a drug addict. One taste of second-level living, and it can become very dangerous. You know I don't *ever* go where all the 'cool' people go."

He touched my cheek. "No, you don't," he said quietly.

"And that's not at all wrong, I've figured out."

"Of course it's not 'wrong.' That's one of the reasons I loved you."

"Well, let's go," I said, pulling on my panties.

"Yeah," he said. "When you're hung over, you need *grease! Hash browns!*" He jumped up and pulled on his jeans.

Even though the Kaimuki Inn was practically down the hill, we, of course, took my car. I didn't really like the way they'd remodeled the Kaimuki Inn: it looked too respectable. Before, it had a sort of low-life look to it, but now it had the blue vinyl look. Definitely better than the Yum-Yum Tree with all the kiddies and their hung-over "cool" parents eating spinach omelets and, even WORSE, people who were FINISHED with their running.

Grant *did* order grease: french fries, hash

browns, and over-easy eggs. "Heavy on the grease," he said to the Japanese waitress, and she laughed as if he had made a good joke. (See what I mean? When you tell people your secret truth, they just laugh.) I ordered some scrambled eggs, and Grant smiled tenderly at me when I dumped about half a bottle of catsup on them. We ate in silence. But it was the good kind of silence: the silence of two lovers eating their breakfast knowing the other is thinking of the passion, the fucking, and the future. We didn't say anything until after I had paid the check.

Finally, I broke the quiet. "What are you going to do, Grant? I mean, now that Mr. Macho is dead, I—"

He put his hand on mine, and his blue eyes looked straight into my gray ones. He slowly smiled and took my hand and put it on his face. "The universe will provide," he said.

Now a little financially practical, I said, "But you can't just hope that—"

Again he interrupted me. His smile got broader. As he gestured to the empty, greasy breakfast plates, he said, "Look, Lola Bloom, the universe just provided."

The baby moved inside me, and I can't end this without Lola Bloom crying one more time, but this time the tears were different. I felt safe, and very far from boring.